QUAINT AND HISTORIC FORTS OF NORTH AMERICA

By Courtesy of the St. Augustine Historical Society

THE ANCIENT WATCH-TOWER OF FORT MARION, ST. AUGUSTINE, FLORIDA

Quaint and Historic Forts of North America

John Martin Hammond

HERITAGE BOOKS
2011

HERITAGE BOOKS
AN IMPRINT OF HERITAGE BOOKS, INC.

Books, CDs, and more—Worldwide

For our listing of thousands of titles see our website
at
www.HeritageBooks.com

A Facsimile Reprint
Published 2011 by
HERITAGE BOOKS, INC.
Publishing Division
100 Railroad Ave. #104
Westminster, Maryland 21157

Copyright © 1915 John Martin Hammond

— Publisher's Notice —
In reprints such as this, it is often not possible to remove blemishes from the original. We feel the contents of this book warrant its reissue despite these blemishes and hope you will agree and read it with pleasure.

International Standard Book Numbers
Paperbound: 978-0-7884-0834-2
Clothbound: 978-0-7884-8884-9

PREFACE

A N account of the most famous fortifications of North America is, in reality, a cross section of the military history of the continent; and whatever ingenuity there may be in this method of presenting the conspicuous deeds of valor of the American people will, it may be hoped, add interest to the following pages.

So many races of men have wrestled for the North American continent in, historically speaking, so brief a space of time! We behold the Indian in possession though we do not know who was his predecessor in holding the land, though the mounds of the Middle West, notably Illinois and Arkansas, point to a race of a higher culture and more developed knowledge of building than the red men had. There come the Spanish with their relentless persecutions of the natives. There come the English, French, Dutch, Swedish. And the claims of each clash, to at length give way—despite the military acumen of the French—to the steady, home-building genius of the English.

Of the strongholds which the Spanish built to maintain their title to this part of the world there remain such substantial relics as the old fort at St. Augustine, annually visited by thousands of people, and that at Pensacola, Florida. The French are best remembered by their

PREFACE

works at Quebec. Of the defensive works of the Dutch, on the Hudson, or the Swedes, on the Delaware, nothing remains. The English were not great builders of forts; they were essentially tillers of the soil. The most important English military work of early Colonial days in America was Castle William (Fort Independence), Boston harbor.

To the French with their restless explorers and indefatigable missionaries to the Indians must be ascribed the credit of most completely grasping the physical conditions of the North American continent and of formulating the most comprehensive scheme for military defense of their holdings. The French forts extended in a well-organized line from the mouth of the Saint Lawrence west and south through the Great Lakes and down the Mississippi to the Gulf of Mexico. They originated and executed, all things considered, the most daring and comprehensive military project ever conceived on the continent of North America.

In the preparation of this work it has given me great pleasure and has clarified to a marked degree my conceptions of the larger movements of American history,—especially in regard to the topographical considerations governing these movements,—to have visited the seats of early empire in this country and the various centres of military renown in its later days. All of the places described in this book are worth a visit by the sightseer as well as the historian—that is, they contain visi-

PREFACE

ble monuments of the Past. I have, myself, taken the greater number of photographs which illustrate the volume. Others have been donated or purchased, as the credit lines will tell.

It is, perhaps, as well to state that this work has been done with the knowledge of the War Department of the United States, which has very kindly allowed me to reproduce some of the pictures in its archives and has greatly helped me with my researches in its public records. When I have visited those few points of historic significance still occupied by the army I have been very courteously shown all points of interest not of present military value and have been allowed to photograph scenes which I desired to record which would have no worth to an enemy of the country.

In carrying forward my work I have freely consulted historical authorities, among which I would like especially to acknowledge indebtedness to the writings of Francis Parkman, who in his many volumes has made the days of Old France in the New World a living reality; to John Fiske, " New France and New England;" to Reuben G. Thwaites, " France in America; " to various publications of the Michigan Pioneer and Historical Society; to Agnes C. Laut, " Canada;" to William Henry Withrow, " Canada; " to Randall Parrish, " Historic Illinois; " to the Hon. Peter A. Porter, " Brief History of Old Fort Niagara;" to Benson John Lossing, " Pictorial Field Book of the Revolution;" to E. G. Bourne, " Spain in

PREFACE

America;" to Charles B. Reynolds, "Old St. Augustine;" to Loyall Farragut, "David Glasgow Farragut;" and to various books of travel and reminiscence, among which I would like to mention: S. A. Drake, "Nooks and Corners of the New England Coast" and "The Pine Tree Coast;" George Champlin Mason, "Reminiscences of Newport;" Irene A. Wright, "Cuba;" A. Hyatt Verrill, "Cuba;" Helen Throop Purdy, "San Francisco;" Ernest Peixotto, "Romantic California;" Adelaide Wilson, "Savannah, Picturesque and Beautiful;" Mrs. St. Julien Ravenel, "Charleston, the Place and the People;" and I have received valuable help in material and suggestions from various State historical societies, which have been uniformly courteous and desirous to be of service.

I wish to express gratitude to various friends and individuals who have helped me with suggestions or photographs, among whom I may mention Messrs. Henry P. Baily, Lloyd Norris, William H. Castle, Edward P. Crummer, Maurice T. Fleisher, James Prescott Martin, Edward H. Smith, and Harold Donaldson Eberlein.

September, 1915.   J. M. H.

CONTENTS

	PAGE
STRONGHOLDS OF THE PAST	1
FORT INDEPENDENCE (CASTLE WILLIAM), CASTLE ISLAND, BOSTON HARBOR	25
FORT COLUMBUS, OR JAY, GOVERNOR'S ISLAND, NEW YORK HARBOR	36
TICONDEROGA, LAKE CHAMPLAIN, NEW YORK	49
CROWN POINT, LAKE CHAMPLAIN, NEW YORK	66
THE HEIGHTS OF QUEBEC (THE CITADEL, CASTLE ST. LOUIS), CANADA	72
FORT ANNAPOLIS ROYAL, ANNAPOLIS, ANNAPOLIS BASIN, NOVA SCOTIA	84
THE CITADEL AT HALIFAX, NOVA SCOTIA	93
FORT GEORGE, CASTINE, MAINE	98
FORT FREDERICK, PEMAQUID, MAINE	105
FORT NIAGARA, AT MOUTH OF NIAGARA RIVER, NEW YORK	113
FORT ONTARIO, OSWEGO, NEW YORK	122
FORT MICHILLIMACKINAC AND FORT HOLMES, MACKINAC ISLAND, MICHIGAN	131
FORT MASSAC, ON THE OHIO, NEAR METROPOLIS, ILLINOIS	141
WEST POINT, ITS ENVIRONS, AND STONY POINT, NEW YORK	147
FORT CONSTITUTION (FORT WILLIAM AND MARY), GREAT ISLAND, NEAR PORTSMOUTH, NEW HAMPSHIRE	161
FORTS TRUMBULL AND GRISWOLD, NEW LONDON AND GROTON, ON THE THAMES, CONNECTICUT	167
FORT MIFFLIN, ON THE DELAWARE, PHILADELPHIA	173
FORT MCHENRY, BALTIMORE	180
FORT MARION, ST. AUGUSTINE, FLORIDA	190
LA FUERZA, MORRO CASTLE, AND OTHER DEFENCES, HAVANA, CUBA	201

CONTENTS

FORT SAN CARLOS DE BARRANCAS, PENSACOLA BAY, FLORIDA	207
THE PRESIDIO OF SAN FRANCISCO, GOLDEN GATE, CALIFORNIA	215
FORT ADAMS AND NEWPORT'S DEFENSIVE RUINS, NEWPORT, RHODE ISLAND	222
FORT MONROE, OLD POINT COMFORT, VIRGINIA	232
FORTS SUMTER AND MOULTRIE, NEAR CHARLESTON, SOUTH CAROLINA	241
FORT PULASKI, AT MOUTH OF SAVANNAH RIVER, GEORGIA	251
FORT MORGAN, MOBILE BAY, ALABAMA	257
FORTS JACKSON AND ST. PHILIP, AT MOUTH OF THE MISSISSIPPI, LOUISIANA	263
FORT SNELLING, NEAR ST. PAUL, MINNESOTA	268
FORT LARAMIE, AT THE FORKS OF THE PLATTE RIVER, WYOMING	273
THE ALAMO AND FORT SAM HOUSTON, SAN ANTONIO, TEXAS	279
OTHER WESTERN FORTS: FORT PHIL KEARNEY, NEBRASKA; FORT LEAVENWORTH, KANSAS; FORT FETTERMAN, WYOMING; FORT BRIDGER, WYOMING; FORT KEOGH, MONTANA; FORT DOUGLAS, UTAH	285
FORT VANCOUVER, ON THE COLUMBIA RIVER, WASHINGTON	290
FORT YUMA, AT HEAD OF NAVIGATION, COLORADO RIVER, CALIFORNIA	295
VALLEY FORGE—YORKTOWN—VICKSBURG—LOOKOUT MOUNTAIN—GETTYSBURG—THE "CRATER"	299
INDEX	305

ILLUSTRATIONS

The Ancient Watch-tower of Fort Marion, St. Augustine, Florida	Frontispiece

(By courtesy of the St. Augustine Historical Society)

Mighty Louisburg To-day, Cape Breton, Nova Scotia:

To Sea from the Ruined Walls	2
All That Remains Standing	2
Water-front of Present-day Detroit	3

Where Indian Canoes and the Palisades of the French Were.

Old Block-house, Fort Pitt, Pittsburgh, Pa	18

(From a Painting in the Collection of the Pennsylvania Historical Society)

Fort Independence from the Water, Boston, Mass	26

Floating Hospital in Foreground

Fort Independence, Castle Island, Boston, Mass.:

Fort Winthrop from Castle Island	27
Main Entrance, Fort Independence	27
Harbor Side, Fort Independence, Boston, Mass	34
Entrance to Fort Columbus (Fort Jay), Governor's Island, New York Harbor	36

Fort Sites in Present-day New York City:

Fort Washington Point. Fort Lee on Opposite Shore	37
Where Was Fort Amsterdam; the Customs House	37
Fort Lafayette, from Fort Hamilton, New York	45
Fort Ticonderoga, Lake Champlain, New York	50

Interior Views of Fort Ticonderoga, N. Y.:

The Mess Hall	51
A Council Room	51

Crown Point, N. Y., in Dead of Winter:

Where the Flag Flew	66
The Ruined Barracks	66
The Heights of Quebec	72

(By courtesy of Detroit Publishing Company)

Guns, Parade and Ancient Officers' Quarters, Fort Annapolis Royal, N. S	84

(By courtesy of The Boston Times)

ILLUSTRATIONS

View from Citadel Hill, Halifax, N. S.	94
Old Martello Tower, near Halifax, N. S.	95
Fort Niagara, on Niagara River, N. Y.	114
The South View of Oswego on Lake Ontario	122
(From William Smith's View of the Province of New York, London Edition, 1757)	
Fort Michillimackinac and State Park, Mackinac Island, Michigan	136
Old Block-house and Mission Point, Fort Michillimackinac Reservation, Mackinac Island, Michigan	137
Fort Massac, on the Ohio (La Belle Riviere):	
Memorial Monument, Erected by Illinois Daughters American Revolution	142
From the River	142
Entrance to Fort Putnam, West Point, N. Y., in Winter	148
Showing Tower of New Academy Chapel in Middle Distance	
Sketch Snap-shots of West Point's Historic Memorials:	
Fort Putnam's Rocky Interior	149
Kosciuszko Monument	149
The North Wall, "Old Put"	149
Fort Constitution (Castle William and Mary), Great Island, near Portsmouth, N. H.	162
A Distant View of Fort Constitution	163
Historic Points on the Thames River, Conn.:	
Fort Griswold, Groton	168
Fort Trumbull, New London	168
Entrance to Fort Mifflin, Philadelphia	174
The Moat in Winter, Fort Mifflin, Philadelphia	175
Fort McHenry, Baltimore, Md.:	
A View from an Aeroplane	180
The Guard-house	180
Fort McHenry, Baltimore, Md.:	
Looking Toward the Lazaretto	181
One of the Old Batteries in Place	181
Fort McHenry, Baltimore, Md.:	
From This Point the Star Spangled Banner Flew	186
The Entrance	186

ILLUSTRATIONS

Col. George Armistead................................	187
In Command of Fort McHenry During the Siege	
Moat and Entrance, Fort Marion, St. Augustine, Fla........	190
(By courtesy of the St. Augustine Historical Society)	
Incline Leading to Ramparts, Fort Marion, St. Augustine, Fla..	191
(By courtesy of the St. Augustine Historical Society)	
Morro Castle, Havana, Cuba.............................	203
Fort San Carlos de Barrancas, near Pensacola, Florida.....	209
(By courtesy of the Pensacola Chamber of Commerce)	
Fort Scott and the Golden Gate, Presidio Reservation, San Francisco, Cal..	216
(By courtesy of R. J. Waters & Co.)	
Lime Rock Light-house, Newport Harbor, Looking Toward Fort Adams...	222
Glimpses of Newport's Historic Defences:	
Parade, Old Fort Adams.............................	223
Present-day Aspect of Fort Greene....................	223
Panorama of Newport Harbor, R. I., Showing Fort Adams at Left Middle Distance............................:	230
Goat Island in Central Distance.	
Fort Dumplings, Conanicut Island, a Revolutionary Relic Near Newport......................................	231
From the Ramparts of Fort Monroe, Looking Toward Hampton Roads...	232
Taken During the Jamestown Celebration by the United States War Department and Reproduced by Special Permission.	
Garden View of One of Monroe's Ante-bellum Residences..	233
Fire!!!...	236
Showing Shells Just Leaving Mortars, Fort Monroe, Va. This Remarkable Photograph Was Taken with Modern High Speed Apparatus by the Corps of Enlisted Specialists Stationed at This Post.	
(By courtesy of the War Department)	
Casemates of Fort Monroe, as They Were During the Civil War...	237
Fort Sumter, a Pile of Stone on a Sandy Shoal............	242

ILLUSTRATIONS

The Deserted Casemates of Fort Pulaski, near Savannah, Ga.	252
Scenes of Desolation at Fort Pulaski, near Savannah, Ga.:	
Parade and Ramparts	253
The Battered Eastern Salient	253
Old Stone Tower at Fort Snelling, near St. Paul, Minn	268
Ruins of the Alamo in 1845	280
From a Sketch Upon Map of the Country in the Vicinity of San Antonio de Bexar Made by J. Edmund Blake, 1st Lieutenant Topographical Engineers, U. S. A.	
(By courtesy of the War Department)	
Fort Keogh, near Miles City, Montana	289
Fort Yuma, California	296
(By courtesy of the War Department)	
Scenes at Valley Forge, Pa.:	
National Memorial Arch	300
Washington's Headquarters	300
Two Views To-day of the "Crater," Petersburg, Va.:	
The Slaughter Hollow	301
The Entrance to the Tunnel	301

QUAINT AND HISTORIC FORTS
OF NORTH AMERICA

STRONGHOLDS OF THE PAST

THE tourist on the coast of Cape Breton Island, Nova Scotia—for in summer hundreds of people seek out this pleasant land for its cheerful climate—may come upon a little bay on the easternmost verge of the land where is a deep land-locked inlet protected from elemental fury by a long rocky arm thrust out from the shore into the sea. He will not be able to surmise from the present aspect of his surroundings that this was the site of mighty Louisburg, the greatest artificial stronghold (Quebec being largely a work of nature) that the French ever had in the New World. Of this massive and menacing fortress, which cost thirty million livres and twenty-five years of toil to build after the designs of the great Vauban, hardly one stone lies placed upon another and grass and rubble have taken the place of the heavy walls. Standing on the ground where New France's greatest leaders stood it is difficult to-day to picture the martial pomp which once must have claimed this spot, to visualize, more particularly, the setting for the farcical onslaught of the zealous New Englanders of 1744, under the doughty Pepperell, in their greatest single military exploit.

The Treaty of Utrecht, which provided a basis of agreement for France and England in the New World for almost half a century, did not establish boundaries between the two countries and the contest to determine the question was unceasing, though not officially recognized. France busied herself in building fortifications and was ready frequently to formally draw the sword; yet it needed the outbreak of the War of The Austrian Succession in 1744, in far distant Europe, to precipitate the American quarrel.

The news of the beginning of this conflict came to Duquesnel, commandant of Louisburg, before it reached the English colonies, however, and it seemed to him an essentially proper thing to do to strike against the English. He accordingly sent out an expedition against the English fishing village of Canseau, at the southern end of the Strait of Canseau, which separates Cape Breton Island from the peninsula of Acadia. With a wooden redoubt defended by eighty Englishmen anticipating no danger, Canseau offered no great resistance and was easily taken, its inhabitants sent to Boston, and its houses burned to the ground. The next blow was an unsuccessful expedition against Annapolis Royal. By these two valueless strokes Duquesnel warned New England that New France was on the aggressive.

Enraged by the attacks upon Canseau and Annapolis and with the easy self-confidence which is a heritage of the children of the hardy north Atlantic coast, the people of Massachusetts were prepared for the suggestion of William Vaughan, of Damariscotta, that with

To sea from the ruined walls

All that remains standing

MIGHTY LOUISBURG TO-DAY, CAPE BRETON, NOVA SCOTIA

WATER-FRONT OF PRESENT-DAY DETROIT
Where Indian canoes and the palisades of the French were

their untrained militia they should attack New France's mightiest stronghold. Vaughan found a willing listener in the governor, William Shirley, who helped the enterprise on its way.

The originator of this astounding project was born at Portsmouth, in 1703, and was a graduate of Harvard College nineteen years thereafter. His father had been lieutenant-governor of New Hampshire. Soon after leaving college Vaughan had betrayed an adventurous disposition by establishing a fishing-station on the island of Matinicus off the coast of Maine. Afterward he became the owner of most of the land on the little river Damariscotta where he built a little wooden fort, established a considerable settlement and built up an extensive trade in fish and timber. Governor Shirley was an English barrister who had come to Massachusetts in 1731 to practise his profession and who had been raised by his own native gifts to the position of highest eminence in the colony.

On the 9th of January, 1745, the General Court of Massachusetts received a message from the governor that he had a communication to make to them so critical that he must swear all of the members to secrecy. Then to their astonishment he proposed that they undertake the reduction of Louisburg. They listened with respect to the governor's suggestion and appointed a committee of two to consider the matter. The committee's report, made in the course of several days, was unfavorable and so was the vote of the court.

Meanwhile intelligence of Governor Shirley's proposal had leaked out despite the pledge of secrecy. It is said that a country member of the court more pious than discreet was overheard praying long and fervently for Divine guidance in the matter. The news flew through the province and public pressure compelled a reconsideration of the project. It was urged against the plan that raw militia were no match for disciplined troops behind ramparts, that the expense would be staggering and that the credit of the colony was already overstrained. The matter was put to a vote and carried by a single vote. This result is said to have been due to one of the opposition falling and breaking his leg while hurrying to the council.

The die was now cast and hesitation vanished. Shirley wrote to all of the colonies as far south as Pennsylvania, but of these only four responded: Connecticut, Rhode Island, New Hampshire and Massachusetts, which blazed with holy zeal as, since the enterprise would be directed against Roman Catholics, it was supposed that heaven would in a peculiar manner favor it. There were prayers in churches and families. New Hampshire provided 500 men, of which number Massachusetts was to pay and provide for 150; Rhode Island voted a sloop carrying fourteen cannon and twelve swivels; Connecticut promised 516 men and officers provided that Roger Wolcott should have second rank in the expedition; and Massachusetts was to provide 3000 men and the commanding officer.

This last condition was one of the hardest to fulfil, for, as Governor Wanton of Rhode Island wrote, there was not in New England " one officer of experience nor even an engineer." The choice fell upon William Pepperell, of Kittery, Maine (then a part of Massachusetts), who though a prosperous trader had had little experience to fit him for commanding an attack upon a great fortress. Pepperell's home is still standing at Kittery and is a substantial structure as befitted its affluent master.

There was staying at Pepperell's house at this time the preacher Whitefield. Pepperell asked his guest for a motto for the expedition. *"Nil Desperandum Christo Duce"* was suggested; and this being adopted gave to the expedition the air of a crusade.

A novel plan was suggested, among others, to Pepperell by one of the zealots of New England. Two trustworthy men, according to this plan, were to be sent out at night before the French ramparts, one of them carrying a wooden mallet with which he was to beat upon the ground. The other was to place his ear to the ground and wherever a concealed mine would give back a hollow sound was to make a cross mark with chalk so that the New England boys would know where not to walk when they attacked the fort. The French sentry meanwhile, it was supposed, would be too confused by the unusual noise of the thumping to take any action.

Within seven weeks after Shirley issued his proclamation preparations for the expedition were complete. The force, all told, numbered about four thousand men. Transports were easily obtained in the harbor of Boston or in the towns adjoining. There was a lack of cannon of large calibre, but it was known that the French possessed cannon of large calibre, so cannon balls and supplies to fit such guns were carried along, it being foreseen that the army would capture sufficient of the French cannon to supply its needs. Of other supplies there was a sufficiency and, to overbalance the lack of any military training whatever in the officers, Governor Shirley had written a long list of instructions for the siege. These instructions, after going into such minute directions as how to make fast the windows of the Governor's apartment at Louisburg, and outlining a complex series of military manœuvres to be undertaken after dark by men who had no idea of the country they would be in, ended with the words, " Notwithstanding the instructions you have received from me I must leave you to act, upon unforeseen emergencies, according to your best discretion."

On Friday, April 5, 1745, the first of the transports arrived at Canseau, the rendezvous, about sixty miles from Louisburg, and this little post which had now a small French garrison changed hands again. Captain

STRONGHOLDS OF THE PAST

Ammi Cutter was put in command with sixty-eight men. On Sunday there was a great open-air concourse at which Parson Moody preached on the text "Thy people shall be willing in the day of Thy power." Parson Moody's sermon was disturbed by the drilling of an awkward squad whose men were learning how to handle a musket.

For three weeks the expedition lay at Canseau waiting for the ice to clear from the northern waters, and then, on the morning of the 29th, it set out expecting to make Louisburg by nine o'clock that evening and to take the French by surprise as Shirley had directed. The French, of course, had been aware all the time of the location of the enemy and had even had intelligence from Boston when the affair was first bruited about. A lull in the wind caused a change in the plan of taking the French by surprise and it was not until the keen light of the following morning that the New Englanders saw Louisburg, no very great sight at that, as the buildings of the town were almost completely hid behind the massive walls which encircled them.

And now how were matters going on inside the mighty walls? Badly, it must be admitted. The garrison consisted of five hundred and sixty regulars, of whom several companies were Swiss, and of about fourteen hundred militia. The regulars were in bad condition and had, indeed, the preceding Christmas, broken into mutiny because of exasperation with bad rations and with having been given no extra pay for work on the fortifications. Some of the officers had lost all confidence in their men and the commandant, Chevalier Duchambon, successor to Duquesnel, was a man of hesitant and capricious mind. It is thus to be seen that the fortress was fatally weak within though in material circumstances it was the strongest on the North American continent.

The landing of the provincial forces was accomplished creditably about three miles below the fortifications. Vaughan then led about four hundred men to the town and saluted it with three cheers, much to the discomfiture of the garrison, which was entirely unused to this kind of warfare. He then marched unresisted to the northeast arm of the harbor where there were magazines of naval stores. These his men set on fire and he the next day set about returning to the main force.

The strongest outlying work of Louisburg was the Grand Battery more than a mile from the town. As Vaughan came near this work he observed therein no signs of life. One of Vaughan's party was a Cape Cod Indian. This red man was bribed by a flask of brandy which Vaughan had in his pocket to undertake a reconnoissance, which he carried through in a unique fashion. Pretending to be drunk, and waving his flask around his head, the Indian staggered toward the battery. There was still no life. The Indian entered through an embrasure and found the place empty. Vaughan took possession and an eighteen-year-old drummer boy climbed the flagstaff and fastened thereon a red shirt as a substitute for the British ensign. Thus also did the Massachusetts men acquire the cannon for which they had been hoping.

It is difficult to understand how it was that the Grand Battery was deserted. " A detachment of the enemy advanced to the neighborhood of the Royal Battery," writes the Habitant de Louisburg in his invaluable narrative retailed by Parkman. " At once we were all seized with fright and on the instant it was proposed to abandon this magnificent battery which would have been our best defence, if one had known how to use it. Various councils were held in a tumultuous way. It would be hard to tell the reasons for such a strange proceeding. Not one shot had been fired at the battery, which the enemy could not take except by making regular approaches as if against the town itself, and by besieging it, so to speak, in form. Some persons remonstrated, but in vain; and so a battery which had cost the King immense sums was abandoned before it was attacked."

The battery contained twenty-eight forty-two pounder cannon and two eighteen-pounders. Several of these guns were opened upon the town the next morning, " which," wrote a soldier of New England in his diary, " damaged the houses and made the women cry."

In this good-natured fashion did the whole siege progress. It is hardly possible to write about the informal procedure in an orderly fashion. Accomplishing incredible tasks in fashions opposed to all of the laws of warfare the New Englanders went on with only rudimentary observance of discipline under their merchant commander. While the cannon boomed in front the men behind the lines wrestled, and ran races, and fired at targets, though ammunition was short, and chased French cannon balls for exercise, bringing back the cannon balls to be used in the guns. Some of the men went fishing about two miles away. Now and then some of the fishermen lost their scalps to Indians who prowled about the camps of the besiegers.

At last the impossible happened. Discouraged by humiliating failures and badly, though not fatally, battered, mighty Louisburg surrendered. The strongest work of man in the New World had fallen to ignorant New England fishermen! The soldiers of France received the ridicule of the whole Old World and an effort was made from Versailles to recover the point lost, but unsuccessfully.

Louisburg was restored to the French Crown in 1748 by the treaty of Aix-la-Chapelle. It was to fall again to English arms in the Seven Years War, which ended with the complete extinction of French power in the New World; but with the account of this siege, which was conducted painfully and formally in accord with the rules of war, we need have no concern. The great fortress was then destroyed block by block and Time has continued the work of demolition which the English began.

STRONGHOLDS OF THE PAST

While Louisburg and Quebec were great eastern strongholds of the French in America, their centre of power in the far west was Fort Chartres on the Mississippi River, at the mouth of the Kaskaskia River, Illinois. Here they held gay sway over a wilderness empire that included many Indian tribes and extended over thousands of miles.

The first Fort Chartres was commenced in 1718 when Lieutenant Pierre Dugue de Boisbriant, a Canadian holding a French commission, accompanied by several officers and a large body of troops, arrived at Kaskaskia by boat from New Orleans. A site was selected about eighteen miles north of that little village and by the spring of 1720 the fort was substantially completed. It was a stockade of wood strengthened with earth between the palisades. Within the enclosure were the commandant's house, a barracks, a store-house and a blacksmith shop, all constructed of hand-sawed lumber.

Almost immediately a village of Indians and traders sprang up around the place and the enterprising Jesuits built a church, St. Anne de Chartres, where many a service was recited for motley congregations of red and white. For thirty-six years this first Fort Chartres flourished and during this time was the setting for dramatic and pregnant happenings. Here, in 1720, came Phillippe Francois de Renault, bringing with him five hundred San Domingo negroes into the wilderness, thus introducing negro slavery into Illinois. In 1721 the post was visited by the famous Father Xavier de Charlevoix, in whose train was a young Canadian officer, Louis St. Ange de Belle Rive, who was destined afterward to be the commandant of the fort. Under the administration of the Sieur de Liette, 1725-1730, a captain in the Royal army, the French forces were engaged in armed pacification of the Fox Indians. Belle Rive succeeded de Liette and under his sway the post became the scene of social gayety.

In 1736 there left Fort Chartres a disastrous expedition against the Chickasaw Indians on the far distant Arkansas River. The result of this expedition was a defeat in which D'Artaguette, the leader, de Vincennes, for whom the little town of Vincennes, Indiana, is named, Father Senat, a Jesuit, and about fifteen other Frenchmen were taken prisoners and held for ransom. The ransom not arriving, the prisoners were roasted at a slow fire by their savage captors. A second expedition against the Chickasaws in 1739 was somewhat more successful.

By 1751 the fort was much out of repair and in this year there came to command it a French major of engineers (Irish by descent) Chevalier Macarty, who was accompanied by nearly a full regiment of grenadiers. In 1753 the second Fort Chartres, a solid structure of stone and one of the strongest fortifications ever erected on the American continent, was commenced by Macarty and his men. In 1756 it was finished. The site chosen

STRONGHOLDS OF THE PAST

was about a mile above the old fort and about half a mile back from the Mississippi River and would seem to have been a strange selection for such a structure, as it was low and marshy.

Of the first Fort Chartres not a sign remains to-day, and its exact site is a matter of disagreement. Of the second Fort Chartres the old powder magazine is to be seen. The fort itself has succumbed to the encroachments of the river, which cut away its bank even so far back as to undermine the walls of the fort itself and, in 1772, to cause the desertion of the structure by its garrison. The quarry from which the limestone of which the walls were constructed was obtained was located in the great bluffs four miles east of the point. The finer stone with which the arches and ornamental parts were faced came from beyond the Mississippi.

The fort covered altogether about four acres and was capable of sheltering a garrison of three hundred men. The expense of its erection was one million dollars, a sum of money only equalled in those days by the expenditure for the fortifications of Louisburg, Quebec, and Crown Point. It is generally believed that large profits went to the commandant and to others interested in its construction.

The command of the point in 1760 passed from Macarty to Nenon de Villiers, who led the French and Indians against Washington at Great Meadows in the skirmish which virtually was the opening engagement of the French and Indian War, a part of his force on this occasion being drawn from the garrison of Fort Chartres.

The veteran St. Ange de Belle Rive, stationed at Vincennes, took charge of the fort in 1764 and had the melancholy distinction of surrendering it to the English, October 10, 1765, when Captain Thomas Stirling came from Fort Pitt with one hundred Highlanders of the 42d British regiment,—a fitting distinction when one remembers that St. Ange had been in command of the first fort shortly after its establishment, and when there was no rival to French power in all of the West.

A predecessor of Fort Chartres in making sure French dominion of the West was Fort St. Louis, on Starved Rock, on the Illinois River, about forty miles southwest of Chicago of to-day and not far distant from the present-day city of Ottawa, Illinois. Of Fort St. Louis there remains not a trace, but to its existence and to La Salle, its intrepid founder, there will for centuries be a natural monument—that great towering crag upon whose flat summit the stronghold was built.

A natural phenomenon of great geologic interest, Starved Rock rises directly from a level river plain. Its sides are as steep as castle wall and attain a height of one hundred feet and more. The river washes its western base and its summit overhangs the stream so that water can be drawn therefrom by means of a bucket and a cord. On three sides the pinnacle of the rock is inaccess-

STRONGHOLDS OF THE PAST

ible and the fourth side might be held by a handful of men against an army. The top of the cliff measures about two hundred feet in diameter and is flat.

On this ideal site, in 1682, the French built Fort St. Louis. In less than three months fourteen thousand Indians lay encamped on the plains of the river within sound of the guns of the fort. To-day the point is a pleasure park.

From Fort St. Louis many an exploring expedition pushed forth into the wilderness and here many a treaty was concluded with savage tribes. While frequently obliged to give up command temporarily Henry de Tonti, La Salle's very faithful lieutenant, was supreme at Fort St. Louis practically from its foundation until its abandonment in 1702. In 1718 a number of French traders were making it their headquarters, but its military history ceased with Tonti's departure.

A predecessor even of Fort St. Louis was Fort Crevecœur—Fort of the Broken Heart—which wore its poetic name for only a few months after its construction in 1680, by La Salle, on the east shore of the Illinois River, not far below Peoria Lake. Fort Crevecœur was destroyed by mutineers during the absence of its commander, Tonti, and was not rebuilt, Fort St. Louis succeeding to its mission. The exact site to-day is a matter of dispute.

Fort Crevecœur was the fourth in La Salle's comprehensive scheme of a chain of fortifications to extend

QUAINT AND HISTORIC FORTS

from Quebec, the centre of French power, up the St. Lawrence, through the Great Lakes, across the portage country which lay between the western lakes and the headwaters of the navigable tributaries of the Mississippi and then down the Mississippi to its mouth, thus hemming in the English to their coast possessions east of the Appalachian range, and ensuring the vast major part of the American continent to the French. The other three of La Salle's fortifications at this date were Fort Frontenac, now Kingston, Ontario, Canada; Fort Niagara, commanding the passage from Lake Ontario to Lake Erie, and Detroit, commanding the passage from Erie to Michigan.

The foundation of the city of Detroit thus needs no further pointing out. Where La Salle's tentative fortifications were the city now presents a busy water-front, with steamers and factories and great buildings where Indian canoes and the palisades of the French once were.

Developments of this plan of La Salle's, which was adhered to tenaciously by the French for almost a century, until they fell before the slow-growing mass of the English, were Michillimackinac and a chain of posts along the Ohio River. Of this Ohio series the most important element was the much fought over Fort Duquesne—the objective of Braddock's fateful march —later Fort Pitt, and now the city of Pittsburgh.

The visitor to Pittsburgh to-day will find on Fourth

street, midway between the Monongahela and Allegheny Rivers, a little block-house, more correctly a redoubt, sixteen by fifteen feet in lateral dimensions and twenty-two feet high. The structure is constructed of brick covered with clapboards and with a layer of double logs, and contains thirty-six port-holes in two layers. This little block-house is all that remains to-day of Fort Pitt. It was built by Colonel Boquet in 1764 and was purchased by private parties in the early days of Pittsburgh. In 1894 the property was deeded by its owner of that generation, Mrs. Mary E. Schenley, of London, to the Pennsylvania Chapter of the Daughters of the American Revolution, and is maintained by this organization to-day for the benefit of the public.

The situation of Fort Pitt and its predecessor, Fort Duquesne, was of immense strategic importance in the early days of the American nation, the considerations which gave it value having operated in the field of commerce in late years to make Pittsburgh notable as a manufacturing and distributing centre. It stood at the gateway to the Ohio River and the rich country which the Ohio waters, and since it commanded the Ohio it commanded the key to the West.

These considerations were appreciated by the Colonial Virginians, and in 1754 Captain William Trent was commissioned by Governor Dinwiddie, of Virginia, to erect a fort at the juncture of the Monongahela and the Allegheny Rivers at the expense of the Ohio Company.

Captain Trent commenced his work in February, 1754, but in April, 1754, surrendered to a detachment of French under Le Mercier.

The French then commenced the erection of a fort of their own on the extreme neck of land between the rivers. They finished their work in the summer of that year and named it Fort Duquesne in honor of Governor-General Duquesne, of Canada.

In the same year a force of English colonists, about 150 strong, made a tentative advance against the work under the leadership of our own George Washington, then a young man. Washington found the post too strong for attack and became himself the object of hostile attention from the French, being forced to fall back to Great Meadows and to erect a temporary triangular earth fortification there which he named Fort Necessity.

In 1755 it was the plan of the British ministry to concentrate its forces in the colonies in three directions of attack against the French. One blow was to be struck at Acadia; a second blow was to be struck at Crown Point, and a third, under General Braddock, an English-born officer of wide Continental experience, at Fort Duquesne.

Braddock's unfortunate march began May 27, 1755, from Fort Cumberland, Maryland (Cumberland, today), and of the details of that disastrous journey little need be told in these pages as the story is already familiar. Braddock had the bravery of his calling and the

From a painting in the collection of the Pennsylvania Historical Society

OLD BLOCK-HOUSE, FORT PITT, PITTSBURGH, PA.

STRONGHOLDS OF THE PAST

arrogance and presumption of the European brought into contact with provincials. He did not believe that anything very good could come out of the colonies and did not hesitate to show this attitude of mind. On the line of march he scorned to send out scouts ahead as was necessary in fighting Indians. He insisted on sending his Continental troops in solid order against an enemy who fought behind trees and stumps in any kind of order that suited his purpose. He committed all of the stupidities that vanity and overweening self-confidence could dictate, and, when the French in a despairing last-minute effort against overwhelming numbers had found easy victory, gave up his life on the field of battle. He was buried beneath the feet of the retreating troops so that their steps should obliterate from the fiendish enemy the location of his last resting place.

The English loss in this battle was 714 men killed and a shattering of their military prestige with all of the Indian people of the borderland. The French loss was 3 white men killed and 27 Indians. The access to their influence amongst the savage tribes because of their unexpected victory was much.

Fort Duquesne fell to the English in 1758 when 7,000 men under Brigadier General John Forbes slowly and circumspectly proceeded against it. The French deserted the post after attempting to destroy it and the English took possession November 25 of that year. A new fort was commenced under Forbes which stood on the Monongahela side of the city at the south end of the present West Street and between West and Liberty Streets. It was occupied in 1760 and was completely finished in the summer of 1761. The stone bomb-proof magazine stood until 1852 when the Pennsylvania Railroad built its freight terminal here.

Of the remainder of the line of French forts along the Ohio River there are no relics left, though memorials have been established at several points. The first of this Ohio River chain was Presque Isle on Lake Erie, now the little city of Erie, Pennsylvania. For some years after French domain in the New World Presque Isle was of importance and, indeed, for some years after the Revolution.

The post was taken by the English in 1759, and in 1763 fell a victim to Indian attack as a corollary to the Pontiac conspiracy which had as its object the complete extinction of English life in the West. The fort, a rectangle of earth and wooden palisades, stood on the west bank of Mill Creek and at the intersection with the shore of the lake. Here the veteran Indian fighter, General Wayne, died in 1796. In 1876 the State of Pennsylvania erected a block-house on the site of the old fort as a memorial. This block-house is now included in the grounds of the Pennsylvania Sailors and Soldiers' Home.

From Presque Isle there was a portage to Fort Le Bœuf, now the little city of Waterford, Pennsylvania.

STRONGHOLDS OF THE PAST

Fort Le Bœuf stood at High and Water Streets, Waterford, though there is at this point no sign of its existence. It was erected in 1753 and fell before Pontiac's far-reaching conspiracy in 1763.

Venango, the next of the French line of forts east of Pittsburgh (Duquesne), was the fore-runner of Franklin, Pennsylvania, and stood at Elk and Eighth Streets. Of Venango, too, no sign remains. It fell to the Indians in 1763.

South of Pittsburgh the English had a post at Brownsville, on the Ohio River, Pennsylvania, built in 1754, and known as Redstone Old Fort. The French had Fort Massac to which about one thousand troopers retired after the evacuation of Fort Duquesne. Later years also saw small fortifications developed on the Ohio River, some holding the potentialities of future greatness such as that at the falls of the Ohio River, which was to be the nucleus of the settlement of the present-day city of Louisville, Kentucky.

At the south end of Lake Erie during the French occupancy of the West stood Fort Sandusky which has given its name to the City of Sandusky of to-day. On the Maumee River, Indiana, was Fort Miamis, Miami of to-day.

In the early days of the French there had been a trading post at the site of the future great city of Chicago, but it remained for the United States, in 1803, to establish a formal fortification here, Fort Dearborn,

QUAINT AND HISTORIC FORTS

of bloody memory. Fort Dearborn, as every good Chicagoan knows, or ought to know, stood at the southern approach to the Rush Street bridge and extended a little across Michigan Avenue and somewhat into the river, as it now is. The ground rose into a little mound yielding a fine view of the surrounding flat prairie land. Here the pioneer soldiers erected a rude stockade of logs fifteen feet in height and enclosing a space sufficiently large to contain a small parade ground, officers' quarters, troop barracks, guard house, magazines and two blockhouses, one at the northwest and the other at the southeast corner of the palisade. This rude structure with its small garrison was the seed of the present-day great city.

Upon the outbreak of the War of 1812 General Hull, who was commanding the American army of the border, ordered the evacuation of Fort Dearborn, as the place was too remote to be adequately defended and as its possession meant no access of strength to the United States. There were at this time in the garrison four officers and fifty-four non-commissioned officers and privates under the leadership of Captain Nathan Heald. The wives of the two senior officers were with them and a number of the privates had, also, their families, so that the stockade contained twelve women and twenty children.

Though an experienced soldier, Captain Heald seems to have misjudged the temper of the hostile

Indians surrounding his post and to have too easily accepted their assurances of non-interference with the garrison as it left the fort. At all events, on August 15, 1812, Captain Heald evacuated his fort, and though the Indians allowed the little company—a long cavalcade—to proceed as far as the end of present-day Eighteenth Street without molestation, they then fell upon men, women and children indiscriminately. Of the company of Americans only a handful survived.

In 1816 Fort Dearborn was rebuilt and regarrisoned but after the Black Hawk war fell into disuse, and in 1837 was abandoned by the army. It was used for various purposes by different departments of the Federal government until 1857, when it was torn down except a small building which stood until the great fire of 1871. A commercial building now occupies the site which is commemorated by a small bronze tablet set into the wall by the Chicago Historical Society in 1880.

At the foot of Eighteenth Street at the point where the attack upon the devoted column commenced, a beautiful bronze monument has been erected depicting a scene from the massacre.

Fort Gage, Illinois, memorable as the first objective of George Rogers Clark in 1778, stood at the historic little village Kaskaskia, of French foundation, on the Kaskaskia River near the confluence of that stream with the Mississippi. In shape an oblong, 280 feet by 251 feet, constructed of squared timbers founded upon heavy earthwork, Fort Gage was never heavily garrisoned. It was the point to which the British retired when the crumbling walls of Fort Chartres would no longer hold them. In 1772 the garrison consisted of one officer and twenty soldiers. In 1778 when Clark reached the spot there was not a British soldier on duty and the fort was in command of a Frenchman.

Fort Clark, Illinois, was erected in 1813 on the site of the future city of Peoria, Illinois, and about where the Rock Island depot now stands. For several years it gave its name to the locality and was a post of importance garrisoned by rangers and United States troops. At one time it sustained a severe Indian attack

The foundation of Cincinnati, Ohio, was Fort Washington, which was in existence until after the War of 1812.

FORT INDEPENDENCE
(CASTLE WILLIAM)
CASTLE ISLAND—BOSTON HARBOR

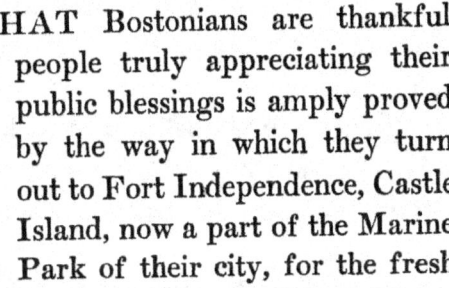HAT Bostonians are thankful people truly appreciating their public blessings is amply proved by the way in which they turn out to Fort Independence, Castle Island, now a part of the Marine Park of their city, for the fresh air and unexciting recreation it offers. Other citizens of other cities create parks from their historic places and, then, content to know that they have them when they want them, allot the day and night watchmen entire seclusion in these domains. With Bostonians it is different: On any bright and cheering day throngs can be found at the old fort, of various classes and of widely sundered poles of thought; but joined together in one great common heritage, a capacity for making use of that which they have and of taking their pleasure in a devout and noiseless manner not to be seen amongst the habitants of any other great American city.

It is a pleasant place, Castle Island, and the air there on a sunny day sweeping in from the great reaches of Boston's environing waters is a true elixir. The views in various directions are entrancing, showing, in one direction, wide expanses of blue with dim islands in the distance and cottony clouds overhead; in another, the shipping and sky-line of Boston harbor and the jumbled city. Geographically stated, Castle Island is a body of hard, rocky land, most of which is occupied by the historic old fort, and it is situated three miles from the head of Boston Harbor and two hundred yards from City Point, South Boston, to which it is connected by a wooden causeway. On the mainland, close at hand, lies Boston's famous Aquarium, where the frying fishes play!

Viewed from the head of the causeway, the fort is a very gay and martial figure though in sober earnest it has never fired a shot in anger in its life. Structurally speaking, it is a pentagonal, five-bastioned enclosure whose granite walls occupy all of the crest of the eminence which makes up the island. To the right, from this stand-point, one sees running off a long thin shallow strip of gravelly sand, which geologists assert has been a gift from the sea since the erection of the fort. Originally, they say, the main portion of the island was larger than it is now; so what was taken from one place seems to have been added on to another.

Passing over the causeway one sees to the left hand, across a ribbon of water, the island which Fort Winthrop crowns in a very modest and inconspicuous fashion. Passing over a draw-bridge one enters the reservation and finds one's self beneath the shadow of the walls of the fort and on the historic ground which its predecessors and itself have held in fief for many, many years.

FORT INDEPENDENCE FROM THE WATER, BOSTON, MASS.
Floating Hospital in Foreground

FORT WINTHROP FROM CASTLE ISLAND

Main Entrance
FORT INDEPENDENCE, CASTLE ISLAND, BOSTON, MASS.

FORT INDEPENDENCE

Benches may be found here and there for the rest-seeking wayfarer, but if one is inspired to wander around the walls he will find many interesting sights, and will be increasingly struck by the strength and formidableness of the abandoned military work, highly suggestive of the time when this island was the seat of military power of his Majesty, the King of England, in his colonies in America.

Historically speaking, Fort Independence is one of the oldest fortified spots in America and it was of exceeding great dignity in the early days of this country. But four years subsequent to the incorporation of the town of Boston, an interesting event which took place in 1630, Governor Winthrop and a party of his Puritans visited the island and, we are told, were detained by the ice without shelter for a day and a night. Nevertheless so well able were they all to detach themselves from their personal petty feelings that they each subscribed five pounds sterling of Great Britain from their own pockets in order to raise the place to the dignity of a fortified point. Two " Platforms " and a fort were to be erected, these platforms being in the nature of bateaux with guns mounted upon them. In the July following their adventure, which had taken place in early spring, they induced the legislature to consent to fortifying the place. The first fort has been described as a " castle with mud walls." The masonry was of lime made from oyster shells.

QUAINT AND HISTORIC FORTS

In 1644 the arrival of a French man-of-war in the harbor of Boston so alarmed the citizens of the province that the fort which had gone into decay was rebuilt at the expense of six neighboring towns. It was now constructed of pine trees, stone and earth, was 50 feet square inside and had walls 10 feet thick.

In 1665 the fort was repaired and enlarged,—the spirit of military preparedness which had been awakened by the Frenchman's arrival having evidently been kept up. A small castle was added with brick walls and three stories in height. There was a dwelling-room on the first floor of this " castle "; a lodging-room above; a gun-room over the latter furnished with " six very good saker guns " and three lesser guns were mounted upon the roof. In this same year occurred an event which gave rise to much curious speculation at the time and is retained in legend. On the 15th of July a stroke of lightning entered one of the rooms of the fort, killed Captain Richard Davenport, the commanding officer, and did not enter the magazine, only a step away, beyond a thin partition, where there was stored enough gunpowder to have blown the fort beyond the seas.

Still the spirit of fire had its due, for in 1673 the fort was burned to the ground. In the year following a new fort of stone was erected. It had four bastions, mounted thirty-eight guns and sixteen culverins, in addition to a water battery of six guns, and was a very imposing work indeed.

FORT INDEPENDENCE

In 1689 the people of Boston, favoring the Cromwellians in England, seized the royal governor, Edmund Andros, and placed him in confinement. They took possession of the castle and appointed Mr. John Fairweather commander to succeed Captain John Pipon.

But all dissension is smoothed down by the hand of Time. Under the administration of Sir Williams Phipps, an appointee of King William, the fort was named Castle William and the Crown donated a large sum of money toward the erection of a stronger structure. The ordnance then became 24 nine-pounders, 12 twenty-four pounders, 18 thirty-two pounders, and 18 forty-eight pounders; and the bastions became known by the names of the "Crown," the "Rose," the "Royal," and the "Elizabeth." This augmentation of strength was the more necessary as a French invasion of the New England colonies was apprehended.

And so we run on through the years: In 1716 Lieutenant Governor William Dummer, a well-known name in the history of Massachusetts, assumed command of Castle William, agreeable to orders from the Crown, and thereby incurred the ill-feeling of the general court of the province which heretofore had had prerogative in the appointment of a commandant. In 1740 the fort was repaired in anticipation of war with France and a new bastion mounting 20 forty-two pounders was created and named Shirley bastion.

Ordnance presented by the King arrived in 1744; a

second magazine was built in 1747; and a third added during Shirley's administration. In 1747 a riot occurred in Boston and the governor took refuge at the Castle. Upon assurance that his authority would be sustained the governor returned to the city two days after his flight.

On the 15th of August, 1757, Governor Pownal arrived to assume the government of the province. Sir William Pepperell, conqueror of Louisburg, held command of Castle William. In accordance with custom Sir William surrendered the key of the castle to the new executive and said, " Sir, I hand you the key of the province." Not outdone at all, Governor Pownal replied, " Sir, the interests of the province are in your heart. I shall always be glad, therefore, to see the key of the province in your hands." Thus the doughty old warrior was maintained in his command until his death in 1759.

In this same year died Captain Lieutenant John Larrabee, who had lived for fifty years on the island in the service of the Crown. In 1764 the Castle was used as an inoculation station during the ravages of a plague of smallpox which swept the little city.

It was about this time that the fort began to take part in the events with which Boston is associated before the outbreak of the American Revolution. Stamps by which revenue was expected to be raised from the colonies were brought to Boston in 1765 and for security

FORT INDEPENDENCE

were lodged in Castle William. Vigorous opposition in America caused the repealment of the act of which they were intended to be the tokens of enforcement and they were taken back to England at the expiration of not many months. These, it will be seen, were not the stamps which figured in the famous Boston Tea Party, but they were of the same nature. The maintenance of a large force of military at Castle William by the Crown in the years immediately following this was a source of irritation to the patriots of the day, and had an influence in determining the events which brought about the separation from the Mother Country.

Captain Sir Thomas Adams, who died on board the frigate *Romney*, was buried on Castle Island October 8, 1772, and his obsequies were conducted with great pomp. In removing earth to Fort Independence thirty years later his corpse, enclosed in a double coffin highly ornamented, but upon which the inscription had become illegible, was dug out, and, no one discovering at the time whose remains the coffin contained, it was committed to the common burying ground at the south point of the island where its resting-place was soon not to be distinguished from that of the common soldiers which surrounded it.

With this coffin necessarily others were removed, and one was favored with an inscription which betrayed, we may assume, either native simplicity or British sarcasm. It read: " Here lies the body of John, aged fifty years, a faithful soldier and a Desperate Good Gardner "!

It does not appear that the force quartered on the island was engaged in the first two battles of the Revolution. The commandant of the castle had been sent in February, 1776, to seize powder and other military stores at Salem; but he was delayed at the ferry by the militia until the objects of the depredation had been moved beyond his reach. He returned peaceably to the island. The same officer was ordered from Castle William at this time with five hundred men to draw the Americans, by a false attack, from their posts at Roxbury. The attack did not succeed and the burning of five or six houses in Dorchester was the only result.

In the meantime a formidable force of Americans was concentrated in the vicinity of Boston under Washington; so General Howe, the successor of General Gage, evacuated the town March 17, and the British fleet dropped below the Castle. The embarkation had been a scene of confusion and distress, it being the 27th of March before the transports were able to put to sea. At their departure the British troops threw into the water iron balls and shot, broke off the trunnions of the ordnance given to Castle William in 1740, destroyed the military stores and battery apparatus which they could not take with them and finally blew up the citadel, leaving the island a mass of ruins. Part of the British fleet lay in the lower harbor until June, when it was harassed by American troops under General Lincoln and raised the blockade of Boston Harbor after the exact duration of two years. With the British troops the seat of the war was removed from Massachusetts, and Castle Island was thenceforth, unmolested, in American possession.

Colonel John Turnbull was the officer sent by General Washington to take possession of the island after the evacuation. Lieutenant Colonel Paul Revere was stationed on the island from 1777 to 1779.

At the conclusion of the Revolution it was enacted by the legislature of Massachusetts that all criminals of the State under sentence of confinement should be removed to Castle Island. Pursuant to this law convicts were sent to the island, and though their number never exceeded ninety their audacity taxed the vigilance of the garrison; they made several bold, fruitless efforts to escape, and in their mutinies some were killed and some wounded. Others met their death while endeavoring to form subterranean passages. Stephen Burroughs, whose extensive forgeries gave him great notoriety, here learned the art of a nailer, and in his published memoirs has publicly boasted of his Castle Island exploits.

It was with reluctance that the legislature of Massachusetts could bring itself to the cession of the Castle to the United States government, but the State was nevertheless willing to sacrifice the partial advantage to the public good and, October, 1798, passed an act by which the transfer was accomplished.

QUAINT AND HISTORIC FORTS

In 1799 President Adams visited the fort and was received with due honors. It was at this time that the name was changed to Independence. With regard to this, Captain Nehemiah Freeman wrote: "The baptism was not indecorous and the godfather (President Adams) is certainly unexceptionable; but Fort Independence must count some years before he can entirely divest his elder brother of his birthright; and though the mess of pottage might have been sold in 1776 yet the title of 'The Castle' is rather endearing to the inhabitants of Massachusetts and is still bestowed by the greater part as the only proper appellation."

A new fort was now planned and constructed under the direction of Lieutenant Colonel Louis Toussard, who was inspector of all of the posts of the Eastern seaboard. The first stone was laid May 7, 1801, and the whole superstructure was raised from an original design not influenced by the structure standing hitherto. On the 23d of June, 1802, the national colors were first displayed at the new fort. The work was a barbette fortification and was not materially different from the present-day structure.

The five bastions of the fort were named, in 1805, as follows: First, "Winthrop" after Governor Winthrop, under whose auspices the first fort was built; second, "Shirley," who repaired Castle William, erected other works and made it the strongest fortified point in British America; third, "Hancock," after the first gov-

HARBOR SIDE, FORT INDEPENDENCE, BOSTON, MASS.

FORT INDEPENDENCE

ernor of the commonwealth of Massachusetts, under whose administration new works were thrown up; fourth, "Adams," after John Adams, who bestowed its present name upon the fort and collected materials for its construction; fifth, "Dearborn," after General Dearborn, Secretary of War, under whose auspices Fort Independence was actually rebuilt.

In 1833 the garrison was withdrawn and the post given over to the Engineers Department for constructing a new work, in effect a modernification and improved edition of the former structure. Work was prosecuted at intervals during the succeeding eighteen years. The post was regarrisoned July 4, 1851. The garrison was finally withdrawn November 25, 1879, and Fort Independence went out of service.

Not long after that the island was deeded to the city by the Federal War Department for use as a public park. That it could ever be of service as a fighting man now in its old age is extremely improbable. The defence of Boston depends upon batteries located at a far greater distance from the city.

To the north from Fort Independence can be seen the island upon which Fort Winthrop is situated and in the distance at the mouth of the harbor can be seen dimly the site of Fort Warren. Both of these posts have reached a dignified age, but neither has years or historical importance approximating that of their big brother.

FORT COLUMBUS, OR JAY
GOVERNOR'S ISLAND—NEW YORK HARBOR

Even Governor's Island, once a smiling garden, appertaining to the sovereigns of the province, was now covered with fortifications, inclosing a tremendous block-house,—so that this once peaceful island resembled a fierce little warrior in a big cocked hat, breathing gunpowder and defiance to the world!—Washington Irving, "Knickerbocker's New York."

THE graceful little island of Washington Irving is described in a recent publication of the government printing office at Washington after the following eloquent fashion: " Irregular in form but approaches nearly the segment of an oblate spheroid, its longest diameter being from north to south, and about 800 yards in length. The transverse diameter is about 500 yards. It has an elevation above high-water mark of 20 feet, and its face is smooth and green, with a rich carpet of grass."

On the top of the highest feature of this smooth, green face with its rich carpet of grass is Fort Columbus, more properly known by its ancient name of Fort Jay.

No doubt you will find it hard to visualize the importance of Fort Jay. It is the head-quarters of the Department of the East of the army of the United States, you may be told. Yes, you will answer indifferently, it is a quiet little place, not nearly so noisy as the roaring forties of Broadway; it keeps to itself and is a sort of annex to the foot of the city to prevent the sea-

ENTRANCE TO FORT COLUMBUS (FORT JAY) GOVERNOR'S ISLAND, NEW YORK HARBOR

Fort Washington Point. Fort Lee on Opposite Shore

Where was Fort Amsterdam; the Customs House
FORT SITES IN PRESENT-DAY NEW YORK CITY

FORT COLUMBUS, OR JAY

ward view from the Battery being without variety! Yet once on a time, not much more than a hundred years ago, Fort Jay was of so great importance to the city that the citizens all, rich men, poor men, beggarmen, and thieves (then, too), turned out in a body to build up the place overnight.

The first point of land ever occupied in New York by the Dutch was Governor's Island, we are told on the excellent authority of Joseph Dankers and Sluyter, of Wueward, in Frusland, in "A Voyage to The American Colonies in 1679-80": "In its mouth (East River) before the city, between the city and Red Hook on Long Island, lies Noten Island (Governor's Island) opposite the fort, the first place the Hollanders ever occupied in the bay. It is now only a farm with a house and a place upon it where the governor keeps a parcel of sheep."

The fort here referred to was not Jay but Fort Amsterdam, later Fort George, of historic memory, which stood on Manhattan where the Customs House of New York City now is. "Red Hook on Long Island" later was fortified, too, forming one of the line of defences captured by the British from the Americans in their descent upon New York in the early days of the Revolution. The Indian name for Governor's Island was Pagganck, and Noten,—as above written,—or Nutten, or Nooten, came about from the abundance of nuts which could be found on the island.

In 1637, the redoubtable Wouter Van Twiller, first

governor of the colony under the New Amsterdam company of which he had been a director, secured for his personal use the island. It is fair to look at this gentleman inquisitively. "The renowned Wouter (or Walter) Van Twiller was descended from a long line of Dutch Burgomasters," says Washington Irving, "who had successively dozed away their lives, and grown fat upon the bench of magistracy in Rotterdam; and who had comported themselves with such singular wisdom and propriety that they were never either heard or talked of— which, next to being universally applauded, should be the object of ambition of all magistrates and rulers. . . . many a dunderpate, like the owl, the stupidest of birds, comes to be considered the very type of wisdom. This, by the way, is a casual remark which I would not for the universe have it thought I apply to Governor Van Twiller. It is true he was a man shut up within himself, like an oyster, and rarely spoke except in monosyllables; but then it was allowed he seldom said a foolish thing. So invincible was his gravity that he was never known to laugh or even to smile through the whole course of a long and prosperous life. Nay, if a joke were uttered in his presence, that set light-minded hearers in a roar, it was observed to throw him into a state of perplexity. Sometimes he would deign to inquire into the matter, and when, after much explanation, the joke was made as plain as a pike-staff, he would continue to smoke his pipe in silence and at length, knocking out the ashes, would exclaim, ' Well, I see nothing in all that to laugh about.'

"The person of this illustrious old gentleman was formed and proportioned as though it had been moulded by the hands of some cunning Dutch statuary, as a model of majesty and lordly grandeur. He was exactly five feet six inches in height, and six feet five inches in circumference. His head was a perfect sphere and of such stupendous dimensions that Dame Nature with all her sex's ingenuity would have been puzzled to construct a neck capable of supporting it; wherefore she wisely declined the attempt and settled it firmly on the top of his backbone just between the shoulders. His body was oblong and particularly capacious at bottom; which was wisely ordained by Providence, seeing that he was a man of sedentary habits and very averse to the idle labor of walking. His legs were short but sturdy in proportion to the weight they had to sustain; so that when erect he had not a little the appearance of a beer-barrel on skids. His face, that infallible index of the mind, presented a vast expanse unfurrowed by any of those lines and angles which disfigure the human countenance with what is termed expression. Two small gray eyes twinkled feebly in the midst, like two stars of lesser magnitude in a hazy firmament, and his full-fed cheeks, which seemed to have taken toll of everything that went into his mouth, were curiously mottled and streaked with dusky red, like a Spitzenberg apple."

QUAINT AND HISTORIC FORTS

After the seizure of the colony by the British in 1664, the island became a perquisite of the governor's office, a sort of retreat from care for the occupant of that harassed position, and was developed into a smiling garden. At this time it became known as Governor's Island, the name that has become its official designation on the charts of the present day.

The first immigrants to New York under the English were assigned by the council to Nutten Island for detention until the presence or non-presence of contagious disease in their ranks could be proved. These immigrants were about fifty Palatines who had been driven from their home land by the war between Louis XIV and Holland and Austria. Subsequently 10,000 followed these first fifty unfortunate exiles. The island thus became the first quarantine station of the city of New York.

During the wars of the Spanish Succession until the Treaty of Utrecht in 1713 the people of the colonies of British North America were in constant dread of attack by the French navy and during this time it was urged continually that Governor's Island should be changed from a garden to a fortified spot. Notwithstanding this fact the successive executives Slaughter, Fletcher and Cornbury did nothing toward carrying out the desires of their subjects.

It was a happy-go-lucky, careless era. Indeed when one looks back upon the perils of the early colonies and how they were survived it is like looking back upon the perils of childhood and wondering how one ever managed to get through. The colonies " just growed," which is true of a variety of things in this world, no doubt.

During Governor Cornbury's administration, fifteen thousand pounds (a value in present day terms of far beyond seventy-five thousand dollars) was appropriated for building a fort upon Governor's Island, but Governor Cornbury used the money to build a pleasure house instead, to which he and succeeding governors might retire from press of business.

Governor Cornbury, we may believe, was an edifying addition to the staid burgher circles of old New York. He was a small, shrimpish man, we are told, and inordinately vain. Being a cousin to her most Christian Majesty, Queen Anne, to which circumstance he owed his appointment, and having been assured that he resembled her hugely in appearance, he was in the habit of dressing himself like a woman and posing upon the balcony of his home,—that New Yorkers might be thrilled by a reflection of royalty. Despite his royal connections his household was most impecunious and his wife gained a reputation for borrowing things which she had no intention of ever giving back. Whenever the executive coach would be seen going the round of the streets on social duties bent, the good wives who might expect visits from her ladyship would say, it is said, " Quick, put away that fancy work and that vase " (or this and that), " Kathrine! Her ladyship is about to call upon us."

QUAINT AND HISTORIC FORTS

Father Time strolled on through the terms of the various royal governors noting their idiosyncrasies and continually hearing the cry that Governor's Island should be fortified, but not by any of these gentlemen did he discover action taken. It was not until after the Continental Congress, October 6, 1775, directed that means should be immediately devised to make New York defensible that the little city one morning woke up to find that there were rudimentary fortifications on Governor's Island. Of course these fortifications were supplementary to the fort on the main island upon which the city chiefly depended, Fort George. This was the name the English had given to Fort Amsterdam's successor, an enlarged and strengthened edition of its original.

Of little avail did all of these works prove, however, for the English, after the battle of Long Island, August 27, 1776, were easily masters of the Americans in that part of the world. On August 30th, Admiral Howe sailed up New York Bay and anchored near the island, and the city of New York passed into British possession, not to be surrendered until the close of the war.

The little force of men on Governor's Island under the command of Colonel Prescott abandoned the place on the approach of the British. One man was injured by a bullet in the arm as they were pulling away from the island. The place was garrisoned by the British during their occupancy of New York and was fortified more extensively than it ever had been before.

FORT COLUMBUS, OR JAY

The site of all of these works was the site of present-day Fort Columbus or Fort Jay.

After the Revolution the value of Governor's Island as a place of fortification was not taken advantage of and the works were allowed to fall into decay. In 1784 Governor Clinton leased the spot to a certain Dr. Price as the site for a hotel and race course. This course was open during 1785 and 1786 and had staged upon it many exciting trials of speed.

We have seen Governor's Island as a flowery retreat for the governors of New York from the cares of office, and we have looked in upon it in the charge of the rough soldiery of England. We now see it as the scene of the dissipations of the rabble and the lusty young sports of the old city. Yet another day is in store for the historic spot.

After the retirement of Washington from the presidency the irritation between France and this country became intense, and fears were entertained of conflict between the European nation and its young former protégé. Agitation began once more in New York for the building up of the defensive works on Governor's Island. Pressing recommendations were made to the federal authorities. The story may be taken up and carried on here in the words of a government report:

"The Secretary of War reported, December 19, 1794, that one bastion commanding two low batteries had been undertaken and was in a considerable state of forwardness, but observed that the works being only sodded would not stand very long. On January 18, 1796, the Secretary reported to the Senate that Governor's Island had been fortified with a fort made of earth and two batteries, under its protection, partly lined with brick masonry; that there had been erected two hot air furnaces, a large powder magazine and a barracks for the garrison; on February 10, 1797, that no alterations had been made since January 1796, except in the repairs and such additions as could be made to the garrison. During this time there had been expended by the general government on the fortifications of the island as follows: 1794, $1,327; in 1795, $6,866.54; in 1796, $1,124.

"But now the apprehension of a French invasion caused such clamor for protection among the people that immediate attention by the general government was bestowed upon properly fortifying Governor's Island. Thirty thousand one hundred and seventeen dollars was at once appropriated to be expended upon the fort, which now became known as Fort Jay. Such was the fervor of the day that the professors and students of Columbia College went in a body to Governor's Island and worked on the fortifications with shovels and wheelbarrows.

"Liberal appropriations were made by Congress in the three succeeding years for completing and improving the fort. In 1799, Congress appropriated $30,116.18; in 1800, $20,124; in 1801, $10,338.05. No further im-

FORT LAFAYETTE FROM FORT HAMILTON, NEW YORK

FORT COLUMBUS, OR JAY

provements were made until 1806, when Fort Jay with the whole of its buildings was demolished except the walled counterscarp, the gate, the sally-port, the magazine, and two barracks; all the rest was removed to give place for a work of durable materials. On the site of the old fort a new one, Fort Columbus, was erected, an inclosed pentagonal work with four bastions of masonry, calculated for one hundred guns, being of the same shape on three sides as Fort Jay, with the addition of fourteen feet on each side, and on the north side of a ravelin, with two retired casemates. Such was Fort Columbus when it was completed in 1809."

Despite the flurried haste of New Yorkers to have the fort completed, despite the unprecedented exertions of the Columbia students with shovels and wheelbarrows, Fort Columbus, or Jay as it has been rebaptized of recent years in military circles, has never been in active service.

Indeed, during the war of 1812, only three years after its completion, the need of a post farther out to sea than this called for the erection of that quaint little brick strong-box just off present-day Fort Hamilton known as Fort Lafayette. It was called originally Fort Diamond but was renamed in honor of the great Frenchman on his visit to this country in 1824. Overshadowed by its great modern neighbor (Fort Hamilton), the little fortification is rarely observed, but it is still in active service and might give good account of itself if called

QUAINT AND HISTORIC FORTS

upon to do so, better account in fact than its sire nestling close to America's greatest city.

Not far from Fort Jay on Governor's Island is a little work whose name is not unfamiliar to New Yorkers. It is Castle Williams. Begun in 1807, it was completed in 1811 and as a military weapon has never been of service to the city which it was created to help protect. As a landmark in the harbor, however, it has acquired some little distinction solely through merit of the years, just as some men live through an entirely commonplace youth and middle age to become in their last years notable figures in their communities as classmates of Father Time.

At about the time that Castle Williams was being constructed, a similar work was in erection just off the Battery, Manhattan, on a ledge of rocks now a part of the city itself. This was Fort Clinton, which is the Castle Garden, or Aquarium, of the present day. Fort Jay and Castle Williams, Fort Clinton and the Battery were the outing places of New Yorkers before the Civil War. To the Island or the Battery did the residents of the city repair for air and recreation on holidays and Sundays. An illuminating picture of this phase of the city's life is drawn by Abram C. Dayton in his "Last Days of Knickerbocker Life in New York."

"Castle Garden, the legend says," he writes, "was created to protect the city against invasion. Whether these invaders were to be New Jersey Indians armed with bows and arrows or Staten Island pirates bent upon destruction with popguns and firecrackers is not related; but it is certain a very limited force would have been required to effect an entrance through its brick walls. About the time we write of its loud-mouthed armament had been removed" (about 1860): "it had been placed by special orders from somewhere on a peace footing. It was neither a concert saloon, an opera house, nor a receptacle for needy immigrants; but the old white-washed barn was devoted to the restaurant business on a very limited scale, as ice cream, lemonade, and sponge cake constituted the list of delicacies from which to select. The ticket of admission required to pass its portcullis cost one shilling; but that was a mere form instituted to guarantee perfect decorum, for it was redeemed as cash in exchange for either of the above specified articles of refreshment. At the close of a summer day its frowning battlements were crowded with listeners eager to catch a strain of martial music wafted from Governor's Island.

"Rabineau's swimming bath was moored to the wooden bridge which connected the old fort with the Battery grounds; and on its roof protected by an awning might be seen, after banking hours on summer afternoons, substantial citizens comfortably seated and refreshing themselves after their bath with the sea breeze, accompanied by mint julep and sherry cobblers."

Prior to 1852, Fort Columbus was for several different short periods of time empty of troops, but since that year it has always contained a garrison. In addition to being the head-quarters of the Department of the East, the old post is now used as a military prison and as a landing-place for the aërial branch of the army.

A visit to Governor's Island to-day is a pleasant excursion for a stranger in new New York and the port would be a new sight for most New Yorkers, so unfamiliar are familiar places to those who are closest to them. One must have a pass from the military authorities at the island to go through the old works, but this can be secured upon written application without great difficulty by any citizen of the United States.

A fine figure of a place Fort Columbus seems to be, —rather a braggart in its way! It spreads out, girded by its "dry moat," over the crest of the hill on which it is placed, in a truly threatening attitude. But one does not need to be told that this is hollow sham. A single shell from a modern engine of war would, no doubt, finish all of its pretensions.

Looking from its sunny interior beyond its battlemented walls one can see the airy fabric of New York's marvellous sky-scrapers against the eastern sky, a poignant contrast to the old stronghold. Age and youth! In this comparison the fort has that advantage which always inheres in years, it has seen youth grow from infancy and it knows the quick passing of all things.

TICONDEROGA
LAKE CHAMPLAIN—NEW YORK

NE could desire to be at the bold promontory of Ticonderoga in 1609, when the virgin woodside gazed anxiously at Samuel Champlain, that intrepid French adventurer, as he fired his bell-mouthed musket against the mystified Iroquois. The echoes of the discharge of this ancient firearm were seldom allowed to die in these wildernesses until the beginning of the Nineteenth Century, until the complete ascendency of white man over red had been established.

Standing upon the ramparts of the old fort one may to-day easily imagine himself in a virgin forest world. Civilization has set her hand upon Lake Champlain, but her work is not obtrusively near to the fort. The hills to the rear are still wooded; the waters, to front and sides, are clear; and the same blue bends over all. The immediate surroundings are little different from those in which Champlain fought his opera-bouffe fight and inaugurated the long struggle between red men and white in this part of the world.

We must remember that in 1609 the French had already taken hold of New France. They had a querulous, contumacious baby of a colony on the Saint Lawrence at Quebec and to this point came many curious red men. With some of these red men the French had formed alliance.

One tribe of these allies had seen the thunderous cannon and guns of the French and had suggested that these weapons be taken out and turned upon some of the ancient enemies of that tribe. The idea had appealed to Champlain as eminently a clever one, and with eleven other Frenchmen armed with arquebuses and clad in light armor he had set out, on the 28th of June, with three hundred amiable red people. The party proceeded up the Saint Lawrence as far as the river which afterward became known as the Richelieu and here paused for feasting and a carouse. During the course of this ceremony three-quarters of the Indians became huffy over a trifle and left for their homes in a hurry, reducing the expedition to eleven Frenchmen and seventy-five Indians.

As the expedition proceeded the Indians consulted their tutelary spirits. A small circular tent would be raised of skins over saplings and into this would crawl the medicine man with shudders and groans. A grand commotion would be heard and then the voice of the spirit would speak in a thin, treble squeak. The tent structure would dance violently around and the savage spectators would feel that their divinity was having a very busy time.

At length the French and Indians approached the lake which was to bear the name of the white chief, and made their way upon it in canoes. They came to a

FORT TICONDEROGA, LAKE CHAMPLAIN, N. Y.

The Mess Hall

A Council Room
INTERIOR VIEWS OF FORT TICONDEROGA, N. Y.

promontory of land which bore the resounding Iroquois name of Ticonderoga, or "meeting of waters," in recognition of the fact that the waters of Lakes George and Champlain come together at the base of the eminence. Here they met a flotilla of skin canoes bearing a large war party of Iroquois and the issue of this little trip of Champlain's may now be said to have been fairly joined.

The Iroquois, not being much given to fighting on water, paddled to land, while the invaders decided to spend the night in their canoes. All night long the air resounded with yells and epithets and bandied menaces, but, at length, morning broke and put an end to the unseemly clamor. The Frenchmen were concealed in the bottoms of canoes until a dramatic moment should arrive to show themselves. Their companions landed and now that they had come to their desire were filled with terror of the Iroquois, calling loudly for Champlain to come forth and destroy his opponents with thunder and lightning. The doughty Frenchman, feeling secure in his armor and his arms, threw aside the skins which covered him, and strode forth like a white god in shining raiment. The gallant Iroquois were filled with consternation at the sight of him. Raising his arquebus, into which he had stuffed four balls, he fired at short range, slaying two chiefs and wounding one. A second shot caused the defenders to break and flee, and this gave Champlain's allies opportunity to kill and capture to their hearts' content.

QUAINT AND HISTORIC FORTS

The expedition made its way back to Quebec filled with exultation. Thus did Ticonderoga come upon the pages of history.

This engagement of Champlain's—incidental as it seems—had far-reaching consequences in the destiny of France in the New World. By the slaughter of the Iroquois Champlain mortally offended the Five Nations, which was an all-powerful Indian confederation, incurring an enmity never remitted. The alliance of the Long House with the English was one of the factors that helped to turn the scale in their favor in the long contest for balance of power which the years brought about between France and England in the New World.

On this very same day of July, 1609, while Champlain's arquebus was frightening the solitudes of this leafy part of the wild New World, a little vessel known as the *Half Moon* was in anchor on the New England coast while the carpenter fitted a new foremast. A few weeks later the *Half Moon* was in the Hudson and had come to anchor above present Troy in the precincts over which the warriors of the Long House kept watch. Thus does the Muse of History play different parts with two hands.

Time passed and French and Indian war parties again and again went by the point of land on which Ticonderoga now stands, bent on marauding and harrying the English villages. Lake Champlain and Lake George had become part of the great highway between

TICONDEROGA

French world and English world. Finally, in 1735, Crown Point, the fore-runner of Ticonderoga, was established by the French as an organized centre of power and an outpost thrown toward the English. Twenty years after this Ticonderoga came into prominence.

The year 1755 was a doleful one for the English colonies. It was the year of Braddock's defeat. In January, Shirley, governor of Massachusetts, proposed an attack on Crown Point. The other colonies were taken with the idea and raised levies of men and funds. A heterogeneous army was the result under the leadership of William Johnson, of New York, with the rank of Major-general, separately bestowed upon him by each of the colonies taking part. His selection was due not only to his immense personal popularity but to his influence in the Long House of the Five Nations as well, no other white man of his time having so much authority with the dwellers in the forest. Of white men he had altogether about eight thousand and he had his Indian allies.

That in an army which included men from Massachusetts, New York, Connecticut, Rhode Island and New Hampshire there should be some bickering and disagreements was inevitable, but, at length, the column reached the foot of Lake George, which had become known to its French acquaintances as Lac le Sacrement. Now it received a new baptism. "I have given it the name of Lake George," wrote Johnson to the Lords of Trade, "not only in honor of His Majesty but to ascertain (assert) his undoubted dominion here." Lake George it has been ever since. A camp was made where, after a time, Fort William Henry was built, and a most unmilitary camp it was, if we can believe the accounts of contemporaries. Though a dense forest gave cover for an enemy to its very borders, no effort was made to clear away the trees. Painted Indians lounged around, traders squabbled together, and New England clergymen preached to the savages long Calvinistic sermons.

Meanwhile the French at Crown Point were preparing a surprise for Johnson. Large forces under the German Baron Dieskau had come up, and Dieskau had assumed command of the united troops. He had no thought of waiting to be attacked. He told his men to be in readiness to move at a moment's notice. Officers were to take nothing with them but one spare shirt, one spare pair of shoes, a blanket, a bearskin and provisions for twelve days. The Indians were to make up their minds not to take scalps until the enemy had been entirely defeated, because the operation of taking a scalp was too lengthy a proceeding, and kept them from killing other men. Then Dieskau moved on to a promontory which commanded both Lake Champlain and Lake George. It was a high wooden mount with a magnificent view of the waters; in short, our old friend Ticonderoga.

The German baron for a time made camp here, the first formal military occupation of this point, but at length, being misinformed by an American prisoner, who had been threatened with torture, as to the force Johnson had, he prepared to move in haste and with deadly intent against the American colonials. News of Braddock's defeat had just then become general information, and throughout the ranks of the ignorant white men of the French party and of all their savage allies ran an unwarranted contempt for English bravery based on accounts of that lamentable massacre. Dieskau left a part of his force at Ticonderoga, and embarking with the rest in canoes and bateaux made his way through the narrow southern part of Lake Champlain to where the town of Whitehall now stands, a point at which they pitched camp.

The close of the next day found them well on toward Johnson and on the day after that the battle of Lake George took place. It is unnecessary to go into detail about this. The first part of the day went against the Americans, who had foolishly sent out against Dieskau, when they received word of his approach, an insufficient number of white and red forces; but the end of the day found the Americans victorious. Dieskau was badly wounded and was a prisoner.

The story goes that a delegation of chiefs waited

upon Johnson while Dieskau was in his cabin. The unwilling guest made some comment about them to his host after their departure. "Yes, they wish to be allowed to burn you," was the response. Johnson took extraordinary pains that the French leader should not fall into the hands of his savages, and Dieskau died a peaceful death as a result of his wounds several years later, midst the civilization of Bath, England, whence he had gone in hopes of being benefited by the waters.

Johnson commenced now to build Fort William Henry at one end of Lake George, and the French, quickly recovering from their set-back, began building at the other end, on the site of Dieskau's camp, the famous Fort Ticonderoga. The building of the French fort consumed the greater part of 1756 and 1757, and was consummated under the reign, in Canada, of Vaudreuil.

The original plan of Fort Ticonderoga was of a bastion fort, but afterwards star-shaped outer walls, following plans of the great Vauban, were added. The French built solidly in their various military works, and Fort Ticonderoga was an enduring and strong construction.

We have seen Fort William Henry and Fort Ticonderoga started as rivals. The survivor of these two was Ticonderoga, and the destruction of Fort William Henry was the occasion of one of the saddest and most horrible massacres in American history. In 1757 the

TICONDEROGA

Marquis de Montcalm, chief of the French king's forces in Canada, was at Ticonderoga and with him was the Chevalier de Levis with about eight thousand regulars, Canadians and Indians. The troopers and the irregular forces were camped around the walls of Ticonderoga near the lake and in the rear of the fort where the eminence of land on which the fort stands continues in a gentle plateau before commencing its descent. A colorful, picturesque camp it was, with its red Indians, its half-breed whites, and its careless soldiery. The officers and gentlemen of consequence were lodged in the fort where they ate in the mess hall and lounged and smoked and drank at leisure.

With his eight thousand men Montcalm set forth on the first of August, 1757, across the little neck of land which divides Lake Champlain from Lake George, leaving a small detachment to hold the fort, and made his way along Lake George to near Fort William Henry. His Britannic Majesty's stronghold was solidly built and was in command of a capable officer, Lieutenant Colonel Munro, a brave Scotchman, but its garrison was insufficient, and reinforcements were never sent. Montcalm attacked.

So well did the little band of beleaguered men contest their position, that when inevitably they surrendered very favorable terms were offered. It was agreed that the English troops should march out with the honors of war and be escorted to Fort Edward by a detachment of French troops; that they should not serve for eighteen months, and that all French prisoners captured in America since the war began should be given up within three months. The stores, munitions, and artillery were to be the prize of the victors, except that the garrison, in recognition of its bravery, was to retain one field-piece. The Indian chiefs were consulted in the making of these terms and agreed to them by shaking of the hands.

When the capitulation took place, a scene very different from that which had been anticipated was to be viewed. The Indians, excited by the presence of so many captives, as they considered the English prisoners of war, were not to be restrained and, though measures were taken to hold them in rein, fell upon the helpless men and women and butchered them mercilessly.

The morning after the massacre soldiers were set to work destroying all that remained of Fort William Henry.

The year that followed the massacre—1758—brought the most formidable looking and least effective of all of the attacks against Ticonderoga. The English, thoroughly incensed at the loss of Fort William Henry, had set themselves with determination to destroy Ticonderoga and to this end had raised a great force of regular soldiery, provincial militia and those invaluable irregular border troops of which Roger's rangers are a good example, and had placed them under the command of General Abercrombie. The whole body lay encamped in June, 1758, at the head of Lake George, within easy striking distance of the terrible French stronghold. It numbered nearly fifteen thousand men, all told. Montcalm's forces were not one-fourth so numerous and the great French leader was sadly sure of disaster to himself and his men.

That disaster did not, indeed, fall upon the French as the outcome of this undertaking on the part of the British is to be ascribed primarily to the unfortunate choice of a leader which they had had made for them and to Providence, which early in the campaign removed from their midst the only military talent which they seem to have possessed. Abercrombie was a political heritage of corrupt powers in England, where the government had undergone a great reconstruction since the horrors of Fort William Henry, and had been kept in authority solely on account of pressure which could be brought to bear at home. Lord Pitt had appointed as second in command of the expedition one of the few military geniuses of his age,—as all of his contemporaries admitted,—the young Lord Howe, elder brother of the more famous Sir William Howe, who later commanded His Majesty's forces in America against the rebellious colonies. "The noblest Englishman that has appeared in my time and the best soldier in the British army," said Wolfe, of him. In a minor skirmish at the very first of the reconnoitring around Ticonderoga

QUAINT AND HISTORIC FORTS

he was killed by an Indian's bullet, and the English troops were left to flounder on from one blunder to another.

The last part of the march against Ticonderoga was commenced on the morning of July 4 and by July 6 the soldiers were at the head of Lake George and in touch with the enemy in Ticonderoga just over a ridge of woods.

The ridge of land on which Ticonderoga is situated continues northwest without the sharp decline that marks its topography in every other direction. Along this spine, then, the English attack might be expected, so in this quarter Montcalm had had barriers built of fallen trees, laid together so as to form a zig-zag parapet nine feet in height and with a platform behind, from which the French soldiers might shoot without exposing themselves. Along the entire front of this barricade the ground was strewn with sharp-pointed boughs. Obviously it was not a position that infantry could take without the aid of artillery.

Yet, under Abercrombie's command, the English advanced against this work without waiting for the cannon which they had with them to be brought up. Between noon and nightfall of July 7 they made six gallant assaults without result. A perfect hades of shot and flame those logs became. The scene has been described by one of Roger's rangers who took part in the action, and his description, found in an old letter, was published a decade ago in Harper's Magazine, by one of his descendants. " The maze of fallen trees with their withered leaves hanging broke their ranks and the French Retrenchment blazed fire and death " he wrote. " They advanced bravely up but all to no good purpose and hundreds there met their death. My dear Joseph I have the will but not the way to tell you all that I saw that awful afternoon. I have since been in many battles and skirmishes but I have never witnessed such slaughter and such wild fighting as the British storm of Ticonderoga. We became mixed up—Highlanders, Grenadiers, Light Troops, Rangers and all, and we beat against that mass of logs and maze of fallen timber and we beat in vain. I was once carried right up to the breastwork, but we were stopped by the bristling mass of sharpened branches, while the French fire swept us front and flank. The ground was covered deep with dying men and, as I think it over now, I can remember nothing but the fruit bourne by the tree of war, for I looked upon so many wondrous things that July day that I could not set them downe at all. We drew off after seeing that no human valour could take that work. We Rangers then skirmished with the French colony troops and the Canada Indians until dark while our people rescued the wounded, and then we fell back. The Army was utterly demoralized and made a headlong retreat during which many wounded men were left to die in the woods."

QUAINT AND HISTORIC FORTS

On the day following his victory Montcalm had a great cross planted in the battle-field bearing words, composed by himself, which have been translated by Parkman as follows:

Soldier and chief and rampart's strength are nought;
Behold the Conquering Cross! 'Tis God the triumph wrought.

The old fort was to fall into English hands the next year, however, when Amherst, commander-in-chief of the English forces in America, advanced against it with a force of British and Americans. Montcalm had hurried to the defence of Quebec with the greater part of his force and Ticonderoga was in the command of Boulemarque, a capable officer, but one no more able than any other man to accomplish the impossible. He could not hold the position with the inconsiderable force he had against that opposed to him. A stroke of Providence was not to be anticipated a second time. So, while the British encamped under the walls of the fort prepared to attack it the next day, Boulemarque set a fuse to the powder magazine and marched his men out. There was a great explosion and a rending of walls, and Ticonderoga's besiegers knew that the fort was their prize.

Through the rest of the French and Indian War, which was from this time forward a tale of uninterrupted success for the British arms, Ticonderoga played no part except that of a garrisoned English possession.

Its walls were repaired where Boulemarque's match had shattered them.

The prestige of the fort had now become such that in the fermenting first days of the outbreak in the colonies against the Mother Country it was conceived that the seizure of the place would have an immense moral effect in the colonies. A sturdy Vermont man, Ethan Allen, with his Green Mountain boys, was given the task of seizing it. In early spring, 1775, Allen approached the old Indian stronghold now held by merely a handful of British, who had no idea that the Americans were in action against them. One cannot depreciate the tenacity of purpose and hardiness which carried Ethan Allen and his men through the inhospitable wilderness to success in their enterprise, but the military valor of the action was not great. With his men Allen crept up to the unsuspecting stronghold, seized the sentry, and, while his men scattered through the fort making prisoners of its inmates, thundered at the door of the commanding officer: " Open in the name of the Great Jehovah and the Continental Congress." While knowing little of the Continental Congress, the officer submitted to the inevitable.

The news of Allen's exploit was spread through the colonies and was a determining influence with many undecided Americans. His resounding phrase has been repeated by school-boys many times since and is perhaps more familiarly associated with the name of Ticonderoga than any of the great exploits which have marked its past.

For a time the Americans held on to the fort. In 1776 a large force was concentrated here, since it guarded that very vital means of access to the heart of the colonies which the British persistently tried to make use of. It was from this point that in 1776 Benedict Arnold set forth with a small fleet of vessels to attack Sir Guy Carleton at Valcour Island. Though the American fleet was almost entirely destroyed, it, nevertheless, set back the plans of the British one year and delayed their projected invasion from the north that long.

In 1777 Burgoyne invested the fort and, by dragging some guns to the top of Mount Defiance, an eminence which commands Ticonderoga, caused General Arthur St. Clair of the American forces to evacuate the place. Burgoyne occupied the fort for a passing visit but was soon on his way into the colonies by the ancient trail which war parties for generations had trod, fortunately, for the colonies, to meet defeat and loss of his army at the battle of Saratoga.

The fort remained in the hands of the British until after the surrender of Yorktown, though Colonel Brown of Massachusetts made a brave effort to take it once more. During the War of 1812 it listened to the guns of McDonough's improvised fleet in action with the

TICONDEROGA

British, but it had no active part in this action or in this war, itself.

In 1806 the property on which the old fort stands was leased from Union and Columbia colleges by William F. Pell of New York, it being a part of a State grant to these institutions. Mr. Pell built a summer cottage for himself and, in 1816, purchased the land. The cottage was destroyed in 1825 and a second building known as the Pavilion was erected. The Pavilion is still in use and has never been out of the Pell family.

The walls of Ticonderoga, the fort, were not greatly prized by the early holders of this Pell tract and it remained for the present head of his generation, Mr. Stephen H. P. Pell, to appreciate the historic value of the old place and to set about a work of restoration and repair. The foundations of the walls were still solid and some of the old buildings were still standing when, in 1909, Mr. Pell began his work of rebuilding. The original plans of the fort were secured from the French government. The work of rehabilitation has been carried forward in strict accordance with authorities. Historic points in the grounds surrounding the fort have been marked with tablets and monuments and each year sees an increasing number of visitors coming to Ticonderoga to inspect this history-filled place.

CROWN POINT
LAKE CHAMPLAIN—NEW YORK

IT would be hard, gazing upon Crown Point to-day, to realize the storms and terrors it let loose upon the English colonists not quite two hundred years ago. Girt by the smiling waters of one of America's most beautiful lakes, overtopped by a verdant mountain, and gazing out upon green fields in the shade of majestic woodlands, all of the atmosphere of the place is one of peace and aloofness from the pain of human suffering. Yet the name "Crown Point" was a sinister thing in the early days of the English colonists, particularly in the northern provinces. The New England matron putting to bed her infant Stephen Brewster or little Praise-the-Lord Jones, or the Dutch vrouw in the country round about Albany with her little Van Rensselaer Tasselwitch, had but to utter this dreadful name, "Crown Point," to bring her child into the most docile state of apprehension. From Crown Point went forth the scalping parties of French, Indian and half-breeds, which preyed upon the borders of the English colonies, carrying wrack and horror wherever they went. A glad and beautiful place, it nourished in its heart an evil spirit.

The settlement of the Crown Point district by the

Where the flag flew

The Ruined Barracks
CROWN POINT, N. Y., IN DEAD OF WINTER

CROWN POINT

French began soon after the opening of the eighteenth century. The beautiful lake which bears the name of its discoverer had been known in France for more than a century, and the country which lay between Lake Champlain and Lake Ontario—all that wilderness stretch of northern New York of to-day—had been charted with a fair degree of exactness, as well. The riches of the region were well sensed. Accordingly, a large and important province was planned by the French political geographers whose eastern boundary should be the Connecticut and whose western boundary should be Lake Ontario. North was the St. Lawrence River, and the southern confine was rather misty, except that it was determined that it should be all that could be kept from the English. The metropolis and capital of this fine project was to be a place situated at that peculiar bend in Lake Champlain where there was a projecting tongue of land, making a fine site for settlement, fortification and development. In other words, it was to be Crown Point, or Pointe de Couronne, as the French had it. A body of settlers was sent over about 1729, and in 1731 a fortification was commenced at the tip of the Crown Point peninsula which was named Fort Saint Frederic. The remains of this fortification are barely visible on the lake side of the point to-day near the Champlain Memorial light-house. And now a few words as to the geography of this part of Lake Champlain.

QUAINT AND HISTORIC FORTS

The lake, as all know, is a long, narrow tongue of water. About mid-way down it is constricted to even more than its usual slender width ("slender" as proportioned to the length) and the water is carried off at a sharp angle to the east. Just before the constriction, however, there is a protuberance, and on the west shore of this protuberance, or bay, there stands to-day the thriving little foundry town of Port Henry. Directly across the water from Port Henry, and at the point where the lake makes a sharp bend to the east, is a long, narrow point of land, and this is Crown Point. Crown Point has water on two sides of it. Though only a short distance from Port Henry by boat, it is quite a long distance by land, for, then, one must drive down to the base of the peninsula and work out to the point along the five-mile extent of the peninsula. The lake on the east side of Crown Point peninsula is so narrow that a cannon could easily fire across it. Behind Port Henry, that is, on the west side of the lake, is a precipitous mountain-side. The Point, therefore, was well protected in the days when cannon were with difficulty to be found in America and when they could not be transported easily through the wilderness of the New World. It could only be approached by water or by the long, narrow strip of land which joined it with the mainland, and either one of these approaches it could master very easily.

The first fort on Crown Point, Fort Saint Frederic,

CROWN POINT

was a little five-pointed star-shaped fort. Though small in size, it played a far larger part in events than the mighty successor which the years brought and which we shall presently come to. Fort Saint Frederic was for twenty-five years the only French stronghold in this part of the world. In 1756 Ticonderoga was begun. In the council-rooms of old Saint Frederic what strange visitors might have been seen, what bizarre juxtapositions of Old World and New, of sophistication and savagery! During all of its life the little fort was a rendezvous for Indians. Here, too, the Baron Dieskau made himself at home before setting out on the expedition, unfortunate for himself, against Johnson on Lake George. Here might have been seen Montcalm and other of the mightiest and craftiest warriors of old France in the new.

Except as a centre for Indians and a council hall for white and red, the little fort did not ever take part in fighting. When the English finally advanced in force against the strongholds on Lake Champlain, Ticonderoga was the point which bore the brunt of the onslaughts. First, Johnson came against these two hornet nests of French and Indians and accomplished little. Then Abercrombie made his futile and disgraceful try ("Mother Nabercrombie" he was long afterward known in the colonies). Finally the two forts fell before the large force which Amherst, in 1757, brought against them and as a result of the need of men at Quebec which had depleted their strength beyond the power of resistance. Fort Saint Frederic, like Ticonderoga, was deserted without a shot being fired, though its departing commander tried to destroy it by fusing the magazines.

Under the British the old French fort was dismantled and allowed to fall into decay. So well did the situation of Crown Point appeal to the British, however, as a place of fortification and so important was a hold upon Lake Champlain deemed, that the British began the construction of a massive fortress, on the most approved model, which was completed as far as it was ever carried within the course of a few years after Amherst's occupation of the point and which cost ten millions of dollars. This is an outlay which would be large even to-day. The jagged ruins of the walls of this fort, which never fired a shot in anger, are what one sees now on Crown Point when paying the old place a visit.

When Ethan Allen took Ticonderoga with his Green Mountain boys, Crown Point also fell to the Americans without resistance. It came passively into English hands again and after the Revolution was allowed to fall into decay.

Not far from the remains of Crown Point fort is the beautiful and large monument to Samuel Champlain, known as the Champlain Memorial. It takes the form of a light-house and is most solidly and durably constructed. Erected through the joint subscription of the States of Vermont and New York, the monument is, as well, a tribute to public spirit. In character the light-house is memorial of the past rather than symbolic of the future; a heroic statue in bronze of Champlain faces the east and at the base of the statue is Rodin's "La France," presented to the States of New York and Vermont for this undertaking by France.

THE HEIGHTS OF QUEBEC
(THE CITADEL, CASTLE ST. LOUIS)
CANADA

HAT hardy mariner, Jacques Cartier, sailed up the St. Lawrence River in 1535, but it was not until 1608, when Champlain's vessel brought the first permanent colonists of New France, that Quebec was founded. The storm-tossed little caravel entered the St. Lawrence in the early summer of that year. Champlain landed his miscellaneous following, built "L'Habitation," as he named the first official residence in Quebec, and laid the foundations of a small fort, an act portentous of the stirring events which the future held calmly waiting their turn and which were to give Quebec so conspicuous a place in the military annals of the New World.

The first fortifications were little more than gun platforms placed at an advantageous position so as to command the river. Their site became the location of Castle St. Louis and is to-day the eastern end of the Dufferin Terrace. So it is easy to remember where Champlain laid the foundations of the new city.

The new seat of power was shortly to see its master exerting his authority in a way not to be lightly mistaken. Treachery was plotted by some among Cham-

THE HEIGHTS OF QUEBEC

By courtesy of Detroit Publishing Company

THE HEIGHTS OF QUEBEC

plain's followers, who planned to assassinate their chief and sell his new city to the Spaniards. News of this move was brought to Champlain's ears. He caused the ringleaders to be seized by his soldiers and hung in the fort until dead. In this fashion the stronghold saw its first acts of violence. Scurvy marked the passage of the first winter in the New World of the little fort's defenders, and by the spring only the most hardy were alive.

The years which came between 1608 and 1629, the date of the first formal siege of Quebec, brought enlargement and strength to both the fort and the city. During this period both had been frequently surrounded by hostile Indians, who feared the white man's guns too much to attempt an attack by storm but who prowled around beneath the very ramparts of the fort seeking for unwary adventurers who might be without the gates. The control of the little colony in France had passed through various hands, but always the chief executive in the New World had been its founder, the rugged Champlain. The year 1629 finds the little colony in the possession of the Company of the 100 Associates, an organization founded by His Excellency, Cardinal Richelieu, and of which His Eminence was himself a member, and the winter of this year finds the colony in its usual desperate straits, beleaguered by winter and by savage foe and deserted in all but name by its sponsors in France.

QUAINT AND HISTORIC FORTS

In the spring of 1629 the inhabitants of Quebec were gladdened by the intelligence that a fleet had been discerned from Cap Tourmente in the mouth of the river and that it was even then approaching the city. It was supposed that this was the long-wished-for squadron of relief ships and that all would be prosperity and good cheer in the town for a time now. The citizens assembled on the walls of the fort to descry the distant sail, when word was brought by a friendly Indian that the looked-for vessels, far from being messengers of peace, were, in fact, emissaries of war; that they were English, and that they had just burned and pillaged a fishing village in a care-free, happy-go-lucky fashion on the way up the river. War had been declared between England and France and Quebec had not received word of it! Joy was changed to woe.

The next day emissaries arrived from Sir David Kirke, the English admiral in command of the fleet, demanding the surrender of the town and the fort, but Champlain, believing that help would soon arrive from France and not being of the temper, anyhow, which quickly gives up, turned these messengers away with words of defiance. The first siege of Quebec was now begun.

To tell the truth it was an informal sort of matter, anyhow, this first siege of Quebec. The English vessels pounded away at the town for a day or two in a casual fashion and then drifted down the river. The French,

THE HEIGHTS OF QUEBEC

on their part, had but fifty pounds of powder and were very careful about wasting any of this. Time passed and still no aid came from distant France. At length the intelligence which Champlain had been dreading was brought to him. The long-awaited French relief ships had entered the mouth of the St. Lawrence only to be overcome and seized by the English blockader. Hope had now departed, and when, in July, three English ships sailed up to the town, Champlain and his sixteen soldiers watched them apathetically because they knew that they, themselves, could do no more. Quebec was surrendered to the English and on July 20, 1629, the English flag for the first time flew over the little settlement. Said one of Kirke's captains: " There was not in the sayde forte at the tyme of the rendition of the same, to this examinate's knowledge, any victuals save only one tubb of bitter roots."

It was not until 1632 that Quebec was restored to the French by the treaty of St. Germain-en-Laye, and during its three years of English occupancy the point had made no progress. The Indians did not like their rough, new associates and trade had languished. Even the fort was in sad condition.

The summer of 1632 saw the little settlement in French hands and under the guidance of Emery de Caen, a fiery French Huguenot. The next year found the colony once more in the direction of the veteran Champlain. It is not clear why de Caen was given

QUAINT AND HISTORIC FORTS

power for this one year. On Christmas Day, 1635, the Father of New France passed peacefully away in the fort which had seen so many of his earthly activities. His body was laid to rest in a " chambre particulier," according to old record. Late investigation inclines to the belief that Champlain's last resting place was a niche hollowed out of the stone half way down Mountain Hill in full view of the strand on which his early " Habitation " was built.

The successor of Champlain, M. de Montmagny, a Knight of Malta, rebuilt of stone Champlain's fort shortly after his arrival in 1636, and Castle St. Louis had now a most martial appearance. Close to the castle was the Jesuit presbytery, this close conjunction of church and Mars well typifying the union of powers which held authority in the colony. All public functions were religious in character and the black-robed priests held the balance of power in the council-room.

Throughout the quarter century following Champlain's death the threat of Iroquois marauding hung over the little city and in 1660 Castle St. Louis witnessed a strange spectacle. It was the burning at the stake by the French of an Iroquois captive as a retaliation against the savages for their outrages. The Indian met his fate with fortitude, but reviled his captors unceasingly and predicted a dire future for the city. At length death put an end to his sufferings and his predictions. His spirit, according to the priests who were

THE HEIGHTS OF QUEBEC

standing by, winged its way to the place of the redeemed, having been freed from sin by the fiery ordeal through which its body had passed.

Time went its way and brought the second siege of Quebec to Castle St. Louis. The bold and impetuous Frontenac was now at the helm of state and it was due to a three-headed expedition of his against the English colonies that this second siege was brought about. Incidentally, this expedition may be looked upon in another light as the opening blow in that long struggle between New France and New England which was to result in the extinguishing of the latter power in the New World. Three war parties set out from the fortifications at Quebec, Montreal and Three Rivers. The first reached the Dutch settlement of Corlaer (Schenectady) on the Hudson and brought about the horrible and historic Schenectady massacre. In similar fashion the other parties fell upon towns in New England. The northern English colonies which had hitherto been kept asunder by jealousies united against a common foe and equipped an expedition which was to set forth from Massachusetts against Quebec.

The vessels of the fleet consisted of thirty-two ships ranging in size from the *Six Friends,* a roisterer of the seas which had been engaged in the dangerous West India trade, and mounted forty-four guns, to humble fishing smacks. The commander was William Phips, afterward Sir William Phips, a strange favorite of

QUAINT AND HISTORIC FORTS

Fortune whose adventurous and large-fisted career carried him through gold-seeking in the Spanish Main, knighthood from the British Crown, and the governorship, by royal appointment, of Massachusetts. Volunteers were called for and nearly four thousand men responded to the call. Provisions were laid in for four months and all was ready for the start.

After waiting so long in Boston for help from England that winter was almost at hand, Sir William at length gave the order to sail and the New England armada was launched upon its career. Its only lacks were a pilot who knew the St. Lawrence River, a sufficiency of gunpowder and a commander competent to direct the expedition. The eventual failure of the undertaking was not hard to forecast.

The fleet anchored a little below Quebec in the autumn of 1690. Frontenac was ready and waiting for it. A messenger was sent from the fleet to the French governor demanding surrender. He was taken in a canoe to the landing place and blindfolded. Then he was directed up the steep streets and crooked stairs of the little city by a devious path to Castle St. Louis where Frontenac, with his aides in full uniform, was waiting to receive him. During his progress onward he was jostled and pushed to make him think that there were immense crowds of people in the little city, and hoarse orders were shouted near his ear to imaginary soldiery. At length he stood in the council-room of our

THE HEIGHTS OF QUEBEC

little fort and the bandage was taken from his eyes. The scene of splendor before him at first filled him with confusion, but he quickly recovered poise and delivered his message.

"No," returned Frontenac, "I will answer your general only by the mouths of cannon, that he may learn that a man like me is not to be summoned in this fashion. Let him do his best and I will do mine!"

During the short and futile siege which followed, the cannonading between the vessels of Sir William's fleet and the French fortification was so terrific that experienced military officers declared that they had heard nothing like it. At length the besiegers sailed away baffled and the furious little fort grumbled down to another season of peace. Phips reached Boston in November, and the rest of his fleet straggled in one by one, such as were not lost in the storms of the perilous Nova Scotia coast. Frontenac, in celebration of the deliverance of Quebec, established the little church of Notre Dame de la Victoire which stands in Quebec as a memorial of those days.

The beginning of the eighteenth century saw the fortifications of Quebec strengthened and enlarged. Vauban, the great engineer, furnished the plans which were carried out under Frontenac's personal supervision. For twenty leagues around, the habitants were pressed into service and even the gentlefolk of the colony volunteered for work with pick and spade, so eager was the

QUAINT AND HISTORIC FORTS

sentiment to carry out Vauban's plans. A line of solid earthworks was extended on the flank of the city from Cape Diamond to the St. Charles River, and now for the first time the summit of Cape Diamond was fortified, this redoubt with sixteen cannon being the foundation of the present-day citadel of Quebec. In the foundation of the new work a copper plate, discovered at the demolition of the old walls in 1854, was buried bearing the following inscription:

In the year of grace 1693 under the reign of the Most August, Most Invincible and Most Christian King, Louis the Great, Fourteenth of that name, the most Excellent and Most Illustrious Lord, Louis de Buade, Count of Frontenac, twice viceroy of all New France, after having three years before repulsed, routed and completely conquered the rebellious inhabitants of New England, who besieged this town of Quebec and who threatened to renew the attack this year, constructed, at the charge of the King, this citadel, with the fortifications therewith connected, for the defence of the country and the safety of the people and for confounding yet again a people perfidious towards God and towards its lawful king. And he has laid this first stone.

In 1709 the sturdy colonists of New England planned another expedition against Quebec. This time the home government had promised to help. But arrangements were delayed and it became late autumn before the expedition was ready to set out. Under the circumstances a fight against the frigid winter of

THE HEIGHTS OF QUEBEC

Quebec as well as its stone strongholds was not to be considered.

The next attempt upon the little city took place in 1711, when a strong fleet under Admiral Sir Hovenden Walker set sail from Boston on the 30th of July. Under a different commander this effort might have resulted in success to the British arms, but Admiral Walker scorned all advice and drove his big frigates on so recklessly amidst the dense fogs and sharp reefs of Newfoundland, that eight battleships were beaten to pieces by the waves and rocks. Eight hundred and eighty-four people, thirty-four of them women, were drowned. Admiral Walker sailed ignominiously back to Boston, and in Quebec the happy French changed the name of their little church of Notre Dame de la Victoire to that of Notre Dame des Victoires.

Yet the persistence of the English was at length to have its way. In 1720 the walls of Quebec were enlarged and made mightier, and the citadel, largely in the form in which it exists to-day, was erected. Vaudreuil, the last governor of New France, loudly proclaimed that the city was impregnable. In 1759 came the expedition of Wolfe against Quebec, the final outcome of which and the method of attack, with Wolfe's heroic death on the Plains of Abraham, is a story that every schoolboy knows.

This conflict was the first in which the citadel took part. The mighty works in which Vaudreuil trusted so loudly had been overcome on their first trial, while the high-perched, precariously-placed little "Castle," which Champlain had first built and which his successors had altered to suit their times, had withstood innumerable Indian attacks and had seen three assaults by Europeans fail against it. The spirit of the men who manned the forts had changed with their times.

There is another tale of siege and Quebec which is not widely familiar and yet which all Americans should know. It is the story of Montgomery's expedition during the Revolution—an expedition in which he lost his life and in which Benedict Arnold played a conspicuous part.

Richard Montgomery was a lieutenant in Wolfe's army and was thoroughly familiar with Quebec. At the outbreak of the War of Independence he was deputized to lead an army up the Hudson and by the familiar approach along the Richelieu River and the St. Lawrence to Quebec. Benedict Arnold led another force through the tangled forests of northern Maine and New Hampshire, reaching Quebec ahead, even, of Montgomery. The combined forces laid siege to the city through the winter, and in the most desperate assault of all, one in which Wolfe's feat of scaling the cliff was attempted, Montgomery lost his life. After six months the United States troops departed, confessing failure.

From that time to this the military history of Quebec has been uneventful. In the early part of the

THE HEIGHTS OF QUEBEC

nineteenth century old Castle St. Louis, which had stood so many storms and assaults, succumbed to fire. The site is now an open square with some relics and a fine view over the river.

The great citadel of Quebec rises three hundred and fifty feet above the river and covers nearly forty acres. The portion of the works overlooking the St. Lawrence is called the Grand Battery, while the surmounting pinnacle of the citadel is known as the King's Bastion. From the King's Bastion a most glorious panorama is spread out before one, embracing the city, the great river, hundreds of miles of forest and farm land, the Laurentian mountains in the distance in one direction and the green hills of Vermont far away in another.

All of the old works of Quebec have been retired from active service in a military sense. The city is protected by modern fortifications in other quarters.

Two memorials record two great events in the history of the citadel. The chief is the Wolfe-Montcalm monument erected just behind the Dufferin Terrace in a little green enclosure known as the Governor's Garden. The second is a simple tablet set up in the face of the cliff on the river-front below the citadel, marking the spot where the United States General Montgomery fell in the winter of 1775.

FORT ANNAPOLIS ROYAL
ANNAPOLIS—ANNAPOLIS BASIN, NOVA SCOTIA

ORE by accident than by design the Sieur de Monts, in 1604, with his oddly assorted band of adventurers on the foggy Bay of Fundy, steered into the rocky entrance which leads into the beautiful landlocked basin of present-day Annapolis in Nova Scotia. One of his followers, the Baron de Potrincourt, was so enchanted by the beauty of the scene that he asked a grant of land here. This was given him, and upon this land in the next year he built himself first a fort, then a house, and then several more houses. This was the beginning of Port Royal, now known as Annapolis, the second oldest fortified place in the Western Hemisphere.

The voyager to-day may repeat de Monts's experience and with no design to do that, too. Fogs wrap the eastern and western coasts of Nova Scotia in an impenetrable blanket most of the time. The traveller who sails,—let us say,—from St. Johns, New Brunswick, for the Annapolis Basin, crosses sparkling waters, and then, as he enters the mountainous cleft which gives entrance to this beautiful bay, comes into the belt of mist which obscures all of the coast. He hears the fog horn on the point at the entrance,—which de Monts did not hear,—and then suddenly, like an apparition,

By Courtesy of The Boston Times

GUNS, PARADE AND ANCIENT OFFICERS' QUARTERS, FORT ANNAPOLIS ROYAL, N. S.

FORT ANNAPOLIS ROYAL

the land looms into view; there is a lane of shrouded, uncertain water, between towering misty headlands; and, then, he is beyond the mists. Annapolis Basin, bright and blue with soft clouds overhead, like a highland lake, lies before him. At the far head of the Basin, where the delicate horizon merges into the sky, is Annapolis. It is not hard to understand Potrincourt's enthusiasm for this beautiful spot. It is hard to understand how de Monts himself could have passed over this locality in favor of the barren Isle St. Croix for his first settlement, for this is what he did.

The winter of 1604 was passed by the little colonizing expedition at St. Croix—the sandy island which is now the boundary line between Canada and Maine. Potrincourt went back to France with de Monts to secure supplies and settlers for his own pet project, whose setting was Annapolis Basin, and returned with his chief in June, 1605, to find that the companions they had left behind them at St. Croix had had a sorry winter. The whole settlement was then moved over to Potrincourt's Port Royal. This was the beginning of Annapolis.

The makeup of de Monts's expedition was thoroughly typical of the colonizing bodies sent out by France in that day. There were men of the noblest blood of France, of whom our Potrincourt was a conspicuous example, and there was, also, the sweeping of the offscouring of the most dissolute cities of the Old

World. The motives which inspired these different men were no doubt as mixed as the character of the men and as pleasant a theme of speculation, but with this we will have nothing to do. The second winter of de Monts's adventurers, even at sheltered Annapolis, was severe, and it was with joy that the men saw the spring of 1606 arrive and bring with it the little ship from France which annually brought supplies and new blood from the Old World.

In this ship there was one arrival who must be given a special consideration. A poet-lawyer,—a strange combination, at that,—Marc Lescarbot eventually was to write his name in fame as the author of one of the earliest histories of New France, one of the most authentic records in existence of the early adventures of the French in the New World; but in our regard of him now we must consider the high spirit and bold emprise which he brought with him to cheer his companions and to help them through the rigors of this early settlement. A rhymester of some skill, he tuned his lyre to the most trivial events to keep his associates in good spirits, and in this last endeavor displayed an ingenuity which cannot help but endear him to all generations which like brave deeds done in blithe ways. He organized the Ordre de la Bon Temps, the only requirements for membership in which were presence in the little colony, and the duties of whose members were on successive days to provide a banquet for their brethren.

FORT ANNAPOLIS ROYAL

There was formality attached to the office, too. Theatrical masques were gotten up and odd tasks were devised for all Knights of the Merry Time. Lescarbot infused a brave spirit into even the most dreary of the odd crew which made up this colony. We can picture the merry adventurers in their rude little fort engaged in their pranks of drollery thousands of miles away from home and with inhospitable wilderness and bleak shores for environs.

The charter of the colony was revoked in 1607, by one of those pleasing inconsistencies of royalty which inspire in the student of the past so thorough a belief in the theory of the divine right of kings, and the brave Order of the Merry Time to a man, with retainers and family vessels, embarked upon the skittish little vessels in which they entrusted themselves to the Atlantic and sailed back to France. It was not for three years that any of them returned, but in 1610 perseverance on de Potrincourt's part had triumphed over royal puddingheadedness once more, and in that year he came back again to his colony. It is related that he found everything in Port Royal exactly as he had left it, not a lock or a bar in the little fort having been disturbed by the Indians, who displayed, in addition to their honesty, another engaging trait of fidelity to friendship by the many manifestations of joy which they made at having with them again their friends, the Frenchmen. Not again was Port Royal to be entirely deserted.

QUAINT AND HISTORIC FORTS

In 1613 the Jesuits of Port Royal, a class to themselves, abandoned the place and attempted the settlement of a picturesque inlet on Mount Desert Island on the coast of present-day Maine, their inlet still bearing the name of Frenchmen's Bay. The freebooting Argall, a piratical seafarer from the new colony of Virginia far south on the Atlantic Coast, heard of this settlement and descended upon it in force. Most of the French were killed after a brave but ineffectual resistance, and fire and axe were given to their settlement. In the following year this Argall heard of the presence of Port Royal, for news travelled slowly in those days, and proceeded against that point after completing his work of pillage at Mount Desert and St. Croix. Taking the little place by surprise with a superior force, he scattered the inhabitants, burned the village, and razed the fort to the ground. Potrincourt, a survivor, returned to France and fell fighting at the siege of Mery in the following year.

From this time until the signing of the treaty of St. Germain-en-Laye in 1632, Port Royal and Acadia were held in the hands of the British, and during this time occurred that odd experiment of Sir William Mackenzie to make of Acadia a New Scotland or Caledonia. The Scottish knight obtained the concession of the Acadian peninsula from King James in 1621 and founded a colony on the site or very near the site of Port Royal, building a fort at this point. Charles I renewed the charter granted by his predecessor, and created an order of minor nobility known as the Knights Baronets of Nova Scotia. It became Mackenzie's idea to establish in the New Caledonia the feudal institutions of the Old World. His colony was not a success even during its short life, and in 1632 Port Royal passed by treaty to the French, thus putting an end effectually to New Caledonia and its Knights Baronets of the dissolute Charles's erection.

The see-saw between French and English was once more to incline in the English favor as regards Acadia. The cession of this peninsula to the French had always been looked on with disfavor by the New England colonists, because it gave their hereditary enemies a secure base from which to send out privateering expeditions against their shipping. In 1654, Cromwell the Protector dispatched a force to ensure the subjugation of the Dutch on the Island of Manhattan. Peace with Holland was concluded by England before this purpose was effected, and it was then determined to turn these arms to the reconquest of Acadia. An expedition was accordingly fitted out secretly in Massachusetts and dispatched upon its mission. The French forts on the Penobscot and at St. John were speedily reduced. Le Borgne was at Port Royal with one hundred and fifty men but he attempted little resistance and the post once more came into English possession.

QUAINT AND HISTORIC FORTS

Until 1667 Port Royal was in the hands of the English, and then by the Treaty of Breda the whole of Acadia was returned to the French. During their occupancy the English had spent large sums repairing the fortifications in Acadia under their control, and in this undertaking the importance of Port Royal was duly recognized.

For the next generation the French made Port Royal their base, and the place acquired an evil reputation with the English because of the marauding sea expeditions which proceeded from out of there. Finally, in 1690, the Commonwealth of Massachusetts raised a levy and empowered Sir William Phips to go against the ancient stronghold. This doughty gentleman was successful in his mission and the port was in English hands again—this time hands of destruction.

After the departure of their enemies the French rebuilt Port Royal and it became, once more, a busy shipping point and the haunt of privateers. It is not difficult to-day to appreciate the fine strategic value of Port Royal, set at the head of its beautiful landlocked basin, but it is difficult, to-day, as the river now stands, to appreciate how vessels of any burthen could go up to its wharves. But at that time, doubtless, the river had not filled up to the degree that it has to-day.

In 1704 and again in 1705, the pertinacious New Englanders went upon futile expeditions against Port Royal, each time being driven off without much loss

FORT ANNAPOLIS ROYAL

and each time evincing a singular lack of spirit in their enterprise, a lack of spirit all the more remarkable when one considers the undertakings which they faced and carried through at other times in their history. The taking of Port Royal seems to have become a sort of obsession with them—a theme for an idle hour, a pet worry which they would take up when all other worries failed them. Finally, in 1710, before the onslaught of a combined force of Her Majesty Queen Anne's soldiery and New England militia, Port Royal fell to the English for the last time, bravely and gallantly fighting against overwhelming odds. Its spirited commandant, M. Subercase, with a famished army of one hundred and fifty men, marched out through the ranks of three thousand five hundred enemies and the red flag of England was raised where the white one of France had flown. Port Royal was renamed Annapolis in honor of the English sovereign, and Colonel Vetch, with four hundred and fifty men, occupied the fort. Though it was endangered by French arms several times thereafter, the little fort was never again out of English possession.

The sod ramparts of the fort have been carefully maintained and are to-day the cherished possession of Annapolis—or Annapolis Port Royal, as its inhabitants, making an odd mixture of its names, prefer to call it. From them one may gaze down the placid little river over a scene very like that upon which its French and

QUAINT AND HISTORIC FORTS

English commanders looked on their separate turns and different generations. It is difficult really to visualize the events through which the little fort has passed, but if one considers that its history goes as far back beyond the days of the American Revolution as the beginning of the twentieth century comes this side of the Revolution, one begins to perceive how big is its historical background as events go in America.

The officers' quarters,—a quaint, sturdy, low building,—and the magazine are still standing in the fort at Port Royal, both very ancient and very suggestive edifices, neither one as ancient as the walls of the little fort.

THE CITADEL AT HALIFAX
NOVA SCOTIA

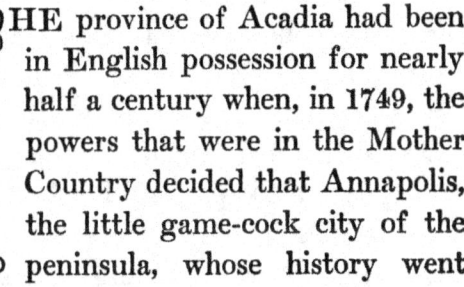THE province of Acadia had been in English possession for nearly half a century when, in 1749, the powers that were in the Mother Country decided that Annapolis, the little game-cock city of the peninsula, whose history went back to 1605, was not a fitting place for the capital of the province. Its harbor, while beautiful and secure, was not large enough for the purposes that England had in mind; moreover, it was on the western side of the peninsula, so that to get to it from Europe one must pass around Cape Sable and up the foggy Bay of Fundy. And so we find that the home authorities projected a new city, which was to be the capital of the province and whose location was to be the magnificent harbor of Chebucto on the east coast of Acadia. That they did not go astray in their anticipations of the future is proved by the present-day Halifax, Nova Scotia's principal city, the child of the plans of these Englishmen of 1749.

The value of Chebucto as a harbor had been known for many years before this time, we may assume. It had been for many years a rendezvous for British vessels in American waters. When D'Anville's misfortuned fleet of French men-of-war was scattered by the elements, its remnants came together in Chebucto Bay. That there was some form of settlement on the shores of the bay ere this time is highly probable, but the existence of human life in any organized form here, if such existence there was, has been completely overshadowed in retrospect by the magnitude of the enterprise by which the present-day Halifax was founded.

As a consequence of its last war there were in England numbers of young and able-bodied men set suddenly at liberty who had been engaged in military or semi-military pursuits. Liberal inducements were offered these people to go to the projected metropolis. A free passage, maintenance for a year was promised, and grants of land varying from fifty to six hundred acres were given. The Imperial Government voted the sum of forty thousand pounds to help defray expenses. This sum was increased to four hundred thousand pounds before five years had passed. The Hon. Edward Cornwallis was appointed and the protection of British institutions and laws was promised.

The fleet on which the colony set sail entered Chebucto Bay in the month of July, 1749. There were thirteen transports, conveying nearly three thousand settlers. These were men of good stock, and the vigor with which they attacked the problems before them was sufficient evidence of this fact. Streets were promptly laid out, a civil government was organized, and the entire population got to work on the practical issue

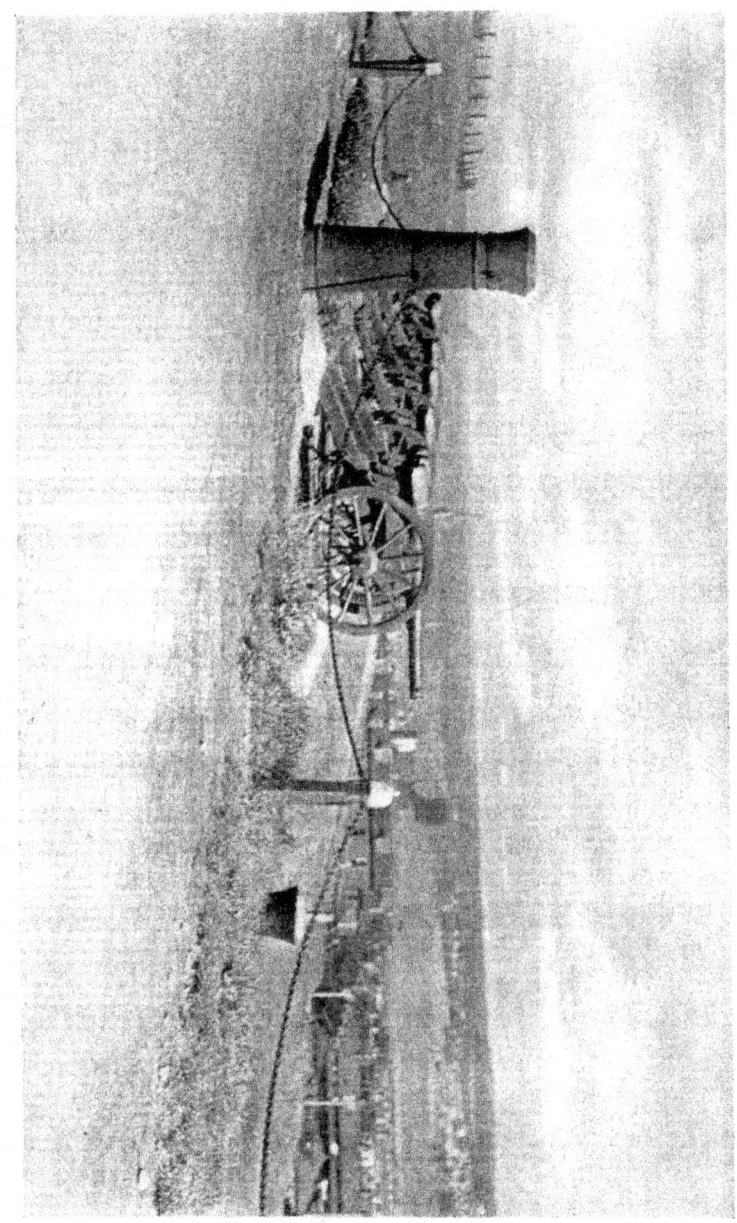

VIEW FROM CITADEL HILL, HALIFAX, N. S.

OLD MARTELLO TOWER, NEAR HALIFAX, N.S.

THE CITADEL AT HALIFAX

of providing shelter for themselves and their families. Houses were built, and, last, but not least, in that day and generation a fort was erected on the rounded top of the hill around which they had plotted their town. This was the forerunner of the citadel of Halifax of to-day. Around the entire settlement was built a high palisade.

The early history of Halifax did not include sieges or sustained attacks by an enemy, but it was in the atmosphere of unrest and conflict from its first days. While the French residents of Acadia had not been molested in their possession of land in Nova Scotia, they had never taken the oath of allegiance to England. Among them were many turbulent spirits who incited the Micmac Indians of the country to outrages against English people and who took part in these outrages themselves in the disguise of savages. Moreover, the French had pressed the boundaries of Canada as close to the boundaries of Acadia as they dared, and they continually tried to foment ill feeling amidst the simple Acadian peasants against the English. The story of the days between the conquest of Acadia by the English and the final peace between France and England in the New World is one of partisan warfare, of forays and minor sieges and attacks by land and water.

All of these things went on around Halifax, and enemy vessels even slipped into her harbor in bold dashes upon rich covey or unsuspecting foe. From

QUAINT AND HISTORIC FORTS

Halifax went forth Lawrence at the order of Governor Cornwallis to oppose the French at Beasejour, now Cumberland, where the French had built a fort on what they claimed was their own ground. Lawrence built another fort on the opposite side of the little stream of Missigouache, which the French claimed to be the boundary between the rival domains, and went back to Halifax for reinforcements. His building the fort was opposed by the French skirmish, and the blood shed in this little skirmish was the first blood to flow in combat between France and England in Old World or New since the treaty of Aix la Chapelle.

In the council rooms of the citadel at Halifax the order to deport the French peasantry, or Acadians, was debated. From the government house here went forth the orders that this act should be done. The story of the deportation of the Acadians and of their sufferings has been told many times in prose and very beautifully by Longfellow in verse.

During the American Revolution and during the War of 1812, Halifax was the centre of activity of the British naval forces, and so it has continued to this day. During the War of the Revolution and the War of 1812 merchant vessels were brought to this port to be sold as prizes. During the great European war of this time of writing merchant vessels suspected of carrying contraband and seized by the British in the American

THE CITADEL AT HALIFAX

Atlantic waters have been taken to Halifax to be passed on by a prize court.

The citadel of Halifax is not one of its prime defences to-day. It has become more of a public park than a strong arm for battle. From its walls magnificent views of the harbor of Halifax can be obtained, one of the most splendid harbors in the world, to-day as stimulating to enterprise as in the days when Chebucto Bay was cast for the part of a great port by the Lords of Trade of England.

FORT GEORGE
CASTINE—MAINE

THE little town of Castine, on the Penobscot River, Maine, is a favorite resort for summer visitors, who are attracted by its fine air, its abundance of sea food, and its accessibility to the interior of the country. These same considerations together with the fine strategic location of Castine Peninsula at the head of Penobscot Bay, guarding the entrance to the Penobscot River, influenced the French adventurers of three hundred and more years ago to plant their settlement of Pentagoet and to build a fort in this very vicinity. Traditions of the settlement and grass-covered ruins of the fort are still to be discovered at Castine.

In the course of the years there came here the British at war with the colonies, and His Majesty's forces built Fort George, an important post in its day and one of the best preserved Revolutionary works in New England. These ruins are the scene of pilgrimage of hundreds of people annually—merry parties from the summer colonies which dot the shores of Penobscot Bay or from Mount Desert Island, around the corner as the land lies from Castine.

The remains of Fort George might even to-day be, with no disproportionate labor, put into condition for

FORT GEORGE

defence. The fort was a square bastioned work protected by a moat excavated down to solid rock. Each bastion was pierced with four embrasures. Though no buildings now remain inside the fortress, the position of the barracks, magazine and guard-house may easily be traced.

Standing on the ruined wall of Fort George, one can easily discern in what features lay its strength and importance. The approach on three sides is by steep ascents, and especially is this the case to the south or seaward, the quarter from which attack might be expected. The shape of the peninsula is seen. Very similar to the peninsula on which Portland is situated, it is a large swollen heart of land hung to the mainland by a cord from the north. To the south the eye has a wide prospect, bounded in the distance by the blue mountains of the Camden range. To the west is Brigadier's Island, and blue water where Belfast lies in the distance. To the north Fort Point can be seen with the granite walls of the never-completed Fort Pownall, begun by Governor Pownall in 1759. North of east is more water and the distant solitary Blue Hill.

The military history of Fort George reflects no great credit on American sagacity, though it throws into strong light the national aggressive spirit. The first four years of the American Revolution passed very peacefully in Maine (then a part of Massachusetts), though its hardy seamen and backwoodsmen were not backward in joining the fighting forces to the south. Then, in 1779, the British powers in Halifax decided to carry the war into the northern colonies. Accordingly, in June of that year, Colonel Francis M'Lean was despatched from the aforesaid port with nine hundred men to seize and fortify the well-known peninsula of Castine or, as it was then known, Penobscot Peninsula. He landed on the 12th of June, and with great energy commenced to establish himself firmly in his position.

The news was immediately carried to the Massachusetts fathers at Boston. Hancock was then Governor and General Gates commanded the Eastern Department of the colonies, with headquarters at Providence. With that cocksureness for which the Puritan colony has been distinguished since its foundation, the rulers of Massachusetts at Boston put their heads together without notifying Gates, the Continental Congress, or the leaders of the war in this country, and resolved to push an expedition against M'Lean. An embargo of forty days was put upon vessels in Massachusetts ports, so that transport possibilities could not put to sea, and a large land and naval force was raised.

The army was commanded by Solomon Lovell; the fleet by Captain Saltonstall of the *Warren,* a fine frigate of thirty-two guns. Peleg Wadsworth was second in command to Lovell, and Paul Revere, of Longfellow's poem, was in charge of the artillery. The

FORT GEORGE

land forces numbered about twelve hundred men, and this number might be augmented by three hundred marines from the fleet. There were enough guns of large calibre and other supplies of war. The fleet was formidable in appearance and equipment, but it was entirely lacking in discipline and co-ordination, as was shortly to be seen.

The force appeared off Castine on the 25th of July, 1779, and found the fort unfinished and thoroughly unprepared for defence. M'Lean despatched messengers to Halifax for aid, and kept busily on with his defences. Two bastions had not been begun and the two remaining, with the curtains, had not been raised more than four or five feet. Captain Mowatt, a thoroughly-hated British naval officer, and the bombarder of defenceless Portland, was in the harbor with three light vessels with which he took position to prevent a landing on the south side of the peninsula. A deep trench was cut across the isthmus connecting with the mainland.

No landing could be made except beneath the precipitous bluff, two hundred feet high, on the west.

On the third day the Americans succeeded in landing and in securing a position on the heights. Instead of making a final assault upon the unfinished fort now, however, they dallied where they stood, threw up earthworks and fought out a wordy battle amongst themselves as to how to go ahead. The commanding officers disagreed on any one plan, so, finally, at this late date, they appealed to General Gates for instructions. Two weeks passed and Sir George Collier arrived with a British fleet to relieve his beleaguered countrymen. The Americans were obliged to take to their heels.

General Wadsworth retired to his home near Thomaston, not a great distance from Castine, and was captured by a British detachment sent out from the fort for the purpose. His escape from the fort with a companion, Major Burton, is one of the interesting minor episodes of the history of that point. Suffice it to say that General Wadsworth on a dark night managed to get over the walls by the aid of a torn blanket and reached the mainland. Eventually he made Portland and safety.

For the remainder of the Revolution the British were at Castine, from whence they went forth on many expeditions of depredation. The loss of this little peninsula became a serious consideration, indeed, to the Americans.

During the War of 1812 Castine once more became a British stronghold, when, in 1814, the American defenders gave up the post to a force which made it a centre for plundering coast towns east and west, levying forced contributions, and destroying ship-yards. At this time Bangor was taken, Belfast visited, and Hampden pillaged. After a stay of eleven months the British left Castine in April, 1815. In the neighborhood of the fort they left a reputation for gayety, their stay having included a round of balls, teas, and dinners.

The history of Castine as a fortified point under New France commences with the re-occupation of Acadia, Nova Scotia, under Richelieu's strong direction. Castine, or Pentagoet, as the French called it, was an extreme outpost against the English and was to be maintained at all costs. In 1654, however, it fell to the conquering hand of Sedgwick, a Massachusetts officer who reduced all French posts in Acadia. Sedgwick describes it as a small well-planned work mounting eight guns. It was not until 1670 that the French flag was again unfurled over Pentagoet, and, at this time, it is shown in old records that the place was considerably enlarged and strengthened, only to fall, in 1674, to buccaneers from San Domingo, who carried off Chambly, the commander, and held him to ransom.

The next Frenchman whom we find at Pentagoet was that strange product of sophistication and savagery, the Baron St. Castine. Vincent, Baron St. Castine, came to America with his regiment in 1665, and the wild life of the great forests seems to have called him from the first. When his regiment was disbanded shortly after its arrival in this country, Castine plunged into the forests and took up life in the fashion that the Indians lived it. He joined the tribe of the Abenakis, a mighty people of that day, and become so high in their favor that he married the daughter of the chief,

QUAINT AND HISTORIC FORTS

Madocawando, an implacable foe of the English. In 1685 we find Castine in command at Pentagoet with his dusky followers around him. He never changed his wife, though we have reason to believe that, like Sir William Johnson, of later times, he found pleasure in many coppery enchantresses. Toward the close of this century his fort and trading post was captured and destroyed by the English, and the Baron himself, it is believed, returned to his native France. His half-breed son, by his Indian wife, for many years carried fire and sword against the English and was a picturesque figure in the wars of the Massachusetts border.

FORT FREDERICK
PEMAQUID—MAINE

HE English clenched hand which answered the brandishing of the French mailed fist at Pentagoet, now Castine, was Fort Frederick at Pemaquid, that anciently-known peninsula which marks the entrance to the Kennebec River. Parts of the walls of old Fort Frederick are still standing, its entire outlines are plainly to be discerned, and it is a favorite point of visit with the many people who make their homes in this part of the Maine coast during the summer months.

Pemaquid, itself, is one of those long arms of rock which are characteristic of the Maine coast. A good word picture of the locality has been painted by S. A. Drake, the chronicler of Maine coast history. "A belt of rusty red granite stretches around it above low water mark," he writes, "and out into the foaming breakers beyond. Pastures pallid from exhaustion and spotted with clumps of melancholy firs spread themselves out over this foundation. In the extreme corner of this threadbare robe there is a light-house. You look about you in vain for the evidences of long occupation which the historic vista has opened to you in advance."

While there have been many wild reports that the settlement on Pemaquid antedated that on Massachusetts Bay, itself, there is lacking weight of historical evidence to support this contention. Pemaquid was visited by Captain John Smith in 1614, but that doughty mariner makes no mention in his account of his visit of having seen any Europeans at the place, as he undoubtedly would have done had his vision encountered any such settlers. William Bradford, the conscientious chronicler of early Plymouth doings, tells us that in 1623 " there were also in this year some scattered beginnings made at Pascataway by Mr. David Thompson, at Monhegan and some other places by sundry others," and it is very conceivable that Pemaquid Point might properly be included amongst these " some other " places. In 1625 we find Samoset, the famous chieftain of Pilgrim days, selling to a certain John Brown land at Pemaquid, the sign-manual Samoset used, according to his custom, being a bended bow with an arrow fitted to the string.

In 1630 there were certainly the beginnings of a settlement at Pemaquid and the foundations of a fortress. Shortly after this time the locality was visited by Dixy Bull, one of the freebooters of that day, who pillaged the place in leisurely and thorough fashion. Another settlement was developed and this shared the fate of its predecessor during the evil days of King Philip's War. But the close of King Philip's War brought better days to Pemaquid, when the government of New York, under royal letters patent, assumed control of that place and constructed a strong timber

FORT FREDERICK

redoubt there with a bastioned outwork. This was to provide a rallying point for the frightened settlers. It was completed in 1677 and garrisoned by soldiers from New York. The fort was known as Fort Charles and the town around it, which was built up on the site of the old settlements, was known as Jamestown. Under the new régime a military government was established, of which the commandant of the post was the head. The free living inhabitants of the post were irked at being under strict martial rule.

Under the terms of the Treaty of Breda, Acadia had been returned to France and with it Pentagoet (Castine) and the possession of the Penobscot River. The French, in the general fashion which they affected, declared that the Kennebec and the country tributary thereto belonged to Acadia. This contention the English disputed. We have, therefore, the rival powers at their two extreme outposts,—the French at Pentagoet and the English at Pemaquid,—in violent opposition to each other.

In 1688, Sir Edmund Andros, Governor of Massachusetts, made a sudden descent upon Castine, the town, and plundered the place. Castine, the man, incited his friends the Abenakis and soon had the border in a blaze. He planned a retaliatory descent upon Pemaquid. Spies were sent to New Harbor, an outpost of Pemaquid, and preparations were made to move in force.

QUAINT AND HISTORIC FORTS

In August, 1689, the war party, led by Castine in person, landed on the eastern shore of Pemaquid Peninsula without being discovered. The attack was planned with care. The main village lay about a quarter of a mile from the fort. The farms where most of the inhabitants were at work were three miles from the fort. One band of the assailants was to throw itself upon the fort and village, and another to cut off the village from the farms.

The plan was carried out without a hitch. The men at the farms ran for the fort and were shot down or taken prisoners. The assailants next turned their attention to the fort. The big rock in back of the fort, which makes so conspicuous a feature of the locality to-day, was occupied by savages, who fired down upon the defenders of the stronghold, and the attack was pressed fiercely from other quarters. For twenty-four hours Weems, the commander, held out. Then, when fourteen out of his garrison of thirty had been wounded, he surrendered on condition that the occupants should be free to leave unmolested. Fort and village were set on fire and Pemaquid for the second time had been swept out of existence.

Under Sir William Phips, who acted by royal instruction, Pemaquid was rebuilt and regarrisoned in 1692. Unlike the old fortress, the new one was built of stone in a most substantial and enduring fashion, and so enlarged as to take in the high ledge of rock which

FORT FREDERICK

had been the vulnerable point of the old defences. The new work was known as Fort William Henry. Cotton Mather, the indefatigable chronicler of that period, speaks of it as follows:

William Henry was built of stone in a quadrangular figure, being about 737 foot in compass without the walls and 108 foot square within the inner ones. Twenty-eight ports it had and fourteen (if not eighteen) guns mounted, whereof six were eighteen-pounders. The wall on the south line, fronting to the sea, was twenty-two foot high and more than six foot thick at the ports, which were eight foot from the ground. The greater flanker, or round tower, at the western end of this line, was twelve foot high. The wall on the east line was twelve foot high, on the north it was ten, on the west it was eighteen.

Impoverished Massachusetts demurred at having to pay the bills for the work, but Phips drove the State to meet the obligation.

The ruler of New France at this time was the energetic and far-sighted Frontenac, who believed that he must reduce the new English fortress or himself lose his hold on his Indian allies. With characteristic promptness he set out about the task that he had visioned. Two ships and some hundreds of savages were despatched to take the fort. The fort had been forewarned through the heroism of a young New Englander, John Nelson, who faced the Bastile or death by the headsman's hands to get word to his brethren in

QUAINT AND HISTORIC FORTS

New England of the expected expedition. The garrison was on its guard and so the expedition miscarried.

Frontenac was not the man to be put off with one reverse, however, as the New Englanders should have realized but did not. In August, 1696, Iberville, with two war-ships and a mixed force of French and Indians, appeared before Fort William Henry and took the garrison completely by surprise.

There were about one hundred men in the fort under the command of Captain Pascho Chubb. Castine and his Indians who are supposed to have landed at New Harbor, two miles away, set up entrenchments in the rear of the fortress (where the cemetery is), thus cutting off the garrison on the land side. Cannon were landed and batteries erected on adjacent shores and islands. With so much energy did the besiegers work that their batteries opened fire at three o'clock of the afternoon following the day on which they appeared before the fort.

To the first summons to surrender Chubb returned a defiant answer, but when the first shells began to burst within his lines he seems to have lost his courage. Intimidated, in addition, by Iberville's threat to show no quarter if he persisted in resistance, he hastened to throw open his gates to the foe. The Indians, hard enough to keep in order, anyhow, found one of their race in irons in the prison of the fortress and immediately began a slaughter of the surrendered English.

FORT FREDERICK

This outbreak was restrained with difficulty, and the English were loaded on ships and sent to Boston.

Two days were consumed by the French in destroying the fortifications at Pemaquid and they then set sail for St. John's River, narrowly escaping destruction by a fleet sent out from Boston in pursuit.

The next attempt to fortify Pemaquid was made in 1729, when Colonel Dunbar was sent over with a royal commission to rebuild the fort at the charge of the English crown. This work he set himself to with a right good will, and he called his fort Fort Frederick in honor of the Prince of Wales, father of George III. Fort Frederick stood until the opening of the Revolutionary War, when the inhabitants of Pemaquid destroyed the works rather than man them, advancing the unique argument that since the people were not strong enough to defend them they were a source of weakness rather than strength!

That the inhabitants of this coast were not lacking in spirit is shown, however, by an incident of the War of 1812, which may be told here. The enemy's cruisers kept the whole coast in alarm because of their frequent depredations against defenceless points. One day one of these cruisers hove to in New Harbor and a barge fully manned put out for shore. A small militia force had been stationed by the Americans at old Fort Frederick and this force was hastily summoned. The English barge drew near. It was hailed by an old fisherman who warned the British officer not to attempt a landing.

"If a gun is fired the whole town will be destroyed," replied the Britisher.

Not a single gun, but a number of them, answered this threat. The rocks of the shore bristled with fowling pieces and ducking-guns and all manner of firearms. The barge drifted helplessly to sea, its occupants badly wounded, and the master of the war-ship, after taking his helpless men on board, sailed away to Halifax.

Old Fort Frederick, in 1814, saw the beginning of the historic combat between the vessels *Boxer* and the *Enterprise,* in which the *Enterprise,* U. S. A., commanded by Lieutenant Burrows, was victorious.

FORT NIAGARA
AT MOUTH OF NIAGARA RIVER—NEW YORK

THE main building of old Fort Niagara, " The Castle," is probably the oldest piece of masonry in the State of New York, having been constructed by the French in 1726. The stone-work of the barracks, a structure 134 by 24 feet with walls only eight feet in height, goes back to 1757, and in this year was, also, built the magazine. The bake-house, replacing a former one on the same site, was put up by the British in 1762 and the two stone block-houses by them in 1771 and 1773.

In the two hundred and eighty-eight and a half acres of the government reservation here one is in touch visibly with the Past. And what deeds of the Past these old stone buildings might tell if they were given power of speech!

The name Niagara is of Iroquois origin, as are so many names of New York State, and is of ancient application to the river and the falls which bear them. The falls of the Niagara are indicated on Champlain's map of 1632 and in 1648 are spoken of by the Jesuit Rugueneau as " a cataract of frightful height." It is certain that the indefatigable emissaries of the order of which he was a member had penetrated to the region of the great falls before this. In 1678 the falls were visited by the Friar Louis Hennepin, who drew a curious picture of them, still preserved, and gave a more curious and exaggerated description.

In the year that the good Friar Hennepin was paying his respects to Nature's great wonder, Robert Cavelier Sieur de la Salle was building his fort at Frontenac, now Kingston, Canada West, and in 1675 King Louis XIV, that brilliant and indefatigable monarch of France, whose legislative labors in opposition to race suicide in Canada justly earned him the title of the Father of Canada, bestowed upon our cavalier a large grant of land near his fort. La Salle, inspired by the brilliant discoveries of Marquette and Joliet in the region farther west than that wherein he had his bailiwick, determined to explore the lands south of Ontario and to connect the territories which he hoped thus to acquire with Quebec by means of a series of posts. Empowered by his royal master with letters warrant to embark upon this form of enterprise, he crossed over Ontario, picked out a settlement point at, or near, the present Lewiston, New York, and commenced the building of a small vessel on Cayuga Creek above the falls, the supplies for this vessel being carried from his little settlement near Lewiston, below the falls, and in the direction of his main base at Fort Frontenac. At the same time he commenced the construction of a small fort at the mouth of the Niagara River, which would guard the approaches to his work farther in the interior and

FORT NIAGARA, ON NIAGARA RIVER, N. Y.

Copyright, Detroit Publishing Company

FORT NIAGARA

would also serve as one of the chain of posts by which he hoped to secure to France the territory which he meant to acquire.

This little fort on Niagara Point at the mouth of the Niagara River was kept up by La Salle during the remainder of his career in the New World, and was continued by the Marquis de Nonville, Governor of New France, who, in 1687, raised it to the dignity of a "fort with four bastions." At this time it was in the command of Troyes with 100 men. Soon after this the little place was besieged by Senecas, and while the four bastions and the other defences beat off the savage foe, the garrison perished almost to a man from the ravages of disease. Shortly after the point was abandoned and allowed to fall into decay. During the succeeding years of misfortune to the French the fort was filled only with weeds and vines and savage visitors,—early prototypes of present-day tourist throngs,—and it was not until 1725 that the place was reoccupied and rehabilitated.

From this time for many years Fort Niagara was a little city in itself and for a long time the greatest point south of Montreal or west of Albany. The fort, proper, covered about eight acres and had its ravines, ditches and pickets, curtains, counterscarps and covered way; stone-towers, laboratory and magazine; mess-house, barracks, bakery and blacksmith shop. For worship there was a chapel with a large dial over the door to mark the course of the sun. "The dungeon of the mess-house, called the black hole, was a strong, dark, and dismal place; and in one corner of the room was fixed the apparatus for strangling such unhappy wretches as fell under the displeasure of the despotic rulers of those days. The walls of this dungeon, from top to bottom, had engraved upon them French names and mementos in that language. That the prisoners were no common persons was clear, as the letters and emblems were chiselled out in good style."

The immense strategic importance of the post was not lost on the English. It guarded approach to the treasured winter regions of the great lakes with their store of furs, and it furnished a fine base for negotiations with the Indians of New York State and the keeping of them in a state of disaffection with the English.

In 1755, during that series of preliminary conflicts which marked the beginning of the great battle royal between France and England for the possession of the New World, an expedition against Niagara was fitted out by Governor Shirley, of Massachusetts, and proceeded under his command as far as Oswego. Thus far it went and no farther, for sickness and desertion thinned the ranks of the men, and unfavorable weather, as well as the presence of the French in strength at Frontenac just across the lake, rendered unwise further advance in the Governor of Massachusetts' project. It was not for four years, 1759, that the arm of the English was used in strength against the busy, ancient fort.

FORT NIAGARA

In this year General Prideaux, a capable officer, with Sir William Johnson, of New York, as his second in command, was despatched with a force of English colonial troops and Indians against the post. Fort Niagara was garrisoned by 600 French soldiers under the command of Captain Pouchot, a chevalier of the order of St. Louis. About a mile up the river was a little wooden stockade commanded by the half-breed Joincaire-Chabert, who with his brother Joincaire-Clauzonne and a clan of Indian relatives had long been a thorn in the side of the English in influencing the powerful Five Nations against them. But Sir William Johnson was beginning to have that ascendency over this savage federation which was to be so great an aid to the English from this time forward and had with him now 900 warriors of this clan to lead against the French. So Joincaire closed up his little stronghold and joined his forces to those of Pouchot, the combined strength of the two by no means being sufficient to beat off the English attack.

There was another resource upon which Pouchot confidently relied, however, and this was prospect of help from the back countries controlled by the French. By order of Vaudreuil, the Governor of New France, the French population of the Illinois, Detroit and other distant posts had come down the Lakes, a motley and picturesque throng, to help maintain the ascendency of France in the New World. They were now gathered at various posts of the French back country, and no sooner did Pouchot learn that the English were about to attack him than he sent messengers to summon all of these forces to Niagara.

The siege began with the clumsy lack of forethought which seemed to mark all military operations of those days, which depended chiefly upon native courage and final enthusiasm of assault to carry through than wise foreplanning. The English trenches were so unskilfully laid out that they were raked by the fire of the fort. However, the English at last got down to business and their batteries commenced to play upon the French. A prematurely bursting shell from one of the coehorns killed Prideaux at almost the first discharges of the bombardment and the command fell upon Sir William Johnson, who proceeded with an enheartening energy to carry on the good work. At the end of three weeks the rampart of Fort Niagara was breached, more than 100 of the soldiery therein had been killed and the garrison was in extremity. Yet Pouchot fought on valiantly, resting upon the arrival of reinforcements from the French and savage forces which he had summoned. At length a distant firing told him that these were near.

Pouchot went with an officer to the bastion next to the river and listened anxiously to the firing which told him that his reinforcements were in conflict with the English and trying to cut a way through to the beleaguered stronghold. For a time he heard the sound of

FORT NIAGARA

battle and then all was still. At length a friendly Indian who had passed unnoticed through the lines of the English came to the French commander. " Your men are defeated," he said in substance. Pouchot would not believe him. Nevertheless it was true and this fact was the death-blow to French hold of Fort Niagara. In the articles of surrender shortly afterward drawn up, it was specially stipulated that the French should be protected from the Indians as they feared that the massacre of Fort William Henry would be avenged upon them. Johnson was able to restrain his lawless allies and, though the fort was given to pillage, no French lives were taken after the surrender.

From this time until the close of the American War of Independence the post remained in English hands. During the Pontiac War of 1763 the Indians made an unsuccessful attack upon it and its garrison frequently took part in small skirmishes with lurking unfriendly Senecas in the woods around the post. Heavily garrisoned by the English during the Revolution, it served as a base for the war parties which frequently devastated the State of New York. Both the expedition led by Colonel Butler, which culminated in the massacre at Wyoming, New York, in 1778, and that which laid waste Cherry Valley in the same year, started from Fort Niagara.

That the American forces were not unaware of the evil dominance of this post on the far western border of

QUAINT AND HISTORIC FORTS

New York, we cannot doubt, as one of the objects of the expedition led by General Sullivan against the Indians in 1779 was the destruction, if possible, of Niagara; but this campaign ended only with the destruction of Indian villages. Subsequent to the declaration of peace between England and America, the point was held by English troops until it was taken over by an American garrison in 1796, probably having the distinction of being the last post surrendered by the English to the Americans in the United States. In 1799, in anticipation of another Indian war, the post was heavily reinforced.

A description of Fort Niagara between 1805 and 1814 has been given by a daughter of Dr. West, surgeon to the post during those years.

> It was then surrounded on three sides with strong pickets of plank, firmly planted in the ground and closely joined together; a heavy gate in front of double plank, closely studded with iron spikes. The fourth side was defended with embankments of earth under which were formerly barracks, affording a safe though somewhat gloomy retreat for the families of soldiers, but which had been abandoned and the entrance closed long before my remembrance, having been so infested with rattlesnakes that had made their dens within that it was hardly safe to walk across the parade.

The last chapter in the history of the fort was not a glorious one, though thoroughly typical of the desultory character of the conflict between Great Britain and the United States which is known as the War of 1812.

FORT NIAGARA

The official declaration of the imminence of hostilities reached Fort Niagara, June 26, 1812, and preparations were immediately undertaken to strengthen and defend the work. The fort was then under the command of Captain Leonard, United States Artillery, with 370 men. During the night of December 19, 1813, the English, 500 strong, under Colonel Murray, crossed the river, captured the sentinels and took the work by surprise, killing 65 of the American garrison and taking prisoner almost all of the remainder, with a loss to themselves of five men killed and wounded. A disgraceful side of the matter is that none of the American officers were at their posts at this time, but were off junketing somewhere in the country near by. Twenty-seven cannon of large calibre, 3000 stand of small arms, and a large amount of clothing, garrison equipage, and commissary stores fell into the hands of the British, who, as well, destroyed the villages of Lewiston and Buffalo, besides all of the dwellings on the lake as far as Eighteen-Mile Creek.

The capture of Fort Niagara was shortly afterwards characterized in the following terms by General Cass who was ordered to the frontier: " The fall of Niagara was owing to the most criminal negligence; the force in it was fully competent for its defence."

The English held Niagara until the close of the war and surrendered it to the United States in March, 1815. The career of the point from that time to the present has been merely one of growing old gracefully.

FORT ONTARIO
OSWEGO—NEW YORK

T was in 1722 that Oswego, New York, was made the site of an armed camp and, at that, it was more through the stubborn determination of Governor Burnet of the colony that the thing should be done than through any willingness of the staid burghers of the State Assembly to co-operate with their executive in schemes leading to future good. As a matter of fact, Governor Burnet is said to have paid the bill for establishing his little fort out of his own pocket, though he may have made this sum up in some other direction—authorities do not tell us this kind of thing! Yet this little post was to become one of the most decisive factors in determining the result of the conflict between France and England for the New World, the flags of three Christian nations were to fly over it at different periods, and warriors white, red, French, English and colonial were to struggle for its possession. So much grows out of so little!

One of the earliest mentions of Oswego in the history of the colonies is that in 1687 the Onondaga Indians presented a petition to the mayor and common council of Albany, that busy little trading post, requesting them to establish a trading post and fort at this

From William Smith's view of the Province of New York, London edition of 1757

FORT ONTARIO

point. The mayor and common council evidently thought that this was too wild an undertaking; for no defences existed there when, in 1696, the restless Frontenac landed at Oswego Point on a punitive expedition against the Five Nations and built himself a little stockade fort before pressing on to fruitless victory into the interior of the country.

The strategic importance of the location to the English was not lost on these astute empire builders, giving access as it does with the Hudson Valley by way of the Oswego River, through Oneida Lake, to the headwaters of the Mohawk River, or giving access to the Susquehanna Valley by way of the Oswego River, Lake Onandaga and the head of the Susquehanna. During the governorship of Lord Bellemont, in the province of New York, the establishment of a post at Oswego was contemplated, and material was even ordered from England for the purpose, but it remained for Governor Bellemont's successor to carry out in effect what had been before done in theory.

In 1727 Governor Burnet called the attention of the councillors of the province to the fact that he had established a post at Oswego (the name was borrowed from the Iroquois), and added that he had sent a captain, two lieutenants and sixty soldiers to the point and that he intended to keep a force there always.

This announcement came to the ear of the governor of New France and so incensed him that he sent a letter to Governor Burnet asking that official why, in opposition to the plain stipulations of the Treaty of Ghent which forbade the erection of works of defence or offence, he had constructed and manned this fort. Governor Burnet replied by calling attention to the French building of "Oneagorah" or Niagara, thus showing that the practice of justifying a soiled pot by pointing to a black kettle is of ancient foundation. Anyhow, Governor Burnet went cheerfully on with his fortifying of Oswego, though Governor Beauharnais sent several expeditions to harass and deter his workmen.

This first fortification at Oswego was of a very simple character. Beauharnais complained that it was "a redoubt with galleries and full of loop-holes and other works belonging to fortifications," but Burnet merely says that the "walls were four feet thick of large good stone" and finds no other details to dilate upon. In 1741 the colony authorized the expenditure of 600 pounds, sterling, to "erect a sufficient stone wall at a proper distance around the trading house at Oswego, either in a triangular or quadrangular form, as the ground will best admit of, with a bastion or block-house in each corner to flank the curtain." Later on we find that complaints were made to the General Assembly that the contractors who had the job in hand were using clay instead of stone and that they were skimping their work fearfully in order to line their pockets generously. This is one of the very earliest public scandals of New York State and one that seems to have eluded the muck-raker so far.

The post was abandoned between the years 1744 and 1755 as, on the outbreak of hostilities with Canada, its occupants feared that they could not in their exposed and unsupported position withstand an attack in force from Quebec.

As the years went on, however, the post of Oswego became increasingly valuable to the English and they in turn became far more able to hold their own. Situated as it was between Niagara and the ocean,—between the back country of the French and their metropolis of Quebec,—it fairly broke the back of the long wriggling French line of settlements, which extended from the mouth of the St. Lawrence to the mouth of the Mississippi.

In 1755 the English authorities agreed upon a plan of invasion of Canada and resolved to make Oswego their base of operations. Accordingly Colonel Shirley, of Massachusetts, with his own and Sir William Pepperell's regiments, with some New Jersey and New York militia, in addition, made his way to Oswego, arriving there about the end of June, 1755. They were prevented by sickness and ill luck from proceeding against Niagara as had been their intention, and the one great thing that they accomplished was the rehabilitation of the old fort. They also commenced a fort on the west side of the river, which they called Fort Ontario, and Fort Ontario has survived to the present day. An extract from the "Gentleman's Magazine" of 1756, New York Colonial Documents, gives an idea of this undertaking:

> When it was determined that the army at Oswego should go into winter quarters, they began a new fort upon the hill upon the east side of the river, about 470 yards from the old one; it is 800 feet in circumference and will command the harbor; it is built of logs from 20 to 30 inches thick; the wall is 14 feet high and is encompassed by a ditch 14 feet broad and 10 feet deep; it is to contain barracks for 300 men. On the other side of the river west from the old fort another new fort is erecting; this is 170 feet square. A hospital of frame-work, 150 feet by 30 feet, is already built and may serve as a barrack for 200 men, and another barrack is preparing of 150 feet by 24.

The second new fort noted in this extract is Fort George, a rude structure and one not fitted long to stand against the elements.

Another result of Shirley's expedition was to cause the French, who had been rather inactive, to bestir themselves. In the fall of 1755 they heavily reinforced their posts, sending to Fort Niagara a lively young Captain named Pouchot. In 1756 this observant man despatched a memorial to his superiors at Quebec, setting forth that the English at Oswego were not on the alert, or in force, and that the capture of the post was a feasibility. The authorities at Quebec thought well of this idea, so well in fact that Montcalm, himself, who was at Fort Frontenac,—newly arrived in New France to take over the command of the military forces of the whole French new world,—took charge of the expedition, which was organized on Captain Pouchot's suggestion.

Before proceeding in force against Oswego, Montcalm ordered De Villiers to proceed with 700 men to the headwaters of the Oswego River and to observe the enemy at Oswego. This force advanced rapidly, surprised and took Fort Bull, on Wood Creek near the head of Oneida Lake, and destroyed a large amount of provisions destined for Oswego. On May 7, 1756, a party of Indians set out from Fort Niagara, made a descent upon some ship carpenters near Oswego, and returned to Niagara with twelve scalps. These repeated successes, joined with Braddock's defeat, produced a profound effect upon the Indians and caused the Iroquois Federation to side for the time with the French. Throughout the early summer of this year Montcalm's men continued to harass the garrison at Oswego, capturing many stores of provisions designed for Fort Ontario. Montcalm hurried his preparations, so that by August he was ready to march against Oswego with 3000 men well equipped. He landed on Four-inch Point, east of Oswego, on August 11, and marched to a swamp a short distance in the rear of Fort Ontario, where he gave charge of the engineering operations now developing upon his expedition to Captain Pouchot.

Pouchot constructed a road through the swamp in one night and opened up with a battery upon Fort Ontario at sixty paces distance. The garrison fled in disorder across the river to the old fort. Montcalm sent a strong force to cross the river above to cut off retreat and opened fire the next morning with a battery on the river bank. Colonel Mercer, the English commander, was killed and his men soon surrendered. The spoils of the conqueror were 120 cannon, 9 vessels of war in process of construction, and a great quantity of provisions and munitions of war.

There now occurred another one of those horrible massacres which fouled the name of the French through their inability to control their savage allies. The prisoners numbered 1700, many of them civilian employees in the ship-yards, and Montcalm had pledged their safety. Notwithstanding this, more than a hundred were killed by the savages, either quickly or by the slow process of torture. The French losses in the siege were 30 killed and wounded, and the English killed in fighting numbered 150.

The artillery of the English forts at Oswego was removed to Fort Niagara and the forts were dismantled. The forts remained unoccupied until 1759, when the English advancing to the attack of Fort Niagara left a force of 500 men here to protect their rear and keep

FORT ONTARIO

open their lines of communication. The French advanced against this small command and would have taken it by surprise had not a priest insisted upon speaking to the troops before they went into battle. The English became apprised of the approach of the French during this delay and sallied out to attack them, with victory in the subsequent battle crowning their efforts.

In 1760 General Amherst strengthened the forts at Oswego and left a large force here which became valuable in the war against Canada. This was one of the few fortunate moves that this general made.

Fort Ontario was also an important base for the British during the war of American Independence. In 1777 the English Colonel St. Leger gathered 700 men here and was joined by Brant with 700 Indians. The combined forces marched to besiege Fort Stanwix at the head of the Mohawk River, but were defeated and pursued back to their base, where they hurriedly embarked for Montreal.

In 1783 General Washington prepared an expedition under Colonel Willett to capture Fort Ontario. The command assembled at Fort Stanwix and marched for Oswego. When within a few miles of the fort their presence was discovered and made known to the British by some wood-cutters, and Colonel Willett, on learning that his chance of taking the post by surprise was gone, marched back to Fort Stanwix without making an attack. Peace was soon declared and no further operations were conducted.

QUAINT AND HISTORIC FORTS

The post was transferred to the United States in 1796, with the other frontier posts which Great Britain had held. From then until the outbreak of the War of 1812 it was allowed to fall into decay, and at the beginning of that conflict was but partially armed and quite unable to withstand an enemy. The English, hearing of its condition, and hearing, moreover, of the presence in the fort of large quantities of stores of all kinds, sent a fleet with 3000 men against the place.

The British force appeared before the town May 5, 1814. The Americans prepared a battery on shore and gallantly repulsed efforts at landing, until at length the British, through pure force of numbers, were able to accomplish this first step. The Americans then retreated up the river in good order, burning the bridges in their rear. Their number was 300. The British, baffled in taking any prisoners, burned the barracks, spiked the guns and retired. The American loss was 6 killed, 38 wounded and 24 missing. The British loss was 235. From that time to the present Fort Ontario has remained in possession of the United States.

The years saw the town of Oswego grow up around Fort Ontario. The fort was rebuilt of wood in 1839 and of stone in 1863. In 1901 the garrison was withdrawn and the old fort is now a public reservation for the use of the citizens of Oswego, its days of military life probably ended forever.

FORT MICHILLIMACKINAC AND FORT HOLMES
MACKINAC ISLAND—MICHIGAN

IT was a conjunction of the Church and the State which began the career of Fort Michillimackinac, more than three centuries ago, at Saint Ignace, a point on the Canadian side of the Straits of Mackinac; the Church in the person of the restless Father Marquette and the State in the form of its indefatigable military servant, the Sieur de la Salle. In 1673 Father Marquette established the mission of Saint Ignace in a thriving village of the Ottawas, who were, Francis Parkman tells us, among the most civilized tribes of the American natives. Two years later La Salle visited the place in the *Griffon,* the first vessel to sail the Great Lakes. This barque the indefatigable Frenchmen had just constructed on Cayuga Creek just above Niagara Falls.

The beginnings of a fort were already made when La Salle came to St. Ignace, that is, a palisade had been erected. Its defenders were Indians. La Salle sent the *Griffon* back to civilization for supplies and rigging for a second sailing vessel. Fortunately for history, which would have lost one of its most picturesque figures, he decided to remain, himself, at Saint Ignace and not to accompany his beloved *Griffon* on its round trip.

QUAINT AND HISTORIC FORTS

That bewildered little ship was overcome by the fury of one of the lakes. At least it never returned, or was heard of, and reasonable surmise is that it found its haven beneath the waters. La Salle filled in his spare hours at Saint Ignace in the casual practice of his profession, by completing and strengthening the puny defences which Father Marquette had caused to be erected. Thus came into existence the first Fort Michillimackinac.

Indian tradition concerning the name Michillimackinac is curious. It relates that Michapous, chief of spirits, sojourned long in the vicinity of the Straits of Huron, on a mountain on the border of the lake. Here he first instructed man to fabricate nets and to take fish therein. On the island of Michillimackinac he left spirits named Imakinakos and from these legendary possessors came the name Michillimackinac which means Great Turtle. The tradition is not altogether clear. Suffice it to be assured that the word is of Indian origin, and doubtless its patient originators were thoroughly well pleased with it.

The next distinguished visitor to Saint Ignace was La Motte Cadillac, whose name is spread so generously around all of this lakeside region of Michigan and whose errand was to strengthen the fort which La Salle had erected on Father Marquette's foundation. Useless labor this proved to be, for the growing importance of Detroit and the determination of the French to build

FORT MICHILLIMACKINAC

up this point at the expense of the more northern and less accessible trading-post caused Saint Ignace to wane in importance and its stockades to be unoccupied.

In 1712 the little setttlement was moved bodily to the southern side of the straits at the point where Mackinaw City now stands and the second Fort Michillimackinac was erected, destined to a far more eventful history than the first. Time ran on. The French lost their grip of the New World and surrendered Michillimackinac with other places to the English. Let us see how the little place looked in English possession. Parkman has well described it:

> Doubling a point he sees before him the red flag of England swelling lazily in the wind and the palisades and wooden bastions of Fort Michillimackinac standing close upon the margin of the lake. On the beach canoes are drawn up and Canadians and Indians are lazily lounging A little beyond the fort is a cluster of the white Canadian houses roofed with bark and protected by fences of strong round pickets The trader enters at the gate, and sees before him an extensive square area surrounded by high palisades. Numerous houses, barracks, and other buildings form a smaller square within, and in the vacant space which they enclose appear the red uniforms of British soldiers, the gray coats of Canadians, and the gaudy Indian blankets mingled in picturesque confusion; while a multitude of squaws with children of every hue stroll restlessly about the place. Such was Fort Michillimackinac in 1763.

A peaceful spot this was for the scene of bloody savagery which was shortly to be enacted in its precincts. The Indians who were neighbors of Michillimackinac had never become reconciled to the Englishman's presence in their wilderness. Many of these savages had fought with the French against the English and had lost relatives or friends in battle, thus laying the foundations for blood feuds which in the Indian custom could only be wiped out with blood. In addition to that, their leaders were conspirators with the great Pontiac in his aim to push the English back beyond the mountains whence they had come and to restore the forests to the savages. When news came in the spring of 1763 of Pontiac's activities around Detroit, the Ojibwas and Ottawas near Michillimackinac determined that they, too, must taste of blood. The massacre of the garrison of this post was planned.

The Indians' plans were laid well but they should not have had the uncontested success that they did have. All accounts point to a great measure of carelessness and lack of sufficient estimation of his neighbors on the part of the unhappy commander of the garrison. This officer was Captain Etherington and with him were about thirty-five men and the full complement of under-officers. Several times Etherington was warned that the red-skins were plotting mischief, and his own observation might have acquainted him with this fact as well. Yet with true British phlegm he waved aside all suggestions that were made to him and even went so far as to threaten to punish any one who disturbed his garrison with stories of impending disaster. It is not remarkable that the Indians found him unprepared.

On the morning of the fourth of June the weather was warm and sultry. It was his majesty King George's birthday and for this reason there were festal arrangements at the fort. The soldiers were allowed liberty to wander where they would, in or out of the stockades, and the Indians had permission to play a game of ball in honor of the day. As time went on the fort became filled with Indians, chiefs and humble followers of the ranks, old hags, young women and children.

The hour for the ball game approached. This game of ball, or baggataway as the red men called it, was a favorite with the Indians. It was very much like the lacrosse of the present day, in fact was the original of that game. There were two goals and the players attempted to toss a ball through one of these two goals with sticks. They were not allowed to use their hands to throw the ball, so the game required a degree of skill as well as agility and endurance.

The Ojibwas and the Sacs, two rivals of long standing, were the contestants and excitement ran high. Captain Etherington, with one of his lieutenants, was lounging at the gate of the fort whooping on the Ojibwas, for he had promised them that he would bet on their side. Suddenly the ball arose in the air in a graceful curve and fell within the walls of the fort. The players, an excited mob, burst after it yelling. Suspecting nothing, Etherington stepped aside with a laugh to let the howling mass sweep in the walls of the citadel.

The Indians' stratagem had been completely successful. Before he knew what was being done, Etherington, with his lieutenant, was seized and bound, while the Indians, reinforced by their comrades amongst the spectators of the game, seized tomahawks which the squaws had concealed beneath their blankets and fell on the hapless members of the little garrison. There commenced one of those familiar scenes of butchery with which border tradition and the accounts of witnesses who escaped have made us familiar. Men were stricken down and held between Indians' knees while they were scalped, still alive. Women and children were slaughtered. Bodies of both sexes were mangled. Frenzied red warriors scooped up handfuls of blood and drank it in gulps. Soon the chapter was ended. Only a few of the little garrison—kept, like Etherington, on account of rank or for some particular reasons —were left alive.

From this day for four years Fort Michillimackinac was without a garrison. Then, with the subjection of the red tribes, the English came back to their border posts and Michillimackinac was once more filled with soldiery. In the early days of the Revolution the walls

Copyright, Detroit Publishing Company

FORT MICHILLIMACKINAC AND STATE PARK, MACKINAC ISLAND, MICHIGAN

Copyright, Detroit Publishing Company
OLD BLOCK-HOUSE AND MISSION POINT, FORT MICHILIMACKINAC RESERVATION, MACKINAC ISLAND, MICHIGAN

FORT MICHILLIMACKINAC

of the fort were strengthened and the garrison was increased.

The strategic location of the fort had never been advantageous for purposes of defence, however, so in November, 1779, Major de Peyster, fearful of attacks by the Americans, moved his garrison over to the little island of Michillimackinac and built the third Fort Michillimackinac, that which is standing to-day. The location which Major de Peyster chose was on the southeastern portion of the island, which is three miles wide and seven miles long, and there is a fine harbor at the point chosen for the location of the fort. This third fort Michillimackinac was occupied by the British on July 15, 1780, but was not used by them during the Revolution. In 1796 it was turned over to an American garrison as the sequel of an extensive correspondence between the young new nation and its tenacious old mother country.

As it was necessary to know what disposition to make of her newly-acquired border forts, the United States at the close of the eighteenth century despatched a certain Uriah Tracy to visit the frontier of the country and report on the condition of the fortifications there. His letter about Michillimackinac, preserved in the War Department files, gives a picture of the place in December, 1800. The body of the letter follows:

QUAINT AND HISTORIC FORTS

Hon. Samuel Dexter, Secretary of War:

In consequence of your predecessor's request to visit post in the Western territory I proceeded to Plattsburg . . . and on to Michillimackinac. Our fort at Michillimackinac is one of our most important posts. It stands on an island in the straits which lead from Lake Michigan into Lake Huron four or five miles from the head of the strait. Fort Michillimackinac is an irregular work partly built with a strong wall and partly with pickets; and the parade ground within it is from 100 to 125 feet above the surface of the water. It contains a well of never-failing water, a boom proof used as a magazine, one stone barracks for the use of the officers, equal if not superior to any building of the kind in the United States, a good guard-house and barracks for soldiers and convenient store-houses for produce, etc., with three strong and convenient block-houses. This post is strong both by nature and by art and the possession of it has a great influence with the Indians in favor of the United States. The whole island on which the fort is situated belongs to the United States and is five or six miles in length and two or three miles in width. On the bank of the strait adjacent to the fort stands a large house which was by the English called Government House and was kept by the British commander of the fort which now belongs to the United States.

The island and the country about it is remarkably healthy and very fertile for so high a northern latitude.

Uriah Tracy.

The breaking out of the War of 1812 found only 57 soldiers under Lieutenant Porter Hanks at Fort Michillimackinac. Moreover, the federal authorities at Washington neglected to notify several of their border forts that war had been declared. Accordingly when

FORT MICHILLIMACKINAC

Captain Roberts, in command of a British force consisting of English soldiers, volunteers and Indians to the number of about 900, descended upon the little post, Michillimackinac was not in the attitude of resistance.

Thus captured by the British, the post was a most important stronghold for them during the continuance of the conflict between the two countries. Not only did it give them a base of great strategic possibilities, but its easy capture had an immense moral effect upon the Indian tribes round about, bringing many of these tribes to the British aid and being the direct cause of much of the Indian trouble that Americans suffered on the western frontier at this time.

The English set to energetically fortifying the point as soon as they had assumed charge. A hill-top back of Fort Michillimackinac became the site for a blockhouse which is standing to this day, and the walls of Mackinac were strengthened and made greater. A letter from R. McDouall, the British commander, of date July 17, 1814, says:

> I am doing my utmost to prepare for their (the American) reception. Our new works on the hill overlooking the old fort are nearly completed and the block-house in the centre will be finished this week, which will make the position one of the strongest in Canada. Its principal defect is the difficulty of finding water near it, but that obviated and a sufficient supply of provisions laid in, no force that the enemy can bring will be able to reduce it.

QUAINT AND HISTORIC FORTS

The Englishman's opinion of the invulnerability to attack of his block-house was proved by events and was evidently shared by the Americans, for, when they came in force against Michillimackinac, they attacked from a different quarter. The American forces were under the command of Colonel Croghan and Major Holmes, who was beloved throughout the American army for his engaging personality and many fine qualities. During the short and unsuccessful attack Holmes was mortally hurt. At the conclusion of the war, when Michillimackinac and its new block-house were surrendered by Great Britain to the United States, the name of this talented young officer was applied to the block-house. The surrender of Michillimackinac took place July 18, 1815.

From the date of its surrender until 1895 Fort Michillimackinac was regularly garrisoned by United States troops, but in this latter year the garrison was withdrawn and the works were left in the charge of a caretaker. The block-houses were in rather dilapidated condition and the grounds had become overgrown when, in 1909, the Mackinac Island State Park Commission of Michigan was created and in the hands of this organization the old fort has fared well. The block-house has been restored and the grounds of the fort and its buildings have been maintained at the public expense. Every year Michillimackinac is visited by sight-seers and the island is a popular summering place for many.

FORT MASSAC
NEAR METROPOLIS—ILLINOIS

THE far too far-seeing French in 1702, in furtherance of their design of dominion in North America, despatched a detachment of about thirty men from Kaskaskia under the temporal command of M. Juchereau de St. Denis and the spiritual direction of fiery Father Mermet to establish a trading post, mission and fort, as near as convenient to the mouth of the Ohio River to guard the southern access to this vital means of travel. The result of this expedition was the establishment of Fort Massac, the site of the future little city of Metropolis, Illinois.

Consider the map as it is to-day, showing Metropolis and the surrounding country, and see the fine position that Fort Massac had in the day of its establishment: It was about thirty-six miles above the mouth of the Ohio, quite far enough up to be out of the reach of any flood of that great torrent and also to be beyond the convenient call of marauding expeditions which might be making the Mississippi their route north; it faced to the south the mouth of the Tennessee River and was not far from where the Cumberland and Wabash rivers joined their courses to the Ohio, and thus it had fine trading advantages. Therefore it is not to be wondered at that for a time the new post flourished mightily. Juchereau traded and Father Mermet preached to satisfied savages and Frenchmen.

Of Father Mermet's work it has been said that his gentle virtues in every-day life and his fervid eloquence in the spiritual rostrum made him beloved and respected by all.

At early dawn his pupils came to church dressed neatly and modestly each in a deer-skin or robe sewn together from several skins. After receiving lessons they chanted canticle; mass was then said in presence of all the Christians, the French and the converts—the women on one side and the men on the other. From prayers and instructions the missionaries proceeded to visit the sick and administer medicine, and their skill as physicians did more than all the rest to win confidence. In the afternoon the catechism was taught in the presence of the young and old, when every one, without distinction of rank or age, answered the questions of the missionary. At evening all would assemble at the chapel for instruction, for prayer and to chant the hymns of the Church. On Sunday and festivals, even after vespers, a homily was pronounced; at the close of the day parties would meet in houses to recite the chaplets in alternate choirs and sing psalms till late at night. Saturday and Sunday were the days appointed for confession and communion and every convert confessed once in a fortnight. The success of this mission was such that marriages of the French immigrants were sometimes solemnized with the daughters of the Illinois according to the rites of the Catholic church.

Tradition says that the site of Massac had been used by de Soto for a palisade in 1542, but whether this is

MEMORIAL MONUMENT
(Erected by Illinois Daughters American Revolution)

From the River
FORT MASSAC, ON THE OHIO (LA BELLE RIVIERE)

true there is no positive evidence to prove. Juchereau's settlement consisted of a palisaded fort, a trading house, several log cottages and the chapel which Mermet christened "Assumption," and this name was applied to the entire settlement for some years. The name "Massac" did not originate until half a century later. For a time, indeed, the point was known as the "Old Cherokee Fort."

Juchereau was removed from Massac and went to the southern waters of the Mississippi, where he found many large "fish to fry" which need not be described in this chapter, and the good Father Mermet was taken back to Kaskaskia. Deprived of its mainsprings in this fashion, the little post began to languish and shortly came to grief because of rising disaffection among the surrounding Indians. The place was abandoned by the French fleeing for their lives and leaving behind them thirteen thousand buffalo skins which were eagerly seized by the Indians from whom they had been purchased at the rate of munificence usual to those days. Tradition has it that the post was re-established by adventurers shortly after its abandonment and was used as a trading centre pure and simple, but the once lively little foundation of Juchereau and Mermet was not again conspicuous in the events of that border until the French and Indian War of 1756-63.

During this time it was a rendezvous for the French on the Ohio River and was their last defence in the campaign of the English which finally wrested La Belle Riviere from the lilies of France. In 1756 French soldiers landed here in force, threw up earthworks and erected a stockade with four bastions mounting eight cannon. Henceforth in French records the site was known as Fort Massac. In 1763, by the terms of the Treaty of Paris, Massac became an English possession together with all of the rest of the French strongholds in North America, but it was not until the spring of 1765 that the troops of France finally marched out from the fort. The English during the thirteen years that they held the Illinois country never occupied the point with troops.

The event in which Fort Massac played a part, which was to have the greatest influence in its section, took place, however, not during its French and Indian days, but later, when the American colonies were asserting their independence of the Mother Country. All of the Illinois country was held then by His Majesty's troops, but it was common information that the French inhabitants of the conquered country were not extraordinarily well disposed to their rulers and that the garrisons of the English strongholds here had been largely reduced to aid the fight on the eastern sea-coast. Accordingly it entered the head of one George Rogers Clark, a daring borderman of twenty-six years, Virginian by birth, that it would not be an impossible task to take from the English by force the country which

FORT MASSAC

they had in this manner seized from the French. June, 1778, saw him landing at Fort Massac, then ungarrisoned, with a small body of men, and this same day probably saw the American flag unfurled for the first time west of the Ohio River, as it is confidently believed that Clark brought a copy of the new standard with him. From Fort Massac the expedition set out and achieved the ends which its commander forevisioned with many deeds of daring. It opened the gates to American settlement of all the northwest country of the United States.

Fort Massac was not occupied by troops until 1794, when, in view of probable collision with Spain and France, Washington despatched Major Thomas Doyle, of the United States Army, to rebuild and occupy the post. This was done and for some years it was of importance. In 1797 about thirty families had settled in the neighborhood, Captain Zebulon Pike being in command of a garrison of eighty-three men. At different times General Anthony Wayne and James Wilkinson occupied the fort as their head-quarters. In 1812 it was garrisoned by a Tennessee volunteer regiment, but at the close of that conflict the fort was evacuated once more.

In 1855, according to an account of Governor Reynolds, of Illinois, Fort Massac was in good condition. The walls, 135 feet square, were strong and at each corner was a stout bastion. A large well of sweet water was within the fortress and the walls were palisaded with earth between the wood.

The site of old Fort Massac is to-day a State park and the Illinois chapter of the Daughters of the American Revolution have restored the old fort as far as possible to the form that it bore at the time of the Revolution. It is additionally interesting as being the sole survivor of that long line of forts with which the French hoped to hold the Ohio River.

ENTRANCE TO FORT PUTNAM, WEST POINT, N. Y., IN WINTER
Showing Tower of New Academy Chapel in Middle Distance

Fort Putnam's Rocky Interior

Kosciuszko Monument

The North Wall, "Old Put"

SKETCH SNAP-SHOTS OF WEST POINT'S HISTORIC MEMORIALS

WEST POINT AND STONY POINT

and hastened to his brother's assistance with such militia as he could gather.

This completes the convocation of the Clintons in this engagement; Sir Henry Clinton, in command of the British forces, General James Clinton, in command of the two western forts; and Governor George Clinton, hastening to the aid of brother James at Fort Clinton.

The approach of the British caused General Putnam to place his Continentals on the eastern shore behind Peekskill and to bring over from the western shore a large force to reinforce his own. The British galleys advanced far enough up the river to prevent communication between the two American bodies, and it then became plain that it had been the hope of the English commander to cause the Americans to divide their forces by making a feint at the eastern shore where Putnam supposed that the strength of the British would be. The Americans had played into his hands. On the morning of the 6th of October Sir Henry Clinton landed his main forces on the western shore, and by sending a detachment around Dunderberg Mountain managed to attack Forts Clinton and Montgomery from the rear while another force engaged them from the south.

The result of this engagement was that while the Americans fought pluckily they were overcome by the British, with a loss of 250 killed, wounded and missing, as opposed to the British casualty list of 40 killed and

QUAINT AND HISTORIC FORTS

150 wounded, and that the two western forts fell into the hands of the English. The boom and chain across the river were destroyed, and the British fleet sailed up the river and attacked Fort Constitution on Constitution Island opposite West Point. Fort Constitution was hastily abandoned.

Such a signal success on Sir Henry Clinton's part should have caused him to push quickly on to effect a junction with Burgoyne, who had written him of his desperate straits at the northern end of the Hudson, but, having done this much, the English knight seemed to think that nothing more was expected of him, for, beyond sending a marauding expedition up the Hudson as far as Kingston, he made no further northern advance and retired to New York with his entire force. Had he joined Burgoyne in time to prevent the capitulation of the latter, it is probable that the whole history of this country would have been written in another fashion from that date.

Fort Constitution, which held so short an argument with the British fleet opposite West Point, was the first fortification of the series of works which lie in the vicinity of West Point. In August, 1775, a committee appointed by the State of New York and consisting of Isaac Sears, John Berrien, Christopher Miller, Captain Samuel Bayard and Captain William Bedlow, began the erection of forts and batteries in the vicinity of West Point. As an adviser to this committee Ber-

WEST POINT AND STONY POINT

nard Romans, an English engineer, was employed, and under his direction Martelaer's rock, now Constitution Island, was chosen for the site of the principal fortification. The fort, which was commenced under Romans's supervision but finished by another military architect, was named Constitution and cost altogether about $25,000. The remains of the fort are still visible on the island, the outlines of the walls being discernible, with the location of the principal point.

After the retreat of Sir Henry Clinton from before West Point,—a voluntary retreat, it should be observed,—the Americans saw that they must strengthen their defences at this place. Anxious to have the passes here strongly guarded, General Washington wrote to General Putnam, asking that he would give his most particular attention to the matter. Duty called Putnam to Connecticut and little was done in the matter until the arrival of General Macdougal, who took command on March 20, 1778, by whom West Point was approved as the location of the principal defences.

There now comes upon the scene the Polish patriot Kosciuszko, who had been appointed to succeed a French engineer, La Radierre, in the Hudson Highlands and who had taken up his new duties coincidentally with the arrival of General Macdougal. Kosciuszko pushed forward the construction of the works with great vigor.

QUAINT AND HISTORIC FORTS

The principal redoubt was constructed of logs and earth, was 600 feet around within the walls, and its embankments were 14 feet high with a base of 21 feet. The work was situated on a cliff which rises 187 feet above the river, and upon its completion in May was named Fort Clinton. The remains of Fort Clinton are carefully preserved to-day and comprise that line of grass-covered mounds which edge the eastern side of the plateau on which West Point Academy is situated. In the midst of these quiet green mounds stands a monument to Kosciuszko, erected by the corps of cadets of 1828. From the ruins a beautiful view of the Hudson is to be obtained, though the new buildings of the Academy cut off much which formerly was contained in the view from this point.

To support Fort Clinton works were constructed and batteries placed on the hills and mountains of West Point. On Mount Independence, which overhangs the military school, a strong fort was built and named, when completed, Fort Putnam, in honor of the sturdy patriot of Connecticut.

The remains of Fort Putnam, or "Old Put," as it came to be known in the neighborhood, were for many years the scene of picnickers' journeys up the steep hill-side whose crest it crowns and for many years were allowed to lie in a condition of disorder and decay. Of recent years the United States Government has taken in hand the old works and has restored them to as near their original condition as can be learned. The walls have been rebuilt where necessary and the brick casemates relaid. The result is that Fort Putnam to-day is the best preserved and most interesting of the souvenirs of the war-like days of West Point.

A rocky, inhospitable looking, irregular stone enclosure, Fort Putnam to-day gives one a very good idea of the stern, rude conditions with which our forefathers labored in the founding of our republic. From the walls of the fort a most enchanting prospect is to be gained from any direction, enchanting to either the lover of beautiful natural scenery or to the lover of historic memorials; for the Hudson Valley and its towering hills lie out before one to any point of the compass. Upon the points of these high hills were located batteries and strong works in the days when Putnam was young, each battery and work with its quota of rough colonial militia determined to fight to the last man against the trained soldiers of Europe. South of Fort Putnam were two small works known as Fort Wyllys and Fort Webb upon the eminences to be seen from " Put." On the crown of Sugar Loaf Mountain was a redoubt known as South Battery.

In addition to the construction of Forts Clinton and Putnam and their supporting batteries, Fort Constitution was strengthened and re-garrisoned, and between West Point and Constitution Island was stretched a huge iron chain, links of which are preserved in the museum at West Point. The chain was manufactured by Peter Townshend, of the Stirling Iron Works, Orange County, and was made of links two feet in length and in weight over 140 pounds each.

At the close of 1779 West Point was considered the strongest military post in America, and a large quantity of gunpowder, provisions and munitions of war was collected there. These considerations, in addition to the strategic value of the place, made of it a great prize for the enemy, who tried in various ways to seize it for his own. Yet the great menace to the place lay not without, where the British soldiers were, but within, and the story of that fact is one of the saddest things of American history.

The treason of Benedict Arnold had its setting at West Point, though its foundations were laid months before he assumed command of this important locale. Indeed, at the moment of Arnold's appointment to the command of West Point, the American general had been in correspondence with Sir Henry Clinton for eighteen months.

It is supposed that the defection of Arnold and his plans for the surrender of West Point began in Philadelphia during the winter of 1778, when he was appointed governor-general of that city after the evacuation by the British. Fond of show and feeling the importance of his station, he began to live in style far beyond his income, and pecuniary embarrassments

WEST POINT AND STONY POINT

began to multiply around him. He lived in the mansion that had once sheltered William Penn (and which is still standing), kept a coach and four, and gave splendid banquets. When impatient creditors began to press him for funds, he resorted to devious ways of raising money. So open did the scandal become of his indecent use of his position for private gain that charges were laid against him before Congress implying abuse of power, and the whole matter was handed over to Washington to have tried before a military tribunal. The verdict in the trial was rendered January 26, 1780, after a lengthy consideration of the case, and two of the four charges against Arnold were sustained. Washington was ordered to reprimand the officer, convicted by a jury of his peers, and did so in as kind a fashion as ever a reprimand was given. Indeed, at the time, Washington, himself, came in for censure because his reprimand was so ambiguously worded that it might be construed to praise the impetuous warrior who had fought for the new republic rather than to reprove the errant administrator. However, from this time it is supposed that Arnold planned to benefit himself and to deal the American cause a vital blow.

The military importance of West Point being plain, it was equally plain that the British would be willing to pay handsomely for its surrender. Arnold settled upon the place as the prize that his treachery should hold out to the English, and by various pieces of wire-pulling succeeded in having himself appointed its commander-in-chief. The general opinion of this American leader then was that he was headstrong and self-willed but not characterless. His impetuosity and violence were esteemed good qualities, which fitted him for the work of the soldier while they unfitted him for administrative duties. His good will toward his fellow-countrymen was not doubted. In August, 1780, Arnold took command of West Point and made his headquarters in a rambling old house which had belonged to Colonel Beverly Robinson, Colonel Robinson having espoused the English side of the quarrel during the Revolutionary War and having been obliged to take refuge in the English lines in consequence.

The chief correspondent of Arnold in the English ranks was Major André, and for a long time Sir Henry Clinton did not know the identity of the American general with whom André was in communication. To his missives Arnold affixed the signature of Gustavus and wrote in the character of a commercial correspondent of a business house. André on his part signed his letters John Anderson.

The general plan by which Clinton was to take possession of West Point through Arnold's connivance had many ramifications, but its chief text as concerns us was that Clinton should make a strong demonstration against the post and that Arnold, after a weak defence, should yield it to him. The final negotiations

WEST POINT AND STONY POINT

which touched the amount of money which Arnold was to receive for his treachery were concluded by Clinton through the intermediation of André, who assumed the guise of a spy in order to carry out his commander's behests. It was while returning from this trip to Arnold's headquarters and but one day before the drama was to be consummated that André fell into the hands of American forces and the papers which he bore were brought to light.

The morning of the 24th, the day set by Arnold for his surrender to Clinton, dawned bright and fine. Washington was expected at Arnold's headquarters from Hartford. As he sat at breakfast Arnold received a message from Colonel Jameson, stationed to the south, which contained the intelligence not that the British were approaching, but that a Major André had been captured. Hastily asking to be excused, Arnold made his way to the room of his young wife, the beautiful Margaret Shippen, of Philadelphia, and bade her a brief farewell; then he let himself out of the house by a back way and took a short path to the water-shore where he summoned a boatman and had himself rowed to the British fleet. Washington arrived at Arnold's headquarters in time to gather up the loose ends of things and prevent the dreadful catastrophe that the loss of the strongest of the American positions would have meant.

It has been claimed that the influence of Arnold's wife, who was of a Tory family and had been an ardent British sympathizer before her marriage, had much to do with Arnold's desertion from the cause he had first embraced. There is no evidence to finally set at rest this conjecture. Margaret Shippen had many friends amongst the British officers and Major André was the chief amongst these friends, but there is no reason to believe that she was base at heart, that she was not devoted to her husband, or that she could not realize how utter would be his undoing. After his downfall she rejoined him in New York and shared with him patiently all of the contempt and odium that were his portion for the rest of his life, from American and English alike.

The military academy at West Point was established by Act of Congress which became law March 16, 1802. The establishment of such a place had been proposed to Congress by Washington in 1793, and even before the close of the Revolution he had suggested such an institution and had even fixed on West Point as the location. Little was done in the matter even after the act of Congress of 1802, until in 1812, by a second enactment, a corps of engineers and teachers was organized and the school actually started. The beautiful buildings of the Academy are the fruit of the last generation's labor.

Stony Point lies south of West Point, separating

WEST POINT AND STONY POINT

Peekskill Bay on the north from Haverstraw Bay on the south. Opposite is Verplanck's Point. The river here is very narrow. In 1779 Clinton had strongly fortified Stony Point, thus cutting off West Point's communications from the south and establishing a strong base from which to proceed against that place. Washington saw that Stony Point must be captured.

To carry out his bold scheme—for the spot was deemed impregnable to assault—he called upon General Anthony Wayne—" Mad " Anthony—and asked him if he would undertake such a commission. " General, I'll storm hell if you'll only plan it," Wayne is said to have replied.

The situation of Stony Point was a fortress in itself. At high tide it was practically an island, the ravine on the shore side through which the railroad passes now-a-days being then a marshy inlet of the river. From the river the rock rose precipitously, and was at its highest point 700 feet above tide.

The assault was made under cover of darkness, July 15, 1779, the American forces advancing secretly under the guidance of an old negro who had learned the watchword of the fort for that night. This watchword was, " The Fort's Our Own." The phrase has been carved above the doorway of the reservation, where it may be seen by all visitors to-day. One by one the sentries were approached and overpowered, and the

QUAINT AND HISTORIC FORTS

Americans were almost within the walls before their presence was discovered. By two o'clock on the morning of July 16 the fort was the possession of the assailants.

The stores of the English were destroyed and the post was evacuated.

Stony Point is now a public reservation of the State of New York. The battle-ground is in charge of the American Scenic and Historic Preservation Society, which has marked the locality of the redoubts and of interesting points.

FORT CONSTITUTION
(FORT WILLIAM AND MARY)
GREAT ISLAND NEAR PORTSMOUTH—NEW HAMPSHIRE

HE records of the War Department at Washington say that Fort Constitution reservation "contains twelve acres. It is situated on a rocky projection in the Piscataqua River at the entrance to the harbor of the City of Portsmouth. It is about three miles below the city on the west side of the river, on the eastern end of 'Great Island,' being the most eastern end of New Hampshire. It was formerly an English fort called 'William and Mary' and was occupied by United States troops in 1806."

The location of Fort Constitution may be fixed more exactly by saying that it is very close to Newcastle, one of the outlying dependencies of Portsmouth. A long low stone structure thrust out on a wave-washed spit of rock, its picturesque appearance stimulates the fancy of every visitor who approaches Portsmouth by water.

Adjoining the fort is a light-house erected in 1771, and on a rocky eminence overlooking the fort is a ruined martello tower of striking aspect.

The history of Fort Constitution goes back to the early beginnings of settlement on the New England coast. In 1665 the commissioners of King Charles II began to erect a fortification on the point here, but were halted by the prohibitions of the Massachusetts fathers. In 1700 there existed a fort on Great Island and probably on the site of the present structure. This fort was visited by the Earl of Bellemont and declared by him incapable of defending the river, notwithstanding the fact that it mounted thirty guns.

A new defensive structure was planned by Colonel Romer, who recommended as additional works a strong tower on the point of Fryer's (Gerrish's) Island and batteries on Wood and Clark's Islands. His main plans were carried out and with slight alterations formed the fortification which was known at the time of the Revolutionary ferment as Castle William and Mary, its name sufficiently emphasizing the period of its conception. While Castle William and Mary had an honorable career in a passive fashion during the French wars by frightening off French descents upon the flourishing little city which it guards, it does not spring into the lime-light until 1774, when it becomes the scene of the first capture of arms made by the Americans in the struggle against the Mother Country.

In the year we have under consideration the Governor of New Hampshire was the able and passionate Sir John Wentworth. An account of the seizure of the supplies at Fort William and Mary may be succinctly given by means of extracts from Sir John's letters of that period, a series of which was published

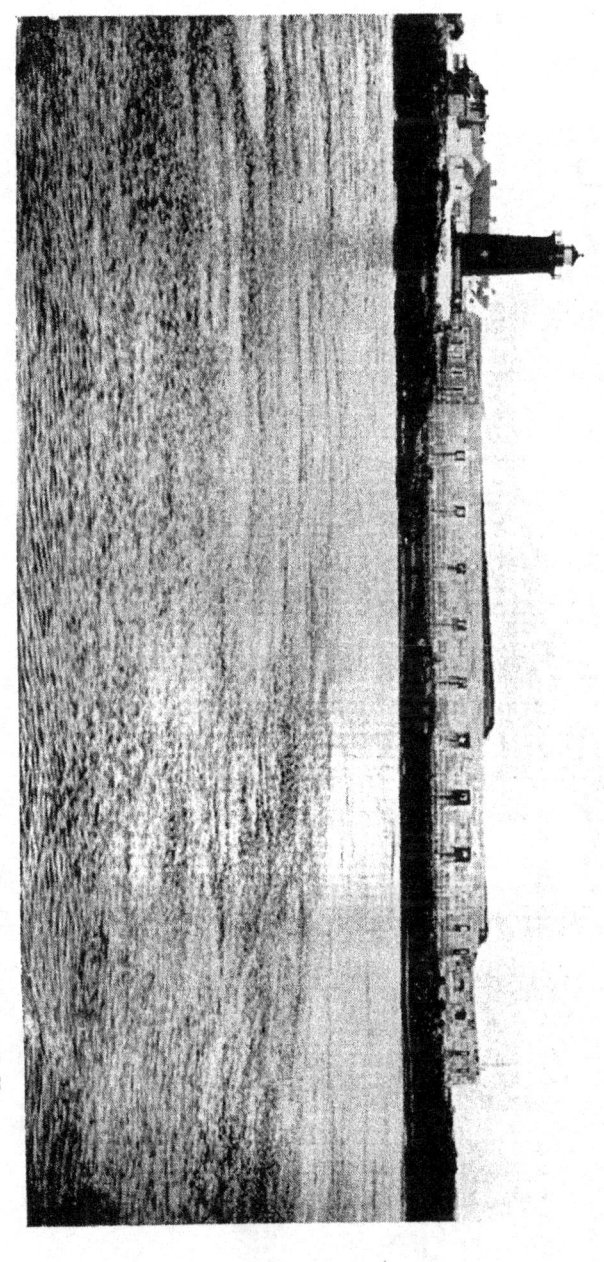

FORT CONSTITUTION (CASTLE WILLIAM AND MARY), GREAT ISLAND, NEAR PORTSMOUTH, N. H.

A DISTANT VIEW OF FORT CONSTITUTION

Copyright, Detroit Publishing Company

in 1869, in the " Historical and Genealogical Register " by the Honorable John Wentworth, of Chicago.

In a letter to the Earl of Dartmouth, dated Portsmouth, December 20, 1774, Governor Wentworth says:

On Tuesday the 13th instant, in the afternoon, one Paul Revere arrived with letters from some of the leaders in Boston to Mr. Samuel Cutts, merchant, of this town. Reports were soon circulated that the Fort at Rhode Island had been dismantled and the Gunpowder and other military stores removed up to Providence and . . . it was also falsely given out that Troops were embarking at Boston to come and take possession of William and Mary Castle in this harbour. These rumors soon raised an alarm in the town; and although I did not expect that the people would be so audacious as to make any attack on the castle yet I sent orders to the captain at the fort to be upon his guard.

On Wednesday news was brought to me that a drum was beating about the town to collect the populace together in order to go and take away the Gunpowder and dismantle the Fort. I immediately sent the Chief Justice of the Province to warn them from engaging in such an attempt. He went to them where they were collected in the centre of the town near the townhouse, explained to them the nature of the offence they proposed to commit, told them it was not short of Rebellion and intreated them to desist from it and to disperse. But all to no purpose. They went to the island and, being joined by the inhabitants of the towns of Newcastle and Rye, formed in a body of about four hundred men and the Castle being in too weak a condition for defence (as I have in former letters explained to your lordship) they forced their entrance in spite of Captain Cochrane who defended it as long as he could; but having only the assistance of five men their numbers overpowered him. After they entered the Fort they seized upon the captain and triumphantly gave three huzzas and hauled down the King's colours. They then put the captain and men under confinement, broke open the Gunpowder magazine and carried off about 100 barrels of Gunpowder but discharged the Captain and men from their confinement before their departure.

On Thursday, the 15th, in the morning a party of men came from the country accompanied by Mr. (Gen. John) Sullivan one of the New Hampshire delegates to the Congress, to take away the cannon from the Fort, also. Mr. Sullivan declared that he had taken pains to prevail upon them to return home again; and said, as there was no certain intelligence of troops being coming to take possession of the Castle, he would still use his utmost endeavors to disperse them.

While the town was thus full of men a committee from them came to me to solicit pardon or a suspension of prosecution against the persons who took away the Gunpowder. I told them I could not promise them any such thing; but if they dispersed and restored the gunpowder, which I most earnestly exhorted them to do, I said I hoped His Majesty may be thereby induced to consider it an alleviation of the offence. They parted from me, in all appearance, perfectly disposed to follow the advice I had given them; and having proceeded directly to the rest of their associates they all publickly voted . . . to return home. . . .

But, instead of dispersing, the people went to the Castle in the night headed by Mr. Sullivan and took away sixteen pieces of cannon, about sixty muskets and other military stores and brought them to the out Borders of the town.

On Friday morning, the 16th, Mr. Folsom, the other delegate, came to town that morning with a great number of armed

FORT CONSTITUTION

men who remained in Town as a guard till the flow of the tide in the evening when the cannon were sent in Gondolas up the river into the country and they all dispersed without having done any personal injury to any body in the town.

On the Fourth of July, 1809, an explosion of powder took place at Fort Constitution in which four men and three boys were killed and a number of bystanders wounded. The cause of the explosion was the carelessness of a sergeant with a lighted fuse, and the unlucky hour that he chose for his celebration was a time when his colonel (Colonel Walbach) had a number of guests to dinner. None of the diners were injured, and a quaint contemporary account tells their natural distress at various of the phenomena around them. "One poor fellow," says this account, "was carried over the roof of the house and the upper half of his body lodged on the opposite side near the window of the dining-room; the limb of another was driven through a thick door over the dining-room leaving a hole in the door the shape of the foot."

The appearance of Fort Constitution to-day is not very warlike and it does not play a very active part in the city's defences. The walls of the older part of the fort are of rough stone topped with brick. Over the arch of the sally-port here is a date, 1808. These walls have been partly enclosed by unfinished walls of granite of later construction.

The martello tower, to which reference has already

been had, was constructed during the War of 1812 and was begun one Sunday morning while two British cruisers were lying off the Isle of Shoals. Its purpose was to prevent a landing on the beach at the south side of the main work. An assault on that work was not attempted at the time, but who can say that the promptness of the New Hampshiremen in thus adding to their defences in the face of the enemy did not have its moral value in forestalling an attack? The tower had three embrasures.

FORTS TRUMBULL AND GRISWOLD
NEW LONDON AND GROTON, ON THE THAMES—CONNECTICUT

HE sunny waters of the Thames at New London, Connecticut, present a smiling aspect, and from the high flag-staff of trig little Fort Trumbull the stars and stripes float gaily. Across the river on the hill above the little town of Groton is the State reservation containing the remains of Fort Griswold, with rough zig-zag paths approaching the summit of the hill. Adjacent to Fort Griswold is the stone monument which commemorates the Fort Griswold massacre. Many sunny years will not wipe out the memory of the bloody deeds of that violent hour.

Fort Trumbull is situated one mile from the mouth of the Thames River and one mile and a half below the little city of New London, with whose history it is associated. A modest work of substantial construction, it covers only thirteen acres and is so restricted for living space that it cannot accommodate a full garrison within its walls. Fort Griswold is a work of far more ancient and rougher construction. It is not garrisoned to-day and has not been garrisoned for many years, though in the fighting days of the two forts it was the more important of the two places.

The little village of New London is a favored water-

QUAINT AND HISTORIC FORTS

ing place for many in summer and its safe and accessible harbor has made it desirable as a haven for the storage of summer light craft during the winter months. These same considerations hold true of Groton on the other side of the river. Thousands of visitors every summer go over the historic defences of Fort Griswold or gaze upon the equally historic site of Fort Trumbull.

The erection of two forts was begun in 1775 by the citizens of New London and Groton, one on the west side of the Thames which was designated in the correspondence of the time as a "block-house with embrasures," and the other, a more pretentious work, on the east side of the river and designated at once "Fort Trumbull." In 1776 Washington directed General Knox to examine the harbor of New London. This gentleman carried out his commission in workmanlike fashion and reported that the harbor was a safe and well-protected retreat for vessels in any wind that blew. The harbor is three miles long and seldom encumbered with ice.

In that same year Captain Shapley was ordered to take command of Fort Trumbull, and Colonel William Ledyard of Fort Griswold on Groton Hill. Later, Ledyard was placed in command of the two positions. In 1777 he revised, strengthened and enlarged Fort Trumbull, and in 1778 performed this same work upon Fort Griswold. Under his direction, in 1779, strong works were thrown up on Town Hill, New London.

Fort Griswold, Groton

Fort Trumbull, New London
HISTORIC POINTS ON THE THAMES RIVER, CONN.

FORT TRUMBULL

Finally, in 1780, the assembly of New London ordered his accounts paid.

The successful operations of the Continental forces in Virginia in 1781 caused Sir Henry Clinton to cast about for some means of distracting his opponents and of recalling Washington from the South, preferably by some deed of enterprise in the North. He fixed on New London as the scene of operations, as he had heard that there were many stores in the little town, and as the leader of the expedition he picked out Benedict Arnold, the traitor, who had just returned from scenes of pillage on the James River, Virginia. The choice of Arnold may have appealed to some saturnine sense of humor in Clinton, as Connecticut, it may be remembered, was Arnold's native State and New London not far from the scenes of his boyhood.

The little works at New London and Groton, despite the conscientious efforts of Colonel Ledyard, were not positions of much consequence. Fort Trumbull, we are told, was merely a strong breastwork of three sides, and open in the rear, mounting eighteen 12-pound guns and three 6-pound guns. Its garrison numbered twenty-three men. Fort Griswold was somewhat more formidable, being "an oblong square with bastions at opposite angles, its longest side fronting the river in a northwest and southeast direction, its walls of stone 10 or 12 feet high on the lower side and surrounded by a ditch; in the wall pickets projected over for 12 feet; above, a parapet with embrasures and within a platform for cannon, with a step to mount to shoot over the parapet with small arms."

In addition to these,—the main defences—there was the little work on the summit of Town Hill, New London, which mounted six small-bore guns and which had become known by the airy title of " Fort Nonsense."

It being manifestly impossible to hold Fort Trumbull with a force of twenty-three men, the Americans, on the approach of Arnold and the British, took all of their forces and placed them in Fort Griswold. At its best the garrison of this point was not as numerous as the attacking body and it was made up of untrained militia gathered at the moment's call.

The result of the battle, when battle was finally given, was a foregone conclusion. The British soldiery landed September 6, 1781, and advanced in force. The plucky American garrison tried desperately to hold back the onslaught, fighting most of the men in sight of their own homes, but without effect. After a sharp engagement the fort was taken and the conclusion of the combat was a signal to Arnold's forces for an indiscriminate slaughter of the Americans, many of whom had thrown down their arms. Of the 160 men making up the garrison all but 40 were killed or wounded, and the vast majority of them after resistance had ceased. The wounded, contemporary testimony asserts, were placed in carts under Arnold's direction and

FORT GRISWOLD

dumped over the edge of the hill here which is very steep.

The British then entered Groton and New London and set them on fire. Arnold finally led his forces back to New York.

To commemorate the gallant defence of Fort Griswold and the terrible scenes which it had witnessed, the State of Connecticut began the erection of a monument on Groton Heights in 1830 and carried the shaft to the height of 127 feet. At this height the monument rested until 1881, when it was carried eight feet higher. On the face of the shaft is a tablet which bears the following inscription:

> This monument was erected under the patronage of the State of Connecticut, A.D. 1830 and in the 55th year of the independence of the United States, in memory of the brave patriots who fell in the massacre at Fort Griswold on this spot on the 6th of September, A.D. 1781, when the British under the command of the traitor Benedict Arnold burnt the towns of New London and Groton and spread desolation and woe throughout this region.

Various spots in the little grounds of the fort have been marked with tablets. The grounds are carefully maintained and are open to visitors at all times.

Though no effort was ever made to rebuild Fort Griswold, a like fate did not befall Fort Trumbull. At the outbreak of the War of 1812 the embankments of Fort Trumbull were nothing but green mounds. A formal work was commenced, leaving the old blockhouse inside the new lines. During this war the fort was often threatened but never attacked.

An anecdote which shows the spirit of the locality is retailed by Lossing:[1]

When the British squadron which drove Decatur into the harbor of New London in 1813 menaced the town with bombardment the military force that manned the forts were deficient in flannel for cannon cartridges. All that could be found in New London was sent to the forts and a Mr. Latham, a neighbor of Mrs. Anna Bailey's, came to her at Groton seeking for more. She started out and collected all the petticoats of little children that she could find in town. " This is not half enough," said Mr. Latham on her return. " You shall have mine too," said Mrs. Bailey as she cut with her scissors the string that fastened it, and taking it off gave it to Latham. He was satisfied, and, hastening to Fort Trumbull, that patriotic contribution was soon made into cartridges. " It was a heavy new one but I did not care for that," said the old lady while her eyes sparkled. " All I wanted was to see it go through the Englishmen's insides." Some of Decatur's men declared that it was a shame to cut that petticoat into cartridge patterns; they would rather see it fluttering at the mast-head of the *United States* or the *Macedonia* as an ensign under which to fight upon the broad ocean.

The present Fort Trumbull was begun in 1839 on the foundations of its two predecessors and finished at a cost of $250,000. Part of the old block-house of the first Fort Trumbull is still preserved in the confines of the present fort.

---

[1] Lossing, vol. i, p. 617.

FORT MIFFLIN
ON THE DELAWARE—PHILADELPHIA

A VISIT to Fort Mifflin, Mud Island, on the Delaware River, Pennsylvania, to-day reveals a star-shaped fort of familiar pattern and of most substantial construction. It has the distinction of being within the corporate limits of one of the largest cities on the continent of North America,—Philadelphia,—yet a more deserted or forlorn looking spot it would be hard to imagine. Without benefit of policemen or any of the familiar marks of a great city, it might well serve in a "movie" for an ancient stronghold in a desert waste and may have been discovered by some enterprising movie manufacturer before these words are in print. Not always quiet, however, Fort Mifflin was the scene of one of the heaviest cannonadings of the War of Independence, when it sturdily held off the combined English naval and land forces until its own walls were reduced to powder.

The ground on which the Fort Mifflin of to-day stands was deeded to the Federal government by the State of Pennsylvania in 1795, and the present works were commenced in 1798. As the strategic advantage and the ease of fortification of the point had been amply demonstrated during the Revolution, a large and strong fortress was built and garrisoned until changing con-

QUAINT AND HISTORIC FORTS

ditions of warfare caused its importance to be a thing of the past and its garrison to be withdrawn in 1853. During the Civil War the fort was garrisoned by a volunteer regiment and served as a detention place for prisoners taken during that conflict, but this structure saw no service in this war and, indeed, has never fired a shot in anger. After the Civil War the place was deserted, though the government has ever since kept a care-taker there. The government land reservation includes over three hundred acres. In other parts of the island are more modern government stations, but in these we have no present interest.

The old fortification is surrounded by a deep moat over which are bridges leading to its three sally-ports. Only one of these entrances is open now. Passing through the thick walls of this entrance, one finds one's self facing a large parade ground, which is surrounded by quaint, old-fashioned structures—the barracks and officers' quarters of a by-gone day. On the south of the parade is a very charming little Georgian chapel, through whose broken window-panes pour in damp winds.

In the casemates of the old fort were confined Morgan's men during the Civil War. It is a dark and dismal trip to the damp rooms in which these men were confined, as one goes through narrow subterranean corridors beneath the thick walls of the fort. One comes to a large cavernous chamber lighted from above by a

ENTRANCE TO FORT MIFFLIN, PHILADELPHIA

THE MOAT IN WINTER, FORT MIFFLIN, PHILADELPHIA

single narrow slit. At one end of this chamber is an open fire-place. On the walls are scribbled numerous names and messages from Morgan's men. It might perhaps be an interesting matter to copy down these names and messages, if one had the patience and time to do so, but hardly a task within the province of this chapter. May be the room was cheerful enough in the days of its use with the big fire-place containing a roaring fire, but it is dismal now, in all conscience!

From the walls of Fort Mifflin there is a fine view of the Delaware River. Natives of the neighborhood say that the marshes round about yield fine gunning during the season. Directly across the Delaware from Fort Mifflin—the river being about a mile wide, here—are the remains of Fort Mercer and the outworks which made up this strong little post in the days of the Revolution. Fort Mercer and its earthworks are preserved by the nation, forming a public reservation which annually receives many visitors.

The ancient Whitall house—a two-story building of red brick—still stands at Fort Mercer, reminding one of the intrepid old lady who occupied it during the battle. Old Mrs. Whitall was urged to flee from the house but refused, saying, "God's arm is strong and will protect me; I may do good by staying." She was left alone in the house and, while the battle was raging and cannon-balls were driving like sleet against her dwelling, calmly plied her spinning-wheel. At length a twelve-pound ball from a vessel in the river, grazing the American flag-staff (a walnut tree), at the fort, passed at the north gable through a heavy brick wall, perforated a partition at the head of the stairs, crossed a recess, and lodged in another partition near where the old lady was sitting. Conceiving Divine protection a little more certain elsewhere after this manifestation of the power of gunpowder, the old lady gathered up her spinning implements and with a step as agile as youth retreated to the cellar, where, not to be pushed out of her house by any circumstance, she continued her spinning as industriously as before. When the wounded and dying were brought to her house to be cared for, she went industriously at the work of succor, not caring whether she tended friend or foe. She scolded the Hessians vigorously for coming to this country on a work of butchery, and at the same time ministered to their sufferings.

The third American redoubt lay farther down the river at Billingsport.

It will be recalled that Howe, with his English regulars and Hessians, spent the winter of 1776–77 in New York with occasional forays from that point. In July, 1777, after a trial of wits with Washington in northern New Jersey, he embarked his troops and set sail to the south. Washington's uneasiness as to the whereabouts of his foe was set at rest after three weeks by hearing of the landing of Howe at the head

FORT MIFFLIN

of the Chesapeake Bay. There then ensued the battle of the Brandywine and that series of skirmishes which ended in Howe's taking possession of Philadelphia, then the capital of the country, with the removal of the American official papers to York.

To secure his position and keep his lines open in Philadelphia, however, it was necessary for Howe to take the American positions at Billingsport, at Fort Mercer and at Fort Mifflin. The works at Billingsport fell quickly before a surprise attack, and it now remained to take Mifflin and Mercer.

The garrison at Mercer consisted of two Rhode Island regiments under Colonel Christopher Greene. At Mifflin there was about the same number of the Maryland line under Lieutenant-Colonel Samuel Smith. The American fleet in the river consisted chiefly of galleys and floating batteries, and was anchored off the present League Island. It was under the command of Commodore Hazlewood.

Count Donop, with 1200 picked Hessians, was sent by Howe to take Fort Mercer. On the morning of October 24, he appeared before the little fort. Though the Americans had only 400 men with fourteen cannon they were not dismayed but stood to their arms. The battle commenced at four o'clock in the afternoon and raged with great fierceness. It resulted in the repulse of the assailants and the death of their commander,

Count Donop, to whom a monument has been erected at Fort Mercer Park.

The firing of the first gun against Fort Mercer was the signal for the British fleet to open upon Fort Mifflin. A heavy cannonade continued until the British were obliged to draw off. A hot shot struck one of their large ships, the *Augusta,* and this vessel burned to the water's edge.

For a season the Americans held undisputed possession of their section of the Delaware, but then the British returned the charge with increased force. Fort Mifflin was made the centre of attack. Batteries were posted upon Province Island,—now a part of the mainland directly off Mud Island on which the little fort stood,—and on this side the fort was not finished. A large floating battery was also brought up the river within forty yards of one angle of the fort. Altogether the British had fourteen strong batteries, in addition to four 64-gun and two 40-gun ships. The engagement opened on the 10th of November and continued for six consecutive days without interruption. In the course of the last day more than a thousand discharges of cannon were made against the little fort on Mud Island. By this time there was little left of its walls and no single chance of the garrison holding out longer. The officer in command escaped to Fort Mercer with the remnants of his force. It is said that the British were preparing to draw away from Fort Mifflin and had made up their minds to give up the siege, but information from a deserter caused them to keep on for the few days necessary to reduce the weakened stronghold.

So strong a force was now sent against Fort Mercer that Colonel Greene was obliged to evacuate that post, leaving behind some guns and ammunition with military stores.

The American fleet sought safety in flight up the Delaware. One brig and two sloops escaped to Burlington. Seventeen other vessels, unable to escape, were abandoned by their crews and burned at Gloucester, just across from the Philadelphia of to-day.

The Delaware River and Philadelphia were now in the hands of Howe. For a long winter he was to lie inactive while Washington took up position at Valley Forge and spent that historic winter with his men of which so much has been written. Instead of working for the future the British spent their time in balls and the Meschianza. Let Americans of to-day be thankful that they found Philadelphia manners and Philadelphia belles so altogether delightful!

FORT McHENRY
BALTIMORE

THE spot whereon the flag-staff stood which bore the stars and stripes that fervid morning upon which Francis Scott Key arose, saw that our flag was still there and jotted down the national anthem on the back of an envelope before going down to breakfast, still conspires with a large and lusty successor of this first staff to keep Old Glory flying in the heavens. The immediate surroundings, the harbor outlook, the busy city now sending its clamor over the point on which the old fort stands, all have changed in the years, but the part of the fort from which the banner of the new republic was sent forth so many years ago has undergone little transformation. A triangle of ground pointing toward open water, and a bare staff, these have little that Time can work wizardry with. The simple focus of Key's inspiration has not been lost in the years, but the rest of the picture which roused his songster's mood is only to be brought back by effort of imagination.

Fort McHenry is now a public park, the last federal trooper having been drawn out of the reservation in the fall of 1913. As such it has been beautified by the City of Baltimore, if the placing of benches in convenient spots, the sodding of terraces, and the clean-

A View from an Aeroplane

The Guard-House
FORT McHENRY, BALTIMORE, MD.

Looking Toward the Lazaretto

One of the Old Batteries in Place
FORT McHENRY, BALTIMORE, MD.

ing of walks are to be considered in the nature of beautification; and it is occasionally used by Baltimoreans as a place of airing. Situated on a point of land separating the two parts of Baltimore's heart-shaped harbor, it gives charming views of the city. Gazing straight ahead from the walls of old Fort McHenry, one can see far down the river (very wide here) into the distance where the river joins the Chesapeake Bay. In the blue of the horizon can be faintly discerned the low squatty outline of the little hexagon of stone built by General Robert E. Lee before the Civil War and known as Fort Carroll.

To the right hand, from this vantage point on the water side of Fort McHenry's parapets, lies Spring Garden, the larger but the less busy part of Baltimore's water-front. To the left is the entrance to "the harbor," as it is affectionately called by Baltimoreans, with entire disregard for that magnificent half-moon of water of more recent development which we have already descried to the right.

The various points of historic interest in the fort and its grounds are marked with tablets and appropriate memorials, this work having been done in recent years by the city, by the Maryland chapter of the Daughters of the American Revolution and by various public-spirited bodies of the municipality.

As one enters the grounds of the old fort, he is confronted first by a long, low, wooden structure with

QUAINT AND HISTORIC FORTS

an archway through which can be gained a glimpse of a broad grass space. This is the parade. On the right of the parade is a row of cottages facing a narrow street, and at the end of this modest thoroughfare can be seen the eastern abutments of the old fort. As one approaches the fort itself the star shape of the walls is plainly observable and its dimensions easily taken in. It is not a large place, this historic old work, and makes no great impression upon the beholder from its material aspect. Batteries of ancient guns are mounted on the walls fronting the river. These were saved from destruction some years ago by the energetic work of some of the historical societies of the city. The reservation is entirely surrounded by a stone sea-wall which makes a very acceptable promenade, and here on summer days may be found couples viewing the beautiful marine prospects, and small boys indefatigably crabbing or fishing, but these energies have a purely legendary interest, for the crabbing and fishing for which the place was once famous are not now what they ought to be.

Seen from the river as one enters Baltimore by steamer the old fort is at its best, for then one sees the long grassy inclines and the level of the parade ground and the soft foliage of trees contrasted sharply with the smoky city in the background. The fort proper is barely visible from the river, its walls not rising above

FORT McHENRY

the crests of the high embankments thrown up in front of it.

The point of land on which Fort McHenry is situated—Whetstone Point, as it was known in old times—was patented in 1662 by Mr. Charles Gorsuch of the Society of Friends, and the stretch that he acquired amounted to about fifty acres. It is thus that it comes upon the pages of history in the possession of one sworn not to use methods of violence. Time passed on, Mr. Gorsuch's tract was divided, and at last came the brewing of the Revolution. It was this which brought Fort McHenry into existence.

A battery was thrown up on the point, and in 1776 a boom was stretched across the river to the Lazaretto, a little projection of land on the northern side of the stream. Two hundred and fifty negroes were employed in this work and their labors extended over a period of almost two years.

Yet this original of Fort McHenry did not see active service during the Revolution. Its greatest days were to be reserved for that short conflict which finally decided the Mother Country in the opinion that the American Colonies were of a right and ought to be free and independent. That so decisive a battle as the repulse of the British fleet before McHenry should have been staged at Baltimore is peculiarly appropriate when we remember the prominence of that type of sailing vessel known as the Baltimore "clipper" in the commerce of the country before the war and the great service these same slim, speedy vessels did as privateers during that conflict. The Baltimore clippers, it is not amiss to note, were built at Fell's Point, about a mile and a half across the river from Fort McHenry, where modern Broadway, a thoroughfare, now has its terminus.

It was before the outbreak of the War of 1812 that the foundations of present-day Fort McHenry were laid. In the closing ten years of the eighteenth century there was much ill feeling against England and war was declared in rumor many times before the actual outbreak of hostilities took place. At one of these periods of apprehension the citizens of Baltimore, at their own expense, started the erection of a star-shaped fort under the direction of John J. Rivardi, engineer. In 1794 this erection, not complete but well started toward completion, passed to the Federal government and was named Fort McHenry in honor of James McHenry, secretary to Washington during the Revolution and Secretary of War from 1796 to 1800. The works were completed in 1805 and the formal cession to the Federal government took place in 1816.

It is hard to over-estimate in the history of the country the importance of the defence of Fort McHenry and of the engagement at North Point,—a corollary of this defence,—though Marylanders themselves have been comparatively indifferent to it until lately. With that pride of race which is a heritage of the South and the feeling which that pride engenders that their men will do well as a matter of course, Marylanders have given this engagement rather casual attention until very recent years. Indeed, up to the last decade, it was not unusual to hear Baltimoreans refer to the heroic defenders of North Point, who checked a force many times more powerful than their own and inflicted terrible injury in mortally wounding the assailants' commanding officer, as the "North Point racers," in humorous appreciation of the nimbleness of foot and ingenuity in evading observation which the men showed when finally they did break ground and retreated to Baltimore. Yet the times were critical enough, Heaven knows, and the part that these same racers and Fort McHenry played a worthy one in the final summing up.

The British, it will be remembered, had proceeded by easy stages up the Chesapeake Bay, burning and pillaging wherever they chose and meeting little opposition. A detachment had crossed to the northwest through Bladensburg and had seized and given to the flames Washington, the capital of the nation, itself; and now the united force was turning its attention to a leisurely march north through Baltimore to the northern cities, where they hoped to complete their subjugation of the country. Their complete reverse at McHenry set back all of their plans, giving the northern cities time to arm and prepare, and demoralized them to a great degree, their demoralization being accompanied by a corresponding enheartening of all American sympathizers. The importance of the action is thus readily seen.

The historic attack upon Fort McHenry began on the morning of September 13, 1814, and continued until 7 o'clock of the next morning. During the engagement more than 1800 shells were fired by the attacking force. The total American loss was four killed and twenty-four wounded. In the land engagement of North Point which preceded the attack by water on the city the American loss was 150 killed and wounded and the British loss about 600.

While Fort McHenry was the main defence of Baltimore, the city showed arms in other directions as well. On the northern side of the harbor (across the river from Fort McHenry) were two long lines of fortifications which extended from Harris Creek, northward across Hampstead's Hill, now Patterson Park,—about a mile in length, along which at short distances were thrown up semicircular batteries. Behind these on more elevated sites were additional batteries, one of which, known as Rodger's Bastion, overlooked Fort McHenry. There were, also, connecting lines of breastworks and rifle-pits running parallel with the northern boundary of the city, connected in turn by inner bastions and batteries, the precise location of which is not known. A four-gun battery was constructed at Lazaretto Point,

From This Point the Star Spangled Banner Flew

The Entrance
FORT McHENRY, BALTIMORE, MD.

COL. GEORGE ARMISTEAD
In command of Fort McHenry during the siege

FORT McHENRY

and between this point and Fort McHenry across the mouth of the harbor a number of vessels were sunk. Southwest of the fort, guarding the middle branch of the Patapsco (known as Spring Garden) against the landing of troops to assail Fort McHenry in the rear, were two redoubts, 500 yards apart, called Fort Covington and the City Battery. In the rear of these upon the high ground of the present Battery Square was a circular battery. A long line of platforms for guns was erected in front of Fort McHenry and was known as the Water Battery.

During the night which followed the unsuccessful afternoon engagement of the 13th a landing party was sent in boats with muffled oars to slip past the City Battery and Fort Covington and to take these works and McHenry in the rear. That this effort was not more successful is due to the presence of a large haystack near one of the American sentries. This sentry, becoming suspicious, touched a match to the hay-stack, and the sudden flames showed the landing party of British. In the engagement that followed the British were repulsed.

It was at dawn of the 14th that Francis Scott Key, who was a prisoner on the British flag-ship, received the inspiration to write " The Star Spangled Banner." He saw that, despite the furies of the night, the American flag still waved over the little fort. The words which he jotted down in the joy of that moment were the subject of some reworking on his part, but, it is understood, had not been materially changed when he showed them to his brother-in-law, Judge Nicholson, after his exchange the next morning. The words were found to fit perfectly to the popular tune "Anacreon in Heaven." Carrying the stanzas to the printing office of Benjamin Edes, copies of it were ordered printed. This was the birth of " The Star Spangled Banner."

The real hero of the attack upon Fort McHenry is not, perhaps, given the acclaim that should be his. It was sturdy Colonel Armistead, commander of the fort. His intrepid spirit and fine ingenuity undoubtedly saved the day.

Among the tributes which were rendered to Colonel Armistead after the engagement may be repeated that of his old friend, the veteran Colonel John Eager Howard, who sent him a brace of ducks and some wine with the words:

> The British are off and the Devil with them. You deserve the thanks of a grateful country. I am sending a brace of ducks and a bottle of Burgundy. I hope you may enjoy them.

During the Civil War Baltimore was again fortified. On the night of May 13, 1861, Major-General Butler occupied Federal Hill, a commanding eminence overlooking the city and harbor. In the following month a strong fort was erected here by General Brewerton, which included the entire crown of the hill and mounted fifty guns. The building of Federal Hill Fort was an answer to the action of a mob in Baltimore in April, 1861, which planned to seize Fort McHenry. This effort was frustrated by the garrison of 100 men under Captain Robinson which put up such a war-like front with such a display of grape and canister, that the enterprise was abandoned.

In September, 1914, during the Star Spangled Banner Centennial, the fort and grounds were loaned to the City of Baltimore by the War Department for use as a public park. It is not to be expected that the old fort will ever again be called into active service.

FORT MARION
ST. AUGUSTINE—FLORIDA

HE ancient city of St. Augustine, the oldest place of European settlement on the North American continent, is on the east coast of Florida at the mouth of the St. Augustine River and at the northern end of a long lagoon formed by Anastatia Island, which separates the waters of the lagoon and of the Atlantic Ocean. Our interest in the quaint spot may be concentrated in Fort Marion, a Spanish bravo which has fought the city's battles for more than three hundred and fifty years. Probably the most picturesque of fortifications in the United States, Fort Marion annually receives thousands of visitors, many drawn from the leisured throng who have made St. Augustine the winter social capital of the American nation.

Fort Marion is situated at the northern end of St. Augustine, where its lonely watch-tower may have a clear view of the shipping channel which leads from the city across the long bar Anastatia Island to the ocean. The fortification is a regular polygon of four equal sides and four bastions. A moat surrounds the structure, but the moat has been dry for many years. The entrance is to the south and is protected by a barbacan, or, less technically, an arrow-shaped out-work. A stationary

By courtesy of the St. Augustine Historical Society

MOAT AND ENTRANCE, FORT MARION, ST. AUGUSTINE, FLA.

By courtesy of the St. Augustine Historical Society

INCLINE LEADING TO RAMPARTS, FORT MARION, ST. AUGUSTINE, FLA.

FORT MARION

bridge leads part way across the moat and the path is then continued on into the fort by a draw-bridge.

Over the entrance is an escutcheon bearing the arms of Spain with gorgeous coloring, which has been much dimmed by the hot sun of Florida. A legend now partially obliterated sets forth that "Don Ferdinand, the VI, being King of Spain and the Field Marshal Don Alonzo Fernando Hereda, being Governor and Captain General of this place, San Augustin of Florida, and its province, this fort was finished in the year 1756. The works were directed by the Captain Engineer Don Pedro de Brozas y Garay."

Passing through the entrance to the fort one finds one's self in a dark passage, on the right and left of which are low doorways, that on the right being the nearer. Glancing through the right door-way one sees three dark chambers, the first of which was used as a bake-room and the two others of which were places of confinement for prisoners. Looking through the dark door-way a few steps forward to the left one gazes into the guard-room.

Walking on one comes into the open court, 103 feet by 109 feet; immediately to the right is the foot of the inclined plane which leads to the upper walls. To the left is the well. On all sides of the court are entrances to casemates. Directly across from the entrance is the ancient chapel, which heard masses sung while the English colonies were just being started. The altar and niches still remain and over the door of this place of worship is a tablet set in the wall by French astronomers, who here once observed the transit of Venus.

Passing up the inclined plane to which allusion has already been made one finds one's self on the ramparts of the fort. A charming view is to be obtained on all sides, but particularly looking out to sea. At each angle of the fort was a sentry-box and that at the northeast corner was also a watch-tower. This tower, probably the most familiar remembrance of old Fort Marion, is twenty-five feet high. The distance from watch-tower to sentry-box (or from corner to corner) of the old fort is 317 feet.

The material of which the fort is constructed is the familiar sea-shell concretion used so largely in Florida and known as "coquina." It was quarried on Anastatia Island, across Matanzas Inlet from the city, and was ferried over to the fort site in large barges. The substance is softer when first dug than when it has been exposed to the air and light for a season, sharing this property with concrete, to which it is analogous in other ways, so the walls of the fort are more solid to-day than when they were built.

The history of Fort Marion takes one back to early bickering between Spanish and French on the North American continent. In 1562 Jean Ribaut, a sturdy French mariner, sailed into the waters of Florida, explored the waters of the St. John's River (at the mouth

FORT MARION

of which busy Jacksonville now stands) and planted a colony and a fort on the St. John's with the name of Fort Caroline. The river he called the River of May, in remembrance of the month in which he first set eyes upon it. In 1564, Laudonierre, a second Frenchman, came with supplies and reinforcements for Fort Caroline, but paused on his passage to investigate an inlet farther south than the mouth of the St. John's River. This inlet he called the River of Dolphins, from the abundance of such creatures at play in the waters here and on the shores of the inlet, which later generations were to know as St. Augustine harbor; he descried an Indian village known as Seloy.

The jealous King of Spain heard of the French settlement in Florida and was displeased. He sent an expedition under Juan Menendez de Aviles to colonize the country with Spaniards and to exterminate the French, who added to the misfortune of not being Spaniards the mistake of not being Catholics. Menendez sailed into Florida waters in September, 1565, reconnoitred the French colony on the St. John's River and then sailed south several days, landing at the Indian village of Seloy. Here he decided to establish the capital of his domain. The large barn-like dwelling of the Indian chief was made into a fort. This was the original of Fort Marion of to-day. Then on September 8, 1565, Menendez took formal possession of the territory, and named his fort San Juan de Pinos.

QUAINT AND HISTORIC FORTS

Of the Sixteenth Century quarrels of Frenchman and Spaniard, of Huguenot and Catholic, there is not space in this chapter to tell. Suffice it to say that even in so broad a land as Florida, which according to the interpretation of the day included all of the present United States and British Canada, there was not room enough for two separated small French and Spanish colonies to subsist together, and for Catholic and Huguenot to be in one world together was beyond all reason. So the next step in the history of our fort is the expedition of Menendez against the French and the perpetration by him of one of the most horrid massacres that has ever stained the New World.

Let us picture a blinding night in September, 1565, at Fort Caroline. The Spanish leader, it is known, has established himself at the River Dolphins. One of the equinoctial tempests to which Florida is subject was raging. The French in their dismantled little post have deemed no enemy hardy enough to venture out in such elemental fury. Laudonierre himself has dismissed the weary sentinels from the wall, secure in the thought that Nature, herself, is his protection. He does not know the tenacity of the Spaniard. Menendez, setting out from his new stronghold with a few hundred men and struggling on against the storm, is even now within striking distance of the doomed French retreat. A sudden rush upon the sleeping garrison and the Spaniards are within the fort. No mercy is shown. One hundred and thirty men are killed with little resistance. One old carpenter escaped to the woods during the mêlée, but surrendered himself to the Spaniards the next morning with pleas for mercy. He was butchered with his prayers upon his lips.

Menendez returned to St. Augustine and in a few days heard that some of the French ships which had fled in disorder during the rout at the fort had landed their crews about twenty miles south of St. Augustine. He immediately set out for the spot with one hundred and fifty men. The hapless French without food and without shelter surrendered themselves to Menendez. All of them (over a hundred in number) with the exception of twelve Breton sailors, who had been kidnapped, and four ships' caulkers who might be useful to the Spaniards, were put to the knife in cold blood. Again, word came to Menendez that castaway Frenchmen were south of St. Augustine. It was the remainder of the French squadron under Ribaut—more than three hundred and fifty in number. Menendez repeated his tactics with this company as well. He allowed them to trust themselves to his mercy and then conclusively proved that there was no mercy in the heart of a Spaniard of the Inquisition by putting the whole company to death ten at a time. The spot where these two butcheries took place is known to this day as Matanzas, or the Place of the Slaughters.

Immediately now the Spaniard began to make himself more secure in Florida. His stronghold at St. Augustine was amplified and Fort Caroline, the luckless French fort, was rebuilt and renamed San Mateo. In 1568 the French under de Gorgues descended upon the Spanish at San Mateo and put the whole garrison to the sword. San Augustin was not attacked, however, and for two hundred years held the Spanish flag supreme in this part of the New World.

For twenty years after its foundation Menendez's little fort of San Juan de Pinos saw no military service, though it was made strong and formidable. Then the clash of arms came to its ears, accompanied by great catastrophe. These were the years of the English sea-kings. Raleigh, Drake, Grenville, Gilbert, Frobisher were sweeping the oceans in their diminutive craft, making anxious the captains of many a Spanish galleon. In September, 1585, Drake sailed on a freebooting voyage from the harbor of Plymouth, England, with more than an ordinarily large number of men and ships, and in May, 1586, this little armada chanced to be in sight of San Augustin. The procedure may now be told in the words of one of Drake's seamen:

> Wee descried on the shore a place built like a Beacon which was indeede a scaffold upon foure long mastes raised on ende. . . . Wee might discover over against us a Fort which newly had bene built by the Spaniards; and some mile or therabout above the Fort was a little Towne or Village without walls, built of wooden houses as the Plot doeth plainely shew.

FORT MARION

Wee forthwith prepared to have ordnance for the batterie; and one peece was a little before the enemie planted, and the first shot being made by the Lieutenant generall himself at their ensigne strake through the Ensigne, as wee afterwards understood by a Frenchman, which came unto us from them. One shot more was then made which strake the foote of the Fort wall which was all massive timber of great trees like Mastes.

And so, in the charming, inconsequential fashion of the times, the narrative goes on, carrying the battle with it. The fort fell into the hands of the English after a stubborn defence by its Spanish occupants and was destroyed. The village was sacked and burned. Drake then sailed on his way.

The fort was rebuilt and stood secure until 1665, when San Augustin was sacked by buccaneers under Captain John Davis and it shared the destruction of the town. Then a substantial structure, the Fort Marion of to-day, was begun. Work was continued for successive generations, until in 1756 the stronghold was declared finished. The new structure was christened San Marco.

During these years the fort was not without service, however. In 1702 and again in 1740 San Augustin was attacked by English forces from the English colonies to the north, and Fort San Marco, even while not complete, bore the brunt of these attacks. The second expedition against San Augustin was under the leadership of Governor Oglethorpe, of Georgia, and arose to the dignity of a siege of the city. For weeks the English forces lay

QUAINT AND HISTORIC FORTS

beyond the city walls and were then driven off by reinforcements brought from Cuba.

With the construction of Fort San Marco the erection of city walls was undertaken, too. The walls of old San Augustin ran from Fort San Marco around the city and were constructed of "coquina." Only the so-called "City Gate" remains of these walls to-day.

In 1763 the warrior which had withstood armed assault fell to the attack of diplomacy, for it was in this year that England made its trade with Spain whereby Spain was given back Cuba, which England had wrested by force of arms from that country, and England was given Florida. The flag of Castile and of Aragon was hauled down from the wall of the old fort and the British lion was raised in its place. Fort San Marco became in British hands Fort St. Mark.

During the American revolution Florida was the only one of the fourteen British colonies which remained loyal to the Mother Country. The fervor of the northern coasts found no kindred spark in old St. Augustine. The town became a haven for Tories. She opened her gates and an oddly-assorted throng came flocking in. There was the Tory colonel Thomas Browne, of Georgia, tar and feathers still sticking to his skin from his experience with the Liberty Boys, of Savannah. There was Rory McIntosh, always attended by Scotch pipers, who paraded the narrow streets breathing out fire and slaughter against the colonies. The Scopholites, so-called from Scophol, their leader, marched down, 600 strong, from the back country of North Carolina, burning and killing in their course through Georgia. With such additions, St. Augustine was not content with passive loyalty and became a centre for military operations against the southern colonies. Many a council did the rooms of Fort St. Mark witness, which had as its result death and privation to the rebellious Americans.

Two expeditions were attempted by the colonists against Fort St. Mark. The first under General Charles Lee fell short because of mismanagement. The second advanced as far as the St. John's River. Consternation in St. Augustine reigned supreme; slaves were impressed to help strengthen the fortifications; citizens ran hither and thither with their valuables. But the Americans were menaced by fever at the St. John's and faced the prospect of a midsummer encampment in Florida, so they turned about and went north. Fort St. Mark was not to leave English hands by force.

In 1783 took place another one of those shuffles between high contracting parties by which each party thinks that he has secured the better of the bargain. England traded Florida to Spain for Jamaica. Spain traded Jamaica to England for Florida. In 1821 Spain ceded Florida to the United States, and in 1825 the name of the fort was changed from Fort St. Mark to Fort Marion in honor of General Francis Marion, of Revolutionary fame.

QUAINT AND HISTORIC FORTS

The Seminole War began in 1835 and continued until 1842, costing the United States two thousand lives, and forty million dollars. Fort Marion was the centre of the military operations of this conflict and it was the scene of the disgraceful episode of treachery by which Osceola and other Indian chieftains were captured. In 1838 General Hernandez, in command of the United States forces, sent word to Osceola that he would be protected if he should come to Fort Marion for talk of peace. With seventy of his followers the Indian came to the conference and was placed in irons. The prisoner was taken to Fort Moultrie, in Charleston harbor, where from much brooding and confinement he died. The same tactics were repeated in another sitting with Coacoochee, the remaining great leader of the Seminoles, and the Seminole War was ended. Coacoochee was confined in Fort Marion, where his cell is pointed out to visitors. His fate became that of an exile, for with his people he was transported to a western reservation.

During the Civil War Fort Marion had a brief flurry of excitement when the fort was seized by Southern sympathizers in 1861. It quickly fell before Federal troops, however, and had no further active part in that war.

The old fort is still government property, but its days of activity are long since past. That it will be maintained for many years as a reminder of the past is, however, well assured.

LA FUERZA, MORRO CASTLE, AND OTHER DEFENCES
HAVANA—CUBA

THE city of Havana was located where it stands to-day in 1519, after a four years' unsatisfactory trial of a site on the opposite, or south, coast of the island. It jogged along comfortably through all of the ordinary perils of that time until 1538, when it was attacked and sacked by a French privateersman. The authorities in the home country determined to provide some means of defence for the baby metropolis, and one Hernando de Soto, an impecunious adventurer who had followed Pizarro to Peru, and had returned enriched with plunder from that unhappy land, was commissioned governor of Cuba and Florida with instructions to build a fortress at Havana.

De Soto came to Havana in the fashion of leisure of the times, and in pursuit of his royal master's instructions, laid the foundations of a fortress. This work was finished under the direction of his lieutenant while he, himself, was searching an El Dorado in Florida and was finding a miserable death by fever on the Mississippi. The structure which de Soto left as his legacy to Havana is the Castillo de la Fuerza, half hidden, to-day, between the Senate and old post-office building on the Plaza de Armes. La Fuerza has been credited with being the oldest inhabitable and inhabited structure in the Western Hemisphere and the claim is not easily disputed. As early as 1544 a royal decree had been given forth that all vessels entering Havana harbor should salute the little fortress with a ceremony not enjoyed by any other city in the New World save Santo Domingo.

The form of la Fuerza is that of a quadrilateral, having a bastion at each of the four corners. The walls are twenty-five feet in height and are double. There is a moat which has not contained water for many years, and arrangements for a draw-bridge which has been replaced by a permanent plank walk. To the seaward is a watch-tower similar in design to that on the fort at St. Augustine, and in this tower is a bell which, tradition says, was rung wildly whenever in the old days a suspicious sail came into the view of the watchman. The little bronze image in the top of the tower is known as "La Habana." When de Soto sailed out from Havana harbor on that storied expedition through the American wilds which was to end in his death, he left la Fuerza, and with it his command as governor, in charge of his bride, Isabel de Bobadilla. For four years Lady Isabel waited for her lord's return, spending anxious hours in the little watch-tower of the fort. Only when the tattered remnants of that splendid army which had accompanied the adventurer were brought back to Havana was her long suspense ended.

The cellars of la Fuerza contain damp dungeons

MORRO CASTLE, HAVANA, CUBA

LA FUERZA

used as receptacles for modern rifles and ammunition, this part of the old fort being given over to the purposes of an armory.

In 1554 Havana was again attacked by the French and partially destroyed and in the following year it fell a victim to pirates. During the wars which marked the reigns of the Emperor Charles V, of Spain, and his son, Philip II, the colony became more and more the object of attack by Spain's enemies, and in 1585, Havana having been seriously menaced by Sir Francis Drake, it was determined to build additional defences for the city. In 1589 Morro Castle, the Castle of the Three Kings and the Bateria de la Punta were begun; by 1597 they were completed.

The word "Morro" means promontory, and Castle del Morro is merely the fortress on the point. The design of Morro is that of the quaint Moorish fortress in the harbor of Lisbon, but it has been changed so much for modern defensive uses that it does not now greatly resemble its original. The work is irregular in shape, is built on solid rock, and rises from 100 to 120 feet above the level of the sea. Its situation on the northern one of the two points of the entrance to the harbor of Havana gives it a great importance. Opposite Morro, across the harbor mouth, is la Punta.

To visit Morro one climbs to the fort by an inclined road cut out of rock, shaded with laurels and royal poincianas. Hedges of cactus hem in the road. The pilgrim reaches at last the moat. This was cut out of solid rock and is seventy feet in depth. Passing over the drawbridge and advancing through the dark walls of the work, one comes to the inner court, from whence there is a passage to the ramparts. Here is a fine outlook over city and harbor, from the seaward side of the ramparts, where there is a battery of twelve guns known as the "Twelve Apostles."

Some of the prison cells in Morro are directly over the water and in one spot a steep chute leads to the sea. Your guide will tell you that from here bodies of prisoners, both living and dead, were shot out to become the food of innumerable sharks waiting below.

The most active service that Morro has seen was in 1762, when Havana was taken by the English under Admiral Pocock and Lord Albemarle. In June of that year, shortly after the outbreak of war between France and Spain as allies against England, a fleet of 44 English men-of-war and 150 lighter vessels, bearing a land force of 15,000 men, appeared off Havana. The Spanish defenders numbered 27,000 men, of whom a sufficient garrison was at Morro. The English landed on the coast to the east of our fortress and worked around to the rear of that structure to an eminence where the fortification of Cabanas now stands. The siege began on June 3 and continued until July 30, when, after a stubborn defence, Morro fell.

The long resistance of the point against an over-

LA FUERZA

whelming force is largely to be credited to the indomitable spirit of its commander, Velasco, who, though he knew that his position had been undermined and his men were deserting him, refused to surrender. The fort was taken after the mines had been sprung and the walls had been battered down. Captain Velasco died of wounds received during the siege, and on the day of his funeral hostilities were suspended by the English in recognition of his bravery.

The authorities in Spain decreed that a ship in the Spanish navy should always bear the name of Velasco, and the vessel so named at the time of the Spanish-American war was sunk in Manila Bay by the Boston.

Havana fell thirteen days after Morro and for a year was in the hands of the enemy.

Stretching along bare hilltop back of Morro is Havana's greatest fortress, built in 1763 after the departure of the unwelcome English guests whose coming had shown the weakness of the city's defences. Cabanas, or to give its full name, Castillo de San Carlos de Cabanas (Saint Charles of the Cabin), is nearly a mile in length with a width of about one-fifth of a mile. Its cost was $14,000,000. When King Charles III of Spain, under whose direction the work was commenced, was told the total of expenditures, it is said that he walked to the window of his study and gazed intently out of it, remarking that such an enormous and expensive construction should be visible from Spain.

QUAINT AND HISTORIC FORTS

Within the fort are innumerable walks, dungeons and secret passages. To the right of the entrance is the famous "Laurel Moat" where unfortunate Cubans and other political prisoners were shot without benefit of trial. The condemned men were compelled to kneel facing a wall, and this wall marked with bullets in a line nearly one hundred feet long is a grim present-day memento of Spain's ruthless rule in the island. The spot has been marked with a bronze tablet which records its history.

Other fortifications in Havana include Principe Castle, built in 1774, and Atares Castle, 1767. There are two ancient little round towers of defence at Chorrera and Cojimar.

FORT SAN CARLOS
PENSACOLA BAY—FLORIDA

PENSACOLA Bay is a lozenge-shaped body of water, the entrance to which from the Gulf is at the southern point of the figure, and the southern side is formed by Santa Rosa Island, which stretches out in a long sandy line here to divide sea and inland water. On the western shore, near the head of the bay, is situated the busy city of Pensacola, one of the most active shipping points on the Gulf and also one of the most ancient. About six miles south of Pensacola, and near the mouth of the bay, is the city's ancient defence, Fort San Carlos de Barrancas, which has gone through ten generations and more of life as humans reckon it and has done valiant service under four flags.

The military (and social) history of Pensacola Bay commences in 1558, when Philip II, of Spain, commissioned Luis de Valesca, viceroy of New Spain, to undertake the settlement of Florida. After a preliminary survey Valesca, in the summer of 1559, sent 1500 soldiers and settlers to make a beginning at Pensacola Bay, this body of water having been adjudged the best roadstead and the most favorable for the support of human life on the Gulf Coast. A tentative settlement was established, but for some reason the site did not please the expedition and its leaders attempted unsuccessfully to find a better one. The winter that followed and the next summer were filled with privation and the colony became much reduced in numbers. During the second summer most of the settlers went with Angel de Villafane to Santa Elena, Port Royal Sound, south on the Atlantic coast (South Carolina, to-day) and the remainder was recalled by Philip II, who thereupon decreed that no further effort should be made to settle the west coast of Florida, a royal promulgation which circumstance and lack of incentive to the contrary conspired to make effective for more than a century. If one accepts this abortive expedition as the beginning of settlement in Florida then Pensacola is the oldest point of European residence in the United States, antedating St. Augustine by seven years.

The Spaniards did not regard La Salle's effort at colonization at the mouth of the Mississippi River with favor and were not at all displeased at his misfortunes. To forestall other efforts of the French they undertook a survey of the coast and established a colony at Pensacola in the last years of the Seventeenth Century. This was the beginning of Pensacola of to-day.

When Iberville, in 1699, sailed from France with several vessels containing colonists for Louisiana and when in due course of time he arrived off Pensacola, he found the Spaniards firmly established with a fort with four bastions and some ships of war. The Frenchmen

By courtesy of the Pensacola Chamber of Commerce
FORT SAN CARLOS DE BARRANCAS, NEAR PENSACOLA, FLORIDA

FORT SAN CARLOS

asked for permission to disembark his forces. His request was refused and he then sailed along the coast until he found a landing to his liking near the present-day Biloxi, Mississippi. The governor of Pensacola at this time—and the first governor of the colony—was Don Andre D'Arriola. The fort was named San Carlos de Barrancas.

There came in 1719 a war against Spain in which France and England were allies opposed to her. The French thereupon sent in this year M. de Serigny with a sufficient force to take possession of Pensacola which was valuable to the French on account of its proximity to Louisiana and its accessibility to the West India Islands. The expedition was entirely successful as, after an attack by land by 700 Canadians, the commander of the Spanish garrison, Don John Peter Matamoras, surrendered with the honors of war.

It is probable that the Spanish stronghold at that time was not the one which has come down to us to-day, though it bore the same name and was, very possibly, built on the same site.

The news of the surrender of Pensacola caused a great stir in Spain, and an expedition was fitted out to recover the lost territory. The command of the expedition was given to Don Alphonse Carracosa and the force consisted of 12 vessels and 850 fighting men. Don Carracosa achieved success, as at the sight of his fleet part of the French garrison deserted and the rest surrendered, to be treated with great severity by the Spanish. Don Matamoras was re-established and an expedition was despatched against the French at Mobile without result satisfactory to the Spanish.

The French were to have their day, again, however. De Bienville invested Pensacola by land and Count de Champmelin by sea. After a stubborn resistance Matamoras surrendered, giving the French between twelve hundred and fifteen hundred prisoners. The French dismembered the greater part of the fort and left a small garrison in the remainder of the structure.

Under the peace of 1720 Pensacola was restored to the Spanish and thus was ended the port's first experience of warfare. Fort San Carlos was rebuilt substantially in the form that it bears to-day, and in 1722 another fortification was built on the point of Santa Rosa Island where Fort Pickens long years afterward was to maintain a gallant defence.

Fort San Carlos is a little semicircular structure most solidly put together but not of great pretension as to size. On account of its fine location, however—having no heights near which could dominate it, and having a fine sweep over the entrance to the bay which it is designed to protect—it was of importance in the days of short-range cannon.

In 1763 the whole of Florida, which, of course, included our brave little fort at Pensacola, passed into the hands of the English by treaty with Spain, and an

FORT SAN CARLOS

English garrison took possession of Fort San Carlos. Upon the outbreak of hostilities again between Spain and England, Galvez, the Spanish governor of Louisiana, sailed from New Orleans in February, 1781, with 1400 men and a sufficient fleet to reduce Pensacola. He was joined by squadrons from Havana and Mobile and in May of that year entered Pensacola Bay. The fort here was in the command of Colonel Campbell with a small garrison of English. After a sufficient resistance Colonel Campbell surrendered and Galvez took charge. In 1783 the whole province of Florida was ceded to Spain, and Pensacola remained under a Spanish ruler for thirty-one years after this latter date.

The next eventful interval in the life of Fort San Carlos had to do with one of the most popular figures of United States history, Andrew Jackson. In 1814, during the progress of the second war of the United States with England, Jackson was made a major-general and was given command of the Gulf Coast region where he had been operating against the Creek Indians. While arranging a treaty with these conquered savages he was informed by them that they had been approached by English officers, through the connivance of the Spanish commander at Pensacola, with offers of supplies and assistance to fight against the Americans. Two British vessels arrived at Pensacola August 4 and Colonel Edward Nicholls in command was allowed to land troops and to arm some Indians. Late in August seven more

British vessels arrived at Pensacola and the mask of Spanish neutrality was thrown aside when Fort San Carlos was turned over to the British, the British being allowed to hoist their ensign thereon, and Colonel Nicholls was entertained by the Spanish governor as his guest.

Jackson was at Mobile, Alabama, not very far distant as the crow flies from Pensacola, and when the intelligence of these happenings had been confirmed immediately set about raising a force of Americans. By November he had 2,000 volunteers and early in that month marched from Fort Montgomery (Montgomery, Alabama) upon Pensacola. November 6 he was two miles from that city. To ascertain the Spaniard's intentions he sent Major Pierre to wait upon the commandant of the city and was rewarded for his pains by having his envoy fired upon. By midnight Jackson had his men in motion against the city, and in the hot engagement which followed the Spanish and British were badly worsted. The British fled down the Bay in their ships, blowing up Fort San Carlos in their retreat and carrying away one of the higher Spanish officers—certainly, on the whole, a not very grateful return for the benefits bestowed upon them by their hosts.

The Creek and Seminole Indians who had begun to rally to the English standard were much impressed by this display of force on the part of the Americans and

FORT SAN CARLOS

esteeming Jackson a very bad medicine, indeed, wisely decided to return to the prosaic paths of peace.

During the Civil War, Fort San Carlos played no conspicuous part. The limelight of fame was thrown on its close neighbor, Fort Pickens, on Santa Rosa Island. This latter post at the outbreak of the war was in charge of Lieutenant Adam J. Slemmer, a Pennsylvanian, who, seeing the conflict impending, concentrated (in Fort Pickens as being the easiest one of them all to defend) the forces in the various forts under his jurisdiction. From January 9 to April 11, 1861, Slemmer was in a state of siege in Fort Pickens and on the latter date was relieved by forces from the North. The point was held by Federal troops throughout the war.

A curious incident which occurred early in 1914 at Fort San Carlos recalled vividly to the officers there the part the little Spanish post played in the days when pirates roamed the Spanish Main and all of this part of the world was new. A stranger came to the fort with an old parchment which he declared showed the location of buried treasure in the old fort. He would not tell how he came by the document, but its evident antiquity aroused interest and for an idle hour's interest the officers of the post decided to dig for the buried treasure. On the parchment was a well drawn plan of the fort with a cross in a particular corner of the parade. This point was located with some little difficulty and men were set to digging. For a time nothing interesting occurred, but after a while one of the men struck a rotten wooden board which proved to be the top of an old well. At the bottom of this covered-over well was discovered a lot of watery mud which, when it had been dug into, revealed the top of an old chest. Darkness fell now and it was not considered worth while to continue operations until the next day. The next morning when the men went back to work they found that the stirring up of the earth and water had caused the object, whatever it was, to sink so deep into the unstable soil of the spot that it could not be recovered!

THE PRESIDIO OF SAN FRANCISCO
GOLDEN GATE—CALIFORNIA

H AND in hand with the Military went the Church during Spain's days of dominion in the New World. Where the soldier walked, there too, came the priest. At first when all of the New World was new, when the hold of the Old World was insecure, it was the soldier who pointed the path, but when Spain's hand had a firm grasp upon her possessions it was the priest who took the lead. The records of Spain on the east coast of America are records of bloodiness and cruel oppression. On the west coast where the friar led the way we find deeds of gentleness and love. Where Florida reveals a memory of hate in two old bastioned fortresses—Marion and San Carlos—with dingy dungeons and rusty chains, California shows its missions with their silvery chimes and its presidios, the two institutions being bound together.

Four presidios were established by Spain in old California to guard its missions; the first, at San Diego; the second, at Monterey; the third, at San Francisco; and the fourth, at Santa Barbara. It is the third which bespeaks our interest in this chapter, owing to its importance in the present day as well as to its historic and natural charm.

The presidio at San Francisco was established in

QUAINT AND HISTORIC FORTS

1776 by an expedition which set out in two parts in June of that year from Monterey; one part to go by land, the other by water. The objective point of the two was a bay which had been discovered in 1769 by an expedition from San Diego. It was named in honor of Saint Francis of Assisi, hence, San Francisco. The land expedition included Friars Palou and Cambon, a few married settlers with large families, and seventeen dragoons under the command of Don Jose Moraga, who was to be the commandant of the new post. It carried garden seed, agricultural implements, horses, mules and sheep. This party reached the neighborhood of the Golden Gate on June 27 and, without waiting for the detachment which was coming by sea, chose a site for the presidio and began work upon the modest buildings of that station. The seed was placed in the ground, the cattle and sheep put out to graze and the horses and mules set to labor. All was activity.

The first part of September saw the buildings of the post substantially complete and on September 17, the feast of the Stigmata of Saint Francis, solemn possession of the Presidio, in the name of the King of Spain, was taken by the grizzled soldier Moraga, while a mass was celebrated by Palou. A Te Deum was sung, a cross was planted and salutes were fired over land and water. Thus was the presidio of San Francisco founded.

It is a far cry from 1776 to the present day (though not so long as from 1776 back to the first day of Spanish

By courtesy of R. J. Waters & Co.

FORT SCOTT AND THE GOLDEN GATE, PRESIDIO RESERVATION, SAN FRANCISCO

THE PRESIDIO

settlement in the future United States), but, while the immediate aspect of the country round about Spain's presidio of 1776 at San Francisco has changed, the situation of the post has remained the same; and the view of land and water here is just as entrancing to-day as it was on that day in 1769 when the expedition from San Diego saw the far-famed Golden Gate.

The Presidio of San Francisco, the most important military station of the Pacific coast, is situated on the northwest rim of the city, north of Golden Gate Park (and north of the exposition grounds of 1915) and connected with that park by a beautiful boulevard one mile long. The grounds comprise more than fifteen hundred acres, developed for military purposes in the most modern fashion. From almost any part of the grounds or the approach thereto enchanting views of the wonderful bay of San Francisco are to be obtained.

A description of the view of the presidio as you approach the place on the boulevard from Golden Gate Park has been given by Ernest Peixotto in his "Romantic California," which may well be repeated here:

In the meantime the city boasts one splendid driveway that, with a connecting link completed, will rank with the famous roadways of the Old World.

Only a decade or two ago the Presidio (it still bears its Spanish appellation) was an isolated military post separated from the city by several miles of barren, sandy thoroughfares.

QUAINT AND HISTORIC FORTS

Now some of the handsomest homes crown the hill tops about it, and owe their chief attraction to the glorious views of bay and shore that they command. To start some fine afternoon toward sunset from one of these homes and take a drive around the cliffs is an experience not soon to be forgotten.

A few blocks run brings you to a stone gateway, its posts topped with eagles; you turn sharply to the right through a grove of eucalypti, swing round a curve and then you stop the motor. From the red Macadam roadway upon which you stand, the hills fall gently in a broad amphitheatre to the barracks and parade grounds laid out symmetrically along the shore, and teeming with soldier life. Beyond, the waters of the bay mirror the azure of the sky—a blue, tinged with green, like those half-dead turquoises that they sell in the marts of Tunis. The North Beach hills, thick-studded with the modest homes of the city's alien population, gleam white against the Contra Costa Mountains—verdant in winter, tawny and dry in summer—with the lumpy silhouette of the Monte Diablo, the Devil's Mountain, poking over the shoulder as if it, too, wished a peep at so fair a prospect.

Across the stretch of intervening water, stern-wheeled river steamers ply northward to San Pablo Bay; on through the Carquinez Straits and up the Sacramento River, their silhouettes varied once in a while by some grim battle-ship or cruiser steaming to the Navy Yard at Mare Island, headquarters, home and hospital for all our ships in the Pacific. Anchored in the middle of the bay, Alcatraz lies terraced with batteries, low, forbidding, while to the north rise the hills of Marin County bathed in purple shadows and clustered around the base of Tamalpais. The whole scene is suffused with the rosy flush of the westering

THE PRESIDIO

sun that gilds the islands, warms the greens of the eastern sky, and blushes the hills with its ardent glances.

One turns from the picture with regret, only to follow on to new vistas. You wind through groves of evergreens and eucalypti out into the open meadows, a riot of flowers in springtime, that top the cliffs above the Golden Gate. The famous straits lie just below, Fort's Point antiquated bastions on their hither shore fronting the white-washed walls of the harbor-light on the Point Bonita bluffs opposite.

To take up the thread of our historical narrative, the presidio remained a possession of Spain's until 1824 when Mexico finally became free from its mother country and the flag of Mexico took the place of the banner of Castile and Aragon at the Golden Gate.

In 1846 the American flag was raised in all of the presidios of California, an interesting chapter of national expansion far too large for abridgment here. In 1849 commenced the era of San Francisco's prosperity and presidio's importance with the discovery of gold in California and the onset of the hordes of gold-seekers who came through the Golden Gate.

The presidio was visited by Richard H. Dana in 1859 and is described by him:

I took a California horse of old style and visited the Presidio. The walls stand as they did, with some changes made to accommodate a small garrison of United States troops. It has a noble situation and I saw from it a clipper ship of the very largest class coming through the Gate under her fore and aft sails. Thence I rode to the fort, now nearly finished, on the southern shore of the Gate, and made an inspection of it. It is very expensive and of the latest style. One of the engineers is Custis Lee, who has just left West Point at the head of his class, a son of Colonel Robert E. Lee who distinguished himself in the Mexican war.

The fort with the "expensive equipment" to which he refers is Fort Winfield Scott, which was seven years building and cost $2,000,000. It is now out of date, but is a picturesque feature of the harbor and is of service to the presidio authorities of the present in various minor capacities.

Opposite Fort Winfield Scott, across the Golden Gate, which is here at its narrowest width of one mile, can be seen the white buildings of Fort Baker. Other defences of San Francisco, visible from the presidio, include Fort Miley, on Point Bonita; Point Lobos, and Alcatraz Island, a picturesque body of land whose Spanish name memorializes the pelicans which once made the place their home.

During the Spanish-American War the presidio was a scene of activity as the point of departure of our soldiers for the Philippines. The national cemetery for the burial of soldiers who have died on duty in the Philippines is situated here, too, and each returning transport brings back its sad burden, far lighter now than in the days when the islands were first feeling the weight of American rule.

THE PRESIDIO

Connected with the history of the presidio is a pretty story which Bret Harte has woven into a familiar one of his poems. It concerns the pathetic love of Dona Concepcion Arguello, daughter of the Spanish Commandant Don Luis Arguello, for Rezanov, chamberlain of the Russian emperor, who came, during the days of Spain's possession of this land, to negotiate for Russian settlements in California. Rezanov won the heart of his host's daughter and sailed away to gain the consent of his emperor to marriage with her. Years passed and no word came from Rezanov. At length Sir George Simpson, the Englishman, in his trip around the world, brought word that Rezanov had been killed by a fall from his horse while crossing Siberia on his homeward journey. Dona Concepcion, who had faithfully waited his return, became a nun and when she died was buried near the old Mission church in the Presidio grounds.

FORT ADAMS AND NEWPORT'S DEFENSIVE RUINS
NEWPORT—RHODE ISLAND

HERE is an odd little cluster of islands on the eastern side of the entrance to Narragansett Bay. The most important of these is Aquidneck and on the southern extremity of Aquidneck Isle is situated Newport. At the southern extremity of Newport is Brenton's Point and on Brenton's Point is Fort Adams. This is the proper way to build up a climax!

Picture to yourself a sunny Fourth of July in 1799; this is the day on which Fort Adams is to be dedicated with imposing ceremonies. From out of the little many-spired city across the sparkling blue waters of Newport Bay winds a little procession around the shore road which leads to the fort. First of all, comes the company of soldiers which is to garrison the post. It is Captain John Henry's company of artillery. After this comes the major-general of the State militia with his staff in gorgeous gold braid. Following him is the famous Newport Artillery Company with two brass field pieces making a brave show. Then there are the Newport Guards with two brass field pieces. Finally there is a company of citizens.

They are all assembled at the fort. Major Tousard,

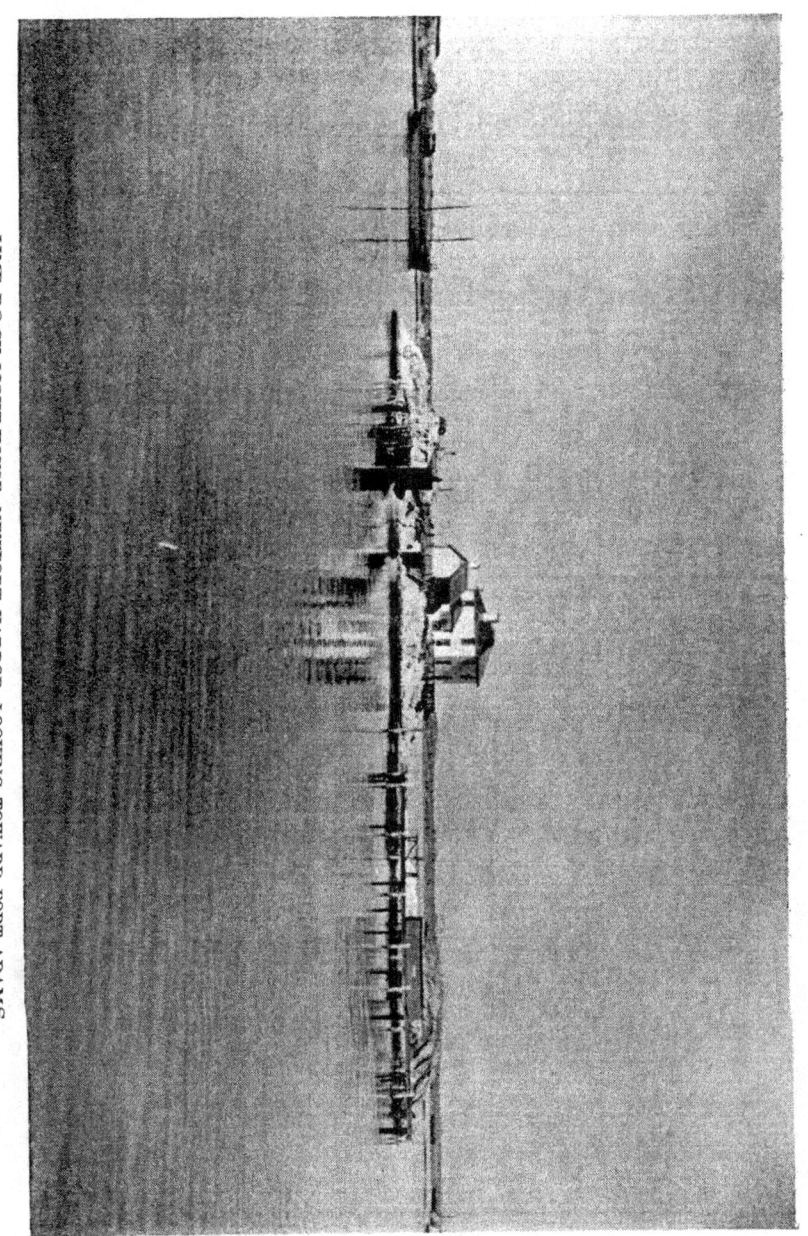

LIME ROCK LIGHT-HOUSE, NEWPORT HARBOR, LOOKING TOWARD FORT ADAMS

Parade, Old Fort Adams

Present-Day Aspect of Fort Greene
GLIMPSES OF NEWPORT'S HISTORIC DEFENCES

of the corps of engineers of the army of the infant republic, is speaking: He says: "Citizens: Happy to improve every occasion to testify my veneration for that highly distinguished citizen who presides over the government of the United States, I have solicited the Secretary of War to name this fortress, Fort Adams. He has gratified my desire. I hope that the brave officers and soldiers who are and shall be honored with its defence will by valor and good conduct render it worthy of its name, which I hereby proclaim Fort Adams." A salute was fired from the four brass field pieces and the great cannon of the new fort. In the distance Fort Wolcott on Goat Island fired guns and the standard of the young United States was unfurled at the head of the flag-staff. Thus was christened one of the most important of American coast defences.

For twenty-five years thereafter Fort Adams was maintained with a small garrison supplied from Fort Wolcott, under whose jurisdiction it was. In 1824 the present Fort Adams was commenced, a star-shaped fortress of grey granite, with outworks, upon an initial appropriation by the Federal government of $50,000. It was finished, under successive appropriations, in 1841. The garrison was withdrawn from 1853 to 1857 and between the years 1859 and 1862, since when it has been continuously occupied. The present area of Fort Adams reservation is about 200 acres, and it contains modern works which need no description.

QUAINT AND HISTORIC FORTS

If one should go back in point of Time beyond the gay little ceremony which marked the beginning of Fort Adams, he would find that Brenton's Point had been a site for martial works before this. Its strategic possibilities for defence were early recognized in the Revolution, as, in the spring of 1776, a light breast-work was thrown up here by the Americans behind which they mounted several guns. In April, 1776, the *Glasgow,* a British war vessel of twenty-nine guns, came into Newport Harbor and anchored near Goat Island. On the following morning such a heavy fire was brought to bear upon the ship from Brenton's Point that it cut its cable and made out to sea. A few days after this the *Scarborough* and the *Scymetar* of His Majesty's service were, likewise, badly battered by fire from these earthworks.

Late in the summer of 1776 the British obtained possession of Aquidneck Island. They made their headquarters at Newport, and erected a temporary barracks on Brenton's Point where the American battery had been. For three years they held possession of Rhode Island and then were removed by orders from their commander-in-chief, embarking October 25, 1779.

The next visitors to Newport were the French. The French fleet, under the command of Admiral de Ternay, appeared in Newport Harbor August 10, 1780. General Rochambeau and his army shortly put ashore. General Heath, in command of the American forces in

FORT ADAMS

Rhode Island, was at the wharf to welcome Rochambeau. There were speeches and the American officers wore cockades of black and white as a courtesy to the allies, the cockade of the formal American uniform being black and that of the French, white. It was not long before the French had been made to feel at home and had settled down to a long stay.

General Rochambeau's defences consisted of a line of earthworks completely enclosing Newport on the north, cutting off access to it by land from any other part of the island. Traces of this line can still be discerned by the inquiring visitor to Newport. Strong temporary fortifications were thrown up at Brenton's Point on the future site of our Fort Adams, and on all of the islands of the harbor were placed guns. The northern water-front of the city was held by a strong redoubt, built by Rochambeau and known as Fort Greene. This was at the site of the present Fort Greene Park, at the head of Washington Street.

Rochambeau was the second visitor to these shores with a French army. The first allies had not made a pleasant impression with the Americans, it must be admitted, chiefly because of their leader's, D'Estaing's, apparent unwillingness to come to grips with the enemy except where such action might directly benefit his own country. Doubtless he acted on orders from Versailles! But General Rochambeau seemed to be under different instructions, for he immediately placed himself under the authority of the American leaders and ingratiated himself with the people. His stay at Newport is a brilliant chapter in the social history of that city.

One of the pleasantest episodes of the French occupation of Newport was the visit of Washington to his French associate in arms. Rochambeau had chosen as his residence and headquarters the comfortable and beautiful dwelling at the corner of Clarke and Mary Streets known as the Vernon House. In March, 1781, Washington, accompanied by his young aide-de-camp, Lafayette, came to Newport and was received here with much formality. The interest with which the French officers regarded their guest is evidenced in some of the journals which they published at the close of the war on their return to their own country. Amongst minor incidents, Washington led a dance with the beautiful Miss Champlin, and French officers, taking the instruments from the musicians' hands, played a minuet, " A Successful Campaign."

A merry time this French occupation of Newport brought about, and traditions of the gayeties and portentous politenesses of the period are still retailed in the little city. A finer body of men than the French army had probably never taken the field. Many had been through the Seven Years War. Officers of the most cultured circles of the Old World embraced a chance of campaigning in the New World with the pleasure of school-boys in a new experience.

FORT ADAMS

One of the officers of the French force was the Viscount de Noailles, in whose regiment Napoleon was afterward a subaltern. Another was Biron, a figure in the French Revolution, and who in 1793, having unsuccessfully commanded the republican armies in La Vendee, was guillotined. There was the Marquis de Chastellux,—an elegant,—whose petits soupers became the talk of every one fortunate enough to be invited. Later Chastellux's " Travels in America " were to become a treasured gallery of pictures of the nation when it was new. There were Talleyrand, Chabannes, Champcenetz, de Melfort, la Touche, de Barras, de Broglie, Vauban, and Berthier, the military confidant of Napoleon, and many others. With such an infusion of genius and culture it is not remarkable that the little city developed an exotic bloom and that the records of this period in Newport are among the gayest in American social history. Nor should one be surprised that the anxious mothers of young daughters of Newport in that time (as we learn now from the betraying evidences of long preserved letters) passed vigilant hours of watchfulness in the sudden maelstrom of French gallantry!

The Chevalier de Ternay, commander at sea of the French forces, died soon after the arrival at Newport and was buried in Trinity church-yard where a slab was erected to his memory.

In 1781 the French marched out of Newport, joined

QUAINT AND HISTORIC FORTS

Washington in his campaign at Yorktown, and the result soon was the surrender of Cornwallis and the virtual end of the War of Independence.

In May, 1794, Governor Fenner addressed the following letter to George Champlin, of Newport:

> Last evening I received a letter from Mr. Rochefontaine the engineer dated New London . . . informing me that he should depart from New London for Newport this day and desiring me to transmit to him my orders and the names of the gentlemen appointed by me to be the agents for the fortifications and to supervise their execution. I have to ask the favor of you to undertake the business with Col. Sherburne until my arrival at Newport, and to wait on the engineer and deliver him my letter of appointment. Give him the necessary information and assistance. Your compliance will render great service to the State and in a particular manner oblige your ob't servant,
>
> A. FENNER.

The building of the new fort was assigned to Major Louis Toussard, and soon it was ready for its dedication. At the time of this ceremony the battery was completed and was mounted with 32-pounders on seacoast carriages.

Strangely enough it was as a protection from the very allies with whom the United States had triumphed against Great Britain that Fort Adams was called into being. It will be recalled by the reader of history that at this period France under the Directory was in constant embroilment with the United States. Citizen

FORT ADAMS

Talleyrand was bent upon turning the new nation to France's ends. In 1798 a French cruiser actually had the impudence, after the capture of several American vessels, to bring her prizes into an American port to escape the more dreaded British. President Adams, as all know, eventually brought the Directoire Exécutif and Citizen Talleyrand to their senses in no uncertain fashion, but for a time affairs between the two countries were in a very unsatisfactory condition.

To President Adams is due, too, the foundation of the present American navy and the increasing importance of Fort Adams. He saw the necessity in the future for a great naval base well located on the coast. A commissioner sent out by him reported that the harbor of Newport most fully answered the specifications he had in mind, and from this time the works on Brenton's Point acquired a new value.

The greater part of the construction of the second Fort Adams, which was begun in 1824, was done under the personal supervision of General J. G. Totten of the United States army in coast defence. It is said that during the progress of the work a full set of plans of the fortress mysteriously disappeared and as mysteriously reappeared after a long interval. Gossip also gratuitously asserts that a copy of these plans could be found in the Admiralty office of Great Britain. However that may be, the plans would be of little value to any one to-day.

Associated with Totten was that General Bernard of the first Napoleon's staff who was raised from the ranks by the Corsican for his skill as a military engineer. Bernard came to the United States in 1816 and offered his services to the infant republic. While his gifts have been generally conceded, his personality must have been far from winning. Colonel McCree, chief of engineers, resigned rather than serve with him, and harmony between the Frenchman and Colonel Totten was only secured by an agreement through which work was divided and each man was bound to accept the other's plans.

There are passages beneath the walls of Fort Adams known only to the engineers. These are always closed, for they are of no use in piping times of peace and might become a trap for curious, unwary visitors. A story is told of an exploring party years ago, before the entrances were barred. This party penetrated far beneath the fort. Suddenly their lantern went out and a scream and a splash from the front showed that one of the party was in distress. A beautiful girl had stepped over the edge of a subterranean reservoir. What could be done! There was a rush and another splash. One of the young men had jumped in the dark into the dank pool beside the drowning girl. He was able to keep himself and his fair charge afloat until a rope reached them. The hero of the tale was the late Washington Van Zandt of the Newport family.

PANORAMA OF NEWPORT HARBOR, R. I., SHOWING FORT ADAMS AT LEFT MIDDLE DISTANCE

Goat Island in Central Distance

FORT DUMPLINGS, CONANICUT ISLAND, A REVOLUTIONARY RELIC NEAR NEWPORT

FORT ADAMS

During the War of 1812 Fort Adams saw no active service, and this is true, too, of the Civil War.

The vicinity of Newport held many fortified points during the Revolutionary War and some of the remains of these can be seen to-day. One of the most interesting of these relics is "Dumplings," at the southern tip of Conanicut Isle. A belligerent little round stone tower, it has as pugnacious an appearance to-day as it had when a few hardy Americans garrisoned it against the English; and it is a favorite picnic point for parties from Newport or from the summer colonies on the west side of Narragansett Bay. Other ruined defences (grass-grown and decayed) are to be found on Conanicut whose history is so obscure that even legend has little to say about them; but they are all a part of the expression of the doughty spirit which moved Newport and its vicinity during the Revolution.

Goat Island in Newport Harbor, now the home of the Fort Wolcott torpedo station, and a naval hospital, was, we are told by Edward Field, in his interesting monograph, "Revolutionary Defences in Rhode Island," the site of a fortification as early as 1700. This early fortification was known as Fort Anna; later Fort George; then, Fort Liberty; and, at the time of the Revolution, Fort Washington.

FORT MONROE
OLD POINT COMFORT—VIRGINIA

ORNING bugle call, the evening gun, grey ships of war stealing in from a misty sea with long plumes of soft black smoke, military uniforms on the streets and trig bright houses are, probably, the average civilian's impressions of a stay at Old Point Comfort where is located Fort Monroe. "Fort" or "Fortress," for the place changes its sex indifferently according to the state of mind of the speaker, it probably satisfies the popular conception of a mighty stronghold of defence more completely than any other such establishment in the United States. And, indeed, it is a great defensive work, guarding one of the most vital points of entrance in this country, menacing hostile approach to the very capital of the country itself.

At the southern limit of the western shore of the Chesapeake Bay is a long sandy peninsula whose extremity in times of flood is cut off from the mainland by a narrow wash of water, and on this sometimes isolated tip of the peninsula is situated Fort Monroe. The grounds of the reservation, which includes all of the residence portion of the little community, too, embrace about 280 acres of almost always dry land. The walls

By courtesy of the War Department

FROM THE RAMPARTS OF FORT MONROE, LOOKING TOWARD HAMPTON ROADS
(Taken during the Jamestown Celebration by the United States War Department and Reproduced by Special Permission.)

GARDEN VIEW OF ONE OF MONROE'S ANTE-BELLUM RESIDENCES

of the fort itself encircle the greater part of this number of acres.

From the summit of these walls one looks out upon a wide prospect of waters. To the south is Hampton Roads, into which empty the waters of the James, the Elizabeth and the Nansemond Rivers. To the east lies the wide expanse of the lower Chesapeake Bay, giving access to the Potomac and the network of other rivers which the bay holds as tributaries. From all directions except from the west pours in upon Old Point a vivifying draught of pure salt air. From the west,—from the mainland,—come all manner of humidities, unpleasantness and mosquitoes, but this is only one of four points of the compass.

It is a healthy place, this Old Point Comfort, so healthy, indeed, that in a grave government report of 1877 the army surgeon at the post tells his superiors in Washington that there is a legend in the army that the air of the place conduces to fecundity in the families stationed there. He adds that from his own professional practice and his observation of the number of children playing in the streets he believes that there is more than fancy in the idea!

The visitor to Fort Monroe will almost invariably come by water, though there is a roundabout way of reaching the post by way of trolley from Newport News —through quaint old Hampton, past Hampton Institute and over a long trestle to the reservation. He will see, first, on putting foot upon the wharf and fighting off the hungry hordes of hackmen and baggage smashers, the red walls of a popular hotel. To the right is a triangular park, on the far side of whose spread of green is a row of modern cottages of pretentious architecture, which are given over to the superior officers stationed at the post. Beyond the roofs of these can be seen, in glimpses, the battlements of the old fort. Perhaps our visitor will penetrate on farther back into the grounds, along the winding main street, until he comes to the main entrance to the fort, faced by an inn much used by officers and the military set. Here there are cottages, of less imposing aspect than those facing the sea, which are given over to the younger officers and their families. Here also one has his first clear view of the fort walls.

Without a doubt it is recollection of the moat that one carries away from Fortress Monroe, primarily. This broad band of water, encircling the high, grey old walls of the place, appeals strongly to one's romantic sense. Ho, warder! to the draw-bridge! And all that sort of thing. There is a draw-bridge, too,—five of them, in fact, at the five entrances to the fort. So, ho, for the draw-bridge and a view inside the fort!

The visitor who crosses the narrow way leading across the moat and penetrates to the interior of Fortress Monroe will not be greatly impressed by show of military works. These are all quietly and modestly ready in the background, somewhere. He will find himself in a charming sort of park which strongly suggests the tropics in its luxuriance of foliage of all kinds. Indeed the air of Old Point, for some reasons, supports tropical plant growth that will not live in the countryside immediately adjoining. One of the effective sights that the visitor sees in the fort are the clumps of fig trees which are to be found, and there are to be found, too, magnolia and rhododendron and crape myrtle.

There is a large parade ground, flanked on the east and north by long barracks. The rest of the grounds, not including the casemates, is given over to residences, to various store-houses and to a building of the Coast Artillery School which has been located at Monroe since 1867.

The casemates of the old fort are used as residences for married private soldiers and for other purposes, not transparently military. The long rows of heavy cannon once to be seen here are to be found no more, their place being taken by modern batteries elsewhere.

There is to be seen the casemate in which Jefferson Davis, president of the Confederate States, was confined after the working out of the destiny of the Lost Cause. It is not different from its neighbors, and is an inconspicuous little compartment in a wall with an ornamental little two-post doorway and one window. Many curious visitors stop before it.

Old Point Comfort and all of this section of the

QUAINT AND HISTORIC FORTS

lower Chesapeake have seen many strange visitors and cargoes in the Past. Doughty old Captain John Smith came to Hampton Roads and wrote about what he saw with that wealth of picturesque detail which those old chroniclers loved to pour forth. The name Point Comfort itself came from the circumstance that Smith was cast into this Hampton Roads on the wings of a storm at sea and that he hailed the first strip of solid land that he saw as a comfort, indeed. At an early period a settlement was made here, as a subsidiary of the Jamestown colony, and, as early as 1611, a fort was built on the point as a defence against Indians and freebooting marauders of buccaneer type. The fort was armed and known as Fort Algernon, in honor of Lord Algernon Percie, one of the directors of the Virginia Company. The greatest fort of the country was once called Algernon!

This little fortification was not of long life, however. It was maintained for a few years by the Jamestown colony but went into decay after the failure of its parent. The strategic value of the Point as a place for defence was not lost sight of, however, in any succeeding generation, though the place was not called into service for many years.

The foundations of Fortress Monroe were laid in 1819, and the works were carried forward actively for ten years. The plans were drawn by the famous Bernard, one-time aide-de-camp of the first Napoleon,

By courtesy of the War Department

FIRE !!!

Showing shells just leaving mortars, Fort Monroe, Va. (This remarkable photograph was taken with modern high speed apparatus by the Corps of Enlisted Specialists stationed at this post)

CASEMATES OF FORT MONROE, AS THEY WERE DURING THE CIVIL WAR

FORT MONROE

and one of his leading engineers. It was Bernard's ambition to construct in the United States (he came to the United States in 1816 and immediately entered the employ of the government) one great fortress like the works of Antwerp, in the fortification of which he had a large share. Fort Monroe, named in honor of the president who did so much to make sure that the coast defences of the country should be adequately founded, was the result of this vision.

It is to be seen that the life of the present fortification begins after the War of 1812, but the military history of the vicinity of Fort Monroe prior to that time is full of interest.

During the Revolution the mouth of the Chesapeake was guarded by British cruisers and a rigorous blockade was maintained. Despite this, during the war no less than 248 privateers were fitted out in the waters of the Chesapeake and managed to gain the high seas by eluding the vigilance of the patrol beyond the capes.

In 1779 General Leslie sailed from New York with 3000 of His Majesty's troopers to land upon the peninsula not far from the site of Fort Monroe and there to await orders from Lord Cornwallis, who was in North Carolina. He entered Hampton Roads and took Norfolk and Portsmouth, fortifying the latter place as a base for future operations. After some weeks of inactivity, he re-embarked and sailed to reinforce Cornwallis at Charleston. In the following year Clinton ordered the traitor Arnold with 50 sail and 1600 soldiers to replace Leslie.

The Arnold expedition proceeded up the James River in 1781 and set the torch to the public buildings of Richmond. After pillaging Petersburg, it returned to Portsmouth and threw up strong intrenchments. Lafayette attempted to stay this destroying band but had not force enough of his own and did not receive expected reinforcement. The fleet which had been sent to augment his numbers was engaged by the British under Admiral Arbuthnot off the capes and compelled, after a hot engagement, to withdraw to Newport. The English thus retained their hold on Hampton Roads and were enabled to send additional forces to General Arnold under General Phillips. In April the combined forces under Arnold moved again up the James River, burning and pillaging.

Cornwallis occupied Portsmouth shortly after this, but soon again moved to Yorktown, where he threw up huge intrenchments, the outlines of which are plainly discernible at the present day. In September, 1781, the French under Comte de Grasse were successful in entering the Chesapeake to co-operate with Washington, Lafayette and Rochambeau. The British fleet under Admiral Graves sturdily contested the capes, but was forced to surrender the hold which it had maintained so effectively. In the ensuing month occurred the historic surrender of Cornwallis.

FORT MONROE

During the War of 1812, a British order in council declared the Chesapeake to be in a state of blockade, and in 1813 Rear-Admiral Cockburn of His Majesty's navy was sent to Lynnhaven Bay, near Norfolk. The Americans had a large flotilla in Hampton Roads, and had constructed Forts Norfolk and Nelson on the Elizabeth River near Norfolk and had thrown up intrenchments on Craney Island, these dispositions all being under the direction of Brigadier General Robert B. Taylor.

At daybreak of June 22, 1813, a determined attack was made by the British under Cockburn from land and sea, which was repulsed. Three days later quiet Hampton was captured after a gallant defence by an inadequate garrison and the town pillaged in barbaric fashion. Soon after, Cockburn withdrew to the coasts of South Carolina and Georgia, but resumed his operations in the lower Chesapeake March 1, 1814. In July, 1814, he was largely reinforced and with a combined land and naval expedition commenced that march up the Chesapeake which culminated in the sacking of Washington and the final repulse of the expedition at Fort McHenry. This was the last important engagement of the War of 1812.

During the Civil War Fortress Monroe saw stirring scenes, though it had no very active part in any of them. In October, 1861, Hampton Roads off the fort was the rendezvous for great land and naval forces under Admiral Dupont and General Sherman designed to capture Hilton Head. In the January following another great force was brought together here for operations on the Carolina coast. In the spring of 1862 McClellan's army arrived at Old Point and went to Yorktown.

In March of 1862 occurred in Hampton Roads the episodes of the *Merrimac*. A watcher on the walls of Fort Monroe would have seen this queer, square vessel, covered with railroad iron, sailing down the blue waters. He might have seen the sinking of the *Cumberland* with the greater part of her crew despite her desperate, impotent efforts against this new kind of adversary. He might have witnessed the destruction of the *Congress* by fire and the partial disabling of the *Minnesota*. He might have heard in the old fort that night the barrack-room gossip of the new giant and whispers of the expected arrival of a United States champion which was to take up the gage of combat. The next day he might have seen from the ramparts the struggle between the *Merrimac* and the *Monitor,* which ushered in a new chapter in naval warfare and began the era of the steel-clad knight of the seas.

Later Old Point Comfort became the base of operation of the Army of the James.

In 1893, during the celebration of the Columbian Exposition, Hampton Roads was the rendezvous under the guns of old Monroe for the vessels of all of the nations of the world. The old fort sees the most important manœuvres of the United States navy of to-day.

FORTS SUMTER AND MOULTRIE
NEAR CHARLESTON—SOUTH CAROLINA

HE bombardment of Fort Sumter from Fort Moultrie began at dawn of April 12, 1861, and continued without remission for about 36 hours, or until noon of the second day. During that time, though shot and shell played havoc with the walls of both the besiegers and the besieged, no human being was hurt,—a strange preliminary, indeed, to the most murderous civil war since the invention of gunpowder in the history of the world.

This has been called the first time in history that two forts waged battle against each other. It was like two strong men, tied by the feet, almost beyond reach of each other, being allowed to strike at each other until one or the other should fall.

To understand something of the conditions which governed this very historic bout between Fort Sumter and Fort Moultrie, one must have some idea of the lay of the land at Charleston. Charleston, itself, it may be pointed out, is situated on a long narrow spit of land at the juncture of the Ashley and Cooper Rivers. The arrow-head formed by these two rivers points almost directly toward the mouth of Charleston Bay, where the waters of the two rivers joined mingle with the Atlantic Ocean. Let us go to the point of the arrow-head upon which Charleston is situated, to the Battery,—that is, Charleston's most famous public park,—and gaze seaward: Five miles away, across a shimmering blue, we see a little geometrical dot almost midway between the jaws which hold Charleston Bay. This is Fort Sumter, a little stone work built by the United States Government in 1828 on a sandy shallow. Fort Moultrie is situated on Sullivan's Island, on the northern one of the two jaws of the bay, a body of land really distinct from the mainland but which seems from this distance to be a part of that land. Of the two fortifications, Fort Moultrie is the older and by long odds the more interesting as to past.

Wise heads of both sections in 1860 saw that war was inevitable between the North and the South, though patriots did their best to prevent armed conflict. But the doctrine of State individualism or State's Rights was too firmly established to be gotten from the body corporate without a purging of blood, just as individual rights in the social structure can never be enforced to the last limit without conflicting with the community purpose. So when, on Christmas night, 1860, Major Anderson, commanding at Fort Moultrie, moved his whole force secretly over to the sub-post, Fort Sumter, and sent his women and children to Charleston, with the request that they be sent north, the citizens of Charleston, at least, knew that the issue had been squarely met, to be settled at the court of last resort.

FORT SUMTER, A PILE OF STONE ON A SANDY SHOAL

Copyright, Detroit Publishing Co.

FORT SUMTER

Mrs. St. Julien Ravenel, in her delightful reminiscences of Charleston, writes:

Doubt and delay were gone. Then came the call to arms . . . January, February, and March were so full of crowded life that they seemed an eternity, yet one dreaded lest eternity should end. End it did when one night at eleven o'clock seven guns thundered out over the town and every man sprang up, seized his rifle and ran to the wharves. It was the signal that the relieving fleet (from the north) was on its way south, and that the whole reserve must hurry to the islands.

During all this time Fort Sumter had been supplied with provisions and necessaries by the citizens of Charleston.

When Major Anderson in command at Fort Sumter accepted Beauregard's terms of surrender and saluted the new flag, he was conveyed, with all the honors of war, in the steamer *Isabel* to the United States fleet which had lain idle in the offing.

From this time until the end of the Civil War Charleston was in a state of siege. There was a short period of preparation on both sides before the Federal fleet appeared, November, 1861, outside the quaint old city. The city maintained its integrity complete against attacks by water, and finally fell to a move in force by land in the last year of the war, when the defenders of Charleston were withdrawn and all of the men of the remnants of the armies of the Confederacy were being concentrated for one last desperate protest against the inevitable.

After the Civil War Fort Sumter was repaired and strengthened and is still a seat of military power as a sub-post of Fort Moultrie.

To reach Fort Moultrie one goes from Charleston by ferry to the northern side of the Cooper River and takes a trolley which leads seaward along the coast across an inlet to Sullivan's Island, which has become a popular summer place with many people of Charleston.

Fort Moultrie, when once it is reached, is not a pretentious place,—the old works, that is,—being simply a star-shaped fort of brownish-red brick on which the hot southern sun pours down in quantity. It overlooks a rumpled beach and the sea on one side and flat uninteresting land on the other. To the seaward one can gaze upon Fort Sumter and find it not more interesting of aspect close at hand than it is at a distance. Beside the gate of Fort Moultrie is a small marble shaft which marks the grave of Osceola, the Seminole chieftain. If one has devoured Indian tales in his youth he will no doubt be more interested in this simple memorial than in the immediate aspect of military things around him. It was in Fort Moultrie that Osceola was jailed after his capture in Florida and it was here that he died,— from a broken heart, if one is still interested in Indian stories!

The present Fort Moultrie was started in 1841 on

FORT MOULTRIE

the site of a famous old palmetto structure of the same name which had stood since early Revolutionary days. In 1903, with the exquisite tact which it displays occasionally, army headquarters in Washington decided to change the name of the fort to Fort Getty in honor of some deserving soldier whose career is recorded in the files of the Army Department, but the loud chorus of indignation that greeted this move carried all the way from Charleston to Washington, and the name of that delightful old Revolutionary character, William H. Moultrie, is still preserved at the spot where his first battle was fought.

The foundations of Fort Moultrie were laid in January, 1776, when a Mr. Dewees, owner of the island which bears his name, was ordered to deliver at Sullivan's Island palmetto logs eighteen to twenty feet long and not less than ten inches in diameter in the middle; and Colonel Moultrie was ordered to superintend the erection of a fort from this material. It was not completed in June when the British came into view. In design a double square pen it was built of palmetto logs piled one upon the other and securely bolted together; the space between the outer and inner pen was about sixteen feet and this was filled in with sand; there were square bastions. The walls were intended to be ten feet high above the gun platforms where were mounted 64 guns.

The British fleet bearing a land force was under

the command of Admiral Sir Peter Parker, and reached Cape Fear early in May, where it was joined by Sir Henry Clinton from New York with a portion of the troops which had participated in the Battle of Bunker Hill. Clinton assumed command of all the land forces. On the 4th of June the fleet appeared off Charleston bar and a small force of men was landed on Long Island, the island just north of Sullivan's Island, and on the 28th of June advanced under Sir Peter Parker to give battle to Fort Sullivan, as Moultrie was then known. There were brought into action in this engagement the following English vessels: The *Bristol* and *Experiment* of 50 guns each; the frigates *Active, Solebay, Acteon, Siren,* and *Sphinx* of 28 guns each; the *Thunderbomb* and *Ranger,* sloops, of 28 guns; and the *Friendship* of 22 guns, in all, a very powerful squadron. The Americans had their unfinished palmetto fort, 64 guns and 1200 men. Several days before the battle the fussy General Charles Lee, whom Washington afterwards in his only recorded uncontrolled exhibition of temper called, at the battle of Monmouth, " a damned poltroon," had removed to another defence of the city half of the small quantity of gunpowder which Moultrie had been given for the defence of his fort.

The command of the defence of Charleston had been given to General Lee by the Continental Congress, and General Lee had appeared in the city on the same day that the British fleet was sighted off the bar. From the first he seems to have been in conflict with Moultrie. Moultrie's fort, he said, was poorly designed, and doubtless it was; Moultrie should provide a means of retreat for his men, and Moultrie replied that they would never use it; and Moultrie this and that. Moultrie himself, his admirers were forced to admit, was "a man of very easy manners, leaving to others many things which he had better have attended to himself."

But the point is that Moultrie carried this same easiness of manner and mental poise into battle with him and was on this account an ideal officer to direct a fight. He had, moreover, the unlimited confidence and affection of his men and he knew the people he was working with.

The British appeared off Fort Sullivan just when the feeling between General Lee and Moultrie was at an acute stage. We find Moultrie now at face with the problem of defending his "slaughter pen" fort against an overwhelming force with the insufficient quantity of gunpowder which General Lee had left him.

The ships formed in double column and poured a terrific fire upon the fort. Moultrie feared that the concussion of the shells would rock his guns off their platforms. "Concentrate upon the Admiral, upon the fifty-gun ships!" This was Moultrie's direction to his men. The Americans, expert marksmen that they were, obeyed his commands and the *Bristol* and the *Experi-*

ment suffered fearfully, the captains of these two great ships being mortally wounded.

The Americans now began to run short of powder. Colonel Moultrie sent a despatch for more. He was in pressing need, but no one would have guessed it from his message which read as follows:

> I think we shall want more powder; at the rate we go on I think we shall. But you can see for yourself; pray send more if you think proper.

Rutledge sent 500 pounds, and Lee, who was at Haddrell's with 5000 pounds he had taken from Fort Sullivan, sent no powder but the message:

> If you should unfortunately expend your ammunition without driving off the enemy spike your guns and retreat with all the order you can. I know you will be careful not to expend your ammunition.

General Lee had an idea that battles were fought with bows and arrows and gunpowder kept to celebrate the victory afterwards with! And he was determined that that retreat should take place, because he had prophesied a retreat by all the laws of war some weeks before.

The cannonade went on, the fire from the fort being at a much slower tempo than that from the ships. And now a new fact was discovered in the art of war: The soft palmetto logs with sand in between were a better bulwark than solid stone. Cannon balls entered them easily and stopped just as easily without sending splinters all around. Shells threw the sand up in the air and the sand fell back again to the spot whence it had risen.

The *Bristol,* the flag-ship, suffered more than any other of the British vessels. At one time Sir Peter was the only man unwounded on the quarter-deck, and he, too, presently was hurt.

The *Acteon* went hard aground on the shoal where Fort Sumter was afterwards to be raised and had to be abandoned, being set on fire before she was deserted.

The rattle-snake flag flying over the American fort was shot down, and Sergeant Jasper, leaping over the parapet, braved the fire of the British to recover the emblem. Sergeant Jasper lost his life at Savannah in an effort to duplicate this same feat.

At length the British drew off beaten. They had lost heavily, on the flag-ship alone 104 men being killed. The American loss was 12 killed and 25 wounded. When the news of this defeat reached England, though the intelligence was given out by the Admiralty in the most politic fashion possible, it was a terrible blow to English pride. " That an English admiral with a well-appointed fleet of 270 guns should be beaten off by a miserable little half-built fort on an uninhabited sand bank was incomprehensible," wrote a correspondent from London. Had Moultrie had powder enough the British loss must have been much heavier than it was.

QUAINT AND HISTORIC FORTS

On the 9th of April, 1780, Fort Moultrie was again in action, when it opened upon Admiral Arbuthnot's fleet which was sailing into the harbor in the course of the operations against Charleston that year. It was unable to prevent the passage of the fleet but it inflicted some damage to the vessels and killed 27 of the enemy. Shortly after Fort Moultrie fell to an overwhelming force of British who attacked by land, and was not again in action during the Revolution.

FORT PULASKI
AT MOUTH, SAVANNAH RIVER—GEORGIA

THE trip from beautiful Savannah to the battered ruins of the once famous brick fortress, Pulaski, takes one through that gold and green country which one comes to associate with the name of this charming southern city. Fort Pulaski is that great hexagon of brick which one sees from incoming steamers on Cockspur Island at the mouth of the muddy Savannah River, and all the country round about is marshy, reedy land, cut up by big and little streams with no hills to be seen and only scraggy pine trees breaking the flat monotony of the horizon.

If one would go to Fort Pulaski from Savannah, he seeks out the little railroad which runs to Tybee, and whose passenger traffic is confined almost exclusively to summer. There he will be received by the hospitable southern trainmen and put off the train near the light-house which graces the northern end of Cockspur Island. Here, if he has been wise and has made his arrangements properly, he will be met by a boat from the light-house and will be carried across to the island.

Arrived at the landing which gives access to the fort, one is struck by the graceful desolation of the scene. The boards and timbers of the wharf have rotted, and

QUAINT AND HISTORIC FORTS

ends of planks hang down toward the water like withered arms. Yet the brilliant Georgia sunshine gives a charm to it all. One does not feel in the presence of decay; one feels only in the presence of something that is passing painlessly away.

This same feeling one carries up the long, straight, muddy path leading to the ruined monument of valor through the marsh which surrounds that work. One comes to a broad ditch now full of mud and weeds and faces the remains of a once sturdy draw-bridge. Passing over this and between the mounds of former outworks one at last faces the entrance to Fort Pulaski.

The walls of this great brick fortress, which cost a million dollars and was one of the greatest brick fortresses of its time, tower over one with great impressiveness. The brick face is pierced by long narrow slits for rifle fire, and these peer at one vacantly. A large ditch, or moat, surrounds the fort, and this still contains water owing to the low elevation of the island above tide, but it is choked with rank vegetation and though horrid of aspect would not be a serious bar to the approach of any storming force.

Crossing the ditch, one passes through a long passage and past massive wooden gates studded with iron bolts and, at length, comes out upon the parade ground. Where brilliant columns once formed and marched in martial evolutions now wave tall saplings except where the solitary care-taker of the fort has cut these growths

THE DESERTED CASEMATES OF FORT PULASKI, NEAR SAVANNAH, GA.

Parade and Ramparts

The Battered Eastern Salient
SCENES OF DESOLATION AT FORT PULASKI, NEAR SAVANNAH, GA.

FORT PULASKI

down to make room for a vegetable garden. The walls go around in a great circle above this parade, the angles of the circumference not being easily perceptible from our vantage point. To the right hand and the left hand stretch casemates in which officers and men dwelt. On the far side of the parade are open casemates fitted for cannon, for this is the quarter from which attack might be expected. Close at hand is a spring whose clear water flows ceaselessly from the rusty iron mouth which the hand of man has provided and neglected.

Passing across the parade to the gun casemates, which occupy the flanks of the fort on three quarters of the compass, one finds the flooring still in good condition, this fact being due to the protected nature of this part of the fort and to the sturdy quality of the planks which are three inches thick and of some close-grained wood—probably cypress. The circular gun-tracks are still visible. Where one can peer through holes in the floor one gazes down into dank, dark depths from which the light is reflected evilly by scummy water.

At the northeast angle of the fort are the remains of one of the magazines. If one cares to prowl in here and is willing to make entrance through a mysterious black hole into an uncanny void, he will be rewarded for his adventure by being able to pick up some rusty grape-shot and smaller odds and ends of murderous looking iron.

Ascending to the parapet of the fort by means of

QUAINT AND HISTORIC FORTS

one of the twisting iron stairs which are to be found at each angle, or by the broad stone stairs adjacent to the habitable casemates, one has a wide view of land and sea. To the east lies the mouth of the Savannah River where this stream joins the Atlantic Ocean. In this direction, too, can be seen long, low, sandy Tybee Point, where Fort Screven, the modern defensive work, lies. To the south are marshes and in the distance the gleam of the river up which the Union forces brought their cannon to attack Fort Pulaski in 1862. To the north and west—more marshes.

The island on which Fort Pulaski is situated was acquired by the government in 1830 by purchase from Alexander Telfair and sisters (an old and wealthy Savannah family) and the title of the government thereto for the purposes of a fortification was confirmed by the State of Georgia by act December 27, 1845. The entire reservation occupies about 150 acres.

The site for the fort was selected by Major General Babcock, United States Corps of Engineers, and work was begun in 1831 under the direction of Major General Mansfield. Sixteen years passed before its mighty walls, containing thirteen millions of bricks, were completed. The name Pulaski was given to the fort in honor of Count Casimir Pulaski, the Polish patriot who lost his life in the siege of Savannah by the Americans during the Revolution, the scene of this sad event being the Spring Hill redoubt near the site of the present Central of Georgia railway station.

FORT PULASKI

The military history of Fort Pulaski does not cover a long period of time. When, in December, 1860, the news reached Savannah of the removal of Major Anderson, in command of the United States forces in Charleston Harbor, from Fort Moultrie to Fort Sumter, there was an open expression of opinion that Georgia should forestall such occupation of the forts on her coast by the forces of the Federal government; and when, on January 2, 1861, it became known that Governor Brown had ordered the seizure and occupation of Fort Pulaski by the military under the command of Colonel A. R. Lawton on the following day, the city was wild with enthusiasm.

Says Adelaide Wilson in her delightful history of Savannah:

Looking back upon the arrangements that were made for the setting out of that first military expedition, there is temptation to smile at the amount of impedimenta that was prepared for the small forces of less than two hundred men. There was scant time between the promulgation of the order and the hour named for its execution, yet when, on the morning of the third, the companies marched down to the wharf to embark on the little steamer *Ida*, it is safe to say that they were encumbered with much more baggage than served later in the war for an entire division in the field. Every man had his cot, every three or four men his mess-chest, with kettles, pots, pans and other cooking utensils in liberal allowance, not to speak of trunks, valises, mattresses, camp-chairs, etc.,—in all a pile large enough to make the heart of a quartermaster sink within him. It was evident that the troops long had anticipated the call upon their services, and also that the mothers, wives and sisters of Savannah had, with anxious forethought, determined that their loved ones should carry into service as many of the comforts of home as possible.

The siege of Pulaski by the Federal troops, April, 1862, was not long at the climax, though it was long in preparation. The Federal forces gathered slowly south of Savannah and then moved to the attack. By means of a channel in the flats to the south of the fort which the Confederates had left unguarded, they were able to post their guns in advantageous positions. As the result of a heavy bombardment the walls of the fort were battered in at the east salient and the garrison was obliged to surrender.

The visitor to Fort Pulaski to-day may see some of the wounds in the walls which the fort sustained on that occasion. The worst injuries were repaired by the United States troops during their occupancy of the fort, and the course of these repairs may be traced by the discerning eye through the different color of the bricks.

Shortly after the Civil War, Fort Pulaski was abandoned. It is still controlled by the government and is in the care of a retired soldier of the United States who lives a life of seclusion, disturbed only by the very infrequent sight-seer or by parties of young men of the neighborhood who find the marshes of the reservation an excellent gunning preserve.

FORT MORGAN
MOBILE BAY—ALABAMA

OBILE BAY, that pear-shaped body of water, with its far-reaching system of water tributaries, has been a scene of settlement and fortification since the early days of French attempts at settlement in the New World. There was, to begin with, Fort Louis de la Mobile, which protected the infant first settlement of Mobile, precursor of the city of to-day. In various guises Fort Louis passed from one to another of the different races of men with which the history of Mobile Bay is associated. Then there are the forts placed on the islands at the mouth of Mobile Bay and the forts at the head of the bay where the big rivers flow in. Finally there is Fort Morgan (Fort Bowyer to begin with) which occupies the point of that long, thin peninsula of land which forms the southern boundary of Mobile Bay, dividing its waters from the waters of the Gulf of Mexico.

Fort Morgan to-day is in ruins and has never been thoroughly rebuilt since its capitulation to Farragut in one of the hottest battles of the Civil War. The governmental reservation of land on which the works are situated contains about 500 acres and is occupied, as well, by modern defences. The view from the point on which the old fort is situated gives a wide prospect

QUAINT AND HISTORIC FORTS

of blue water and sky. Across the ship channel is historic Dauphine Island, on which Fort Morgan's sister fort, Fort Gaines, was situated, and where the government to-day maintains extensive batteries. To the right are the waters of Mobile Bay, with the smoke of the city thirty miles to the north. To the left are the sunny waves of the Gulf.

The first that we hear of Mobile Point as a place of fortification was in 1812, when the Spanish evacuated Mobile. General Wilkinson, in command of the United States forces in the southwest, put nine guns as a battery on Mobile Point and made his way on up to the city, where he commenced to fortify the perdido. Subsequently Mobile Point appealed to him as a better place for defensive works than a spot so far up the bay, and he placed a fortification here, which was called Fort Bowyer in honor of Lieutenant-Colonel Bowyer.

The next occupant of Fort Bowyer was a more picturesque personage than General Wilkinson, none other than Andrew Jackson. Upon his retirement from Pensacola in 1814, Jackson stopped at Fort Bowyer and left a force there of 130 men under the leadership of Major William Lawrence. On September 12 the British appeared before the fort with land and naval strength and demanded the surrender of the little structure. Major Lawrence refused to surrender.

The British strength on this occasion consisted of the *Hermes* of 22 guns, the *Sophia* of 18 guns, the *Caron* of 20 guns, *Anaconda* of 18 guns, all vessels of

FORT MORGAN

large size, under the command of Captain Percy. It was a squadron which Jackson had driven from Pensacola Bay and it was thirsting for revenge. There was, in addition, a land force under Colonel Nichols of a few marines and about 600 Indians which assailed Fort Bowyer from the rear.

The battle began early on the morning of the 15th. The word for the day in the American ranks was "Don't give up the fort," and this originated an oft-repeated phrase. A heavy cannonade continued without interruption until 5.30 o'clock in the afternoon. The flag-staff of the *Hermes,* Captain Percy's flag-ship, was shot away and Lawrence gave the order to cease firing while he hailed the vessel to find out whether she had lowered her colors. The only answer was a murderous volley of grape-shot from another quarter. The flag-staff of the fort then happened to be struck, and the Indians and British on shore, thinking that the plucky little garrison had surrendered, ran forward with terrible cries. They were met by a terrific hail of lead which drove them back for good.

Finally the battered English vessels drew off. The *Hermes* was found to be in such bad shape that she was set on fire by her crew and abandoned. Her destruction was completed by the explosion of her magazine. The British loss was 232, of which number 163 were killed. The American loss was 4 killed and 4 wounded. The British in this engagement outnumbered the Americans more than six times.

QUAINT AND HISTORIC FORTS

The great adventure of Fort Morgan's life, however, was in the Civil War at the time of the taking of Mobile. The stronghold had been considerably enlarged and strengthened and had been re-christened by its Confederate possessors at the outbreak of that disastrous struggle between brother and brother. It is described in official records of the time as a pentagonal bastioned work, with a full scarp brick wall, 4 feet 8 inches thick, its armament consisting of 86 guns of various calibres. The garrison, including officers and men, numbered 640.

The force under Farragut consisted of fourteen large wooden steam vessels of war and four iron-clads of which the *Tecumseh* arrived from Pensacola just in time for the engagement. The wooden vessels were lashed together in pairs and the whole column was headed by the iron-clads.

It was on the morning of August 5, 1864, that Farragut commenced his passage into Mobile Bay. Long before the break of day through the whole fleet could be heard the boatswain's whistles and the cheery cries of " all hands " and " up all hammocks." The wind was west-southwest, just where Farragut wanted it, as it would blow the smoke of the guns on Fort Morgan. At four o'clock the fleet set in motion, led by the four monitors. At 6.47 the booming of the *Tecumseh's* guns was heard and shortly afterward Morgan replied. The story may now be taken up in the words of an officer on board the flag-ship *Hartford:*

FORT MORGAN

The order was to "go slowly, go slowly" and receive the fire of Fort Morgan. At six minutes past seven the fort opened, having allowed us to get into such short range that we apprehended some snare; in fact, I heard the order passed for our guns to be elevated for fourteen hundred yards some time before one was fired. The calmness of the scene was sublime. No impatience, no irritation, no anxiety, except for the fort to open; and after it did open full five minutes elapsed before we answered. In the meantime the guns were trained as if at a target and all the sounds I could hear were "steady boys, steady! Left tackle a little! So, so!" Then the roar of a broadside and the eager cheer as the enemy were driven from their water battery. Don't imagine they were frightened; no man could stand under that iron shower; and the brave fellows returned to their guns as soon as it lulled, only to be driven off again.

At twenty minutes past seven we had come within range of the enemy's gunboats which opened their fire upon the *Hartford*, and as the Admiral afterward told me made her their special target. First they struck our foremast and then lodged a shot of 120 pounds in our mainmast. By degrees they got better elevation; and I have saved a splinter from the hammock netting to show how they felt their way lower. Splinters after that came by cords, and in size sometimes were like logs of wood. No longer came the cheering cry "Nobody hurt yet." The *Hartford* by some unavoidable chance fought the enemy's fleet and fort together for twenty minutes by herself, timbers crashing and wounded pouring down,—cries never to be forgotten.

By half past seven the iron-clad *Tecumseh* was well up with the fort and drawing slowly by, when suddenly she reeled to port and went down straightway with almost every soul on board. She had struck a mine.

For a time this appalling disaster spread confusion in the fleet.

"What's the matter?" was shouted from the flagship to the *Brooklyn* just ahead.

"Torpedoes," was the response.

"Damn the torpedoes," said Farragut, "go ahead."

Go ahead the fleet did and at length had passed Fort Morgan and was in the sheltering waters of the bay. The cost of this operation in the Union fleet was 335 men. Of the 130 men in the *Tecumseh* when she was struck only 17 were saved.

Fort Gaines, the works on the western side of the channel, now surrendered. But Fort Morgan kept on fighting. The Union vessels were in Mobile Bay, but they had not yet forced the indomitable fort on Mobile Point to its knees. Admiral Farragut wrote to a friend:

> We are now tightening the cords around Fort Morgan. Page is as surly as a bull-dog and says that he will die in his ditch. . . . .
>
> How little people know the risks of life. Drayton made his clerk stay below because he was a young married man. All my staff,—Watson, McKinley and Brownell,—were in an exposed position on the poop deck but escaped unhurt while poor Heginbotham was killed.

For seventeen days Fort Morgan held out, though bombarded continuously. Then at length she surrendered, her citadel destroyed and her walls nearly blown to pieces. It is this pathetic shell that now greets the visitor's eye on Mobile Point.

FORTS JACKSON AND ST. PHILIP
AT THE MOUTH OF THE MISSISSIPPI—LOUISIANA

THE two forts which were the scene of Farragut's first brilliant exploit in running by the enemy's works with wooden vessels have not been regularly garrisoned since 1871 and have been maintained only in a casual sort of a fashion. Stronger and newer defences have taken their place, though these two spots have had a long and honorable existence in the defence of the mouth of America's greatest river and of its picturesque French-Spanish-American chief city, New Orleans. Situated 32 nautical miles by river from the Gulf of Mexico and about 22 miles from the light-house at the head of the passes of the Mississippi, they occupy the first habitable ground bordering the river, at a sharp bend known as English Turn. Fort St. Philip is on the northern bank of the river, Fort Jackson on the southern. Though so far from the Gulf by river, Fort St. Philip, owing to the peculiar formation of the mouth of the Mississippi, with long fingers spread out into the sea, is only a short distance from the Gulf as the crow flies.

About a mile above the site of Fort Jackson there stood an ancient French fortification known as Fort Bourbon, which gradually yielded to the encroachments of time so that now there is of it nothing left. Fort

St. Philip, itself, was founded by the French and was surrendered to the United States in 1803 with the purchase of the Louisiana territory.

The situation of the two forts was early recognized by the United States as possessing much military value, and in 1812–1815 St. Philip was made over by the United States authorities and Fort Jackson was built. Fort St. Philip at the time of the Civil War consisted of a quadrangular earthwork with brick scarp rising 19 feet above the level of the river and a wet ditch with exterior batteries above and below. Fort Jackson, largely added to between 1824 and 1832, was a pentagonal bastioned fortification built of brick with casemates, glacis and wet ditch; and of the two was the more formidable work.

The two forts saw service in 1814 against the British. At this time the name Jackson was applied to the southern fort in honor of the fiery American commander whose defence of that city has become an inspiring legend.

The Confederate Government had early taken possession of the forts and had put them in complete order. When Farragut's fleet appeared, early in the spring of 1862, Fort Jackson with its water battery mounted 75 guns and Fort St. Philip about 40. The works were garrisoned by about 1500 men, commanded by Brigadier General J. K. Duncan; St. Philip being under the direct command of Lieutenant-Colonel Edward Hig-

FORT JACKSON

gins. Just above the forts the Confederates had placed a fleet of 15 vessels, including the iron-clad ram *Manassas*. Below Fort Jackson they had obstructed the river with a heavy chain brought from Pensacola. This chain was pinned to the under side of a row of cypress logs which were 30 feet long and four or five feet in diameter. The spring freshets caused this chain to break and it was replaced by two lighter chains supported in similar fashion.

As a first move against the Confederate strongholds, Farragut sent Commander Porter with his fleet of mortar vessels to bombard the forts. The bombardment opened on the 18th of April and continued without remission for six days, but though breaches were made in the walls and the levee was broken at one place so that the beleaguered men had a difficult task to keep the waters of the Mississippi from drowning them out, the action was inconclusive.

It was then that Farragut determined upon the bold move (later duplicated at Mobile) which was so great an element of his fame. At two o'clock on the morning of April 24, 1862, he set his fleet in motion up the river. The chain barriers were cut and the fleet contrived to get past the fort without serious damage or loss of life. Thus was accomplished the feat of passing, with wooden vessels in a stream half a mile wide, two forts specially prepared to resist such an effort. The Confederate fleet was met beyond the forts and repulsed after a sharp engagement.

Farragut now passed on to New Orleans to make sure of the rich prize of a city whose export business at that time was the greatest in the world, while Porter was left behind with a sufficient squadron to continue the bombardment of the forts. After being under continuous fire until the 28th of the month the forts surrendered, and have never since been in active service.

The reservation of Fort Jackson contains 557.6 acres and that of Fort St. Philip 1108.85 acres. The reservations consist entirely of swamp lands, during season of high water being almost completely inundated. Those portions containing the forts, quarters and other buildings are leveed on all sides, but notwithstanding the protection thus afforded there are times when the water rises so high as to become a source of great inconvenience in going about. This is especially the case when rain is added to the water which percolates through the levees.

Any account of Fort Jackson would be incomplete without allusion to its alligators. These reptiles constitute one of the principal objects of interest to visitors and may be seen in numbers floating in the moats or basking on shore in the sunlight. They are from five to fifteen feet in length and possess great strength. It was customary to feed them with bread and crackers from the bridges over the moats, calling them up by whistling,

FORT ST. PHILIP

and from frequent occurrence of this act they seemed to become accustomed to the signal and responded to it just as might dogs.

The rattlesnakes of the vicinity are numerous and formidable. One was caught here measuring $11\frac{1}{2}$ feet and having 27 rattles. Black snakes are large but rare. Moccasins, of which there are two varieties, attain a large size and are frequently very venomous.

The mosquitoes constitute a serious obstacle to the enjoyment of life to the infrequent garrisons at this post, for they not only ply their calling with great diligence during the night but in summer are equally zealous throughout the day. Various expedients are adopted to avoid and drive them away. The smudge is brought into frequent and useful requisition. Gloves are worn and covering of mosquito netting is frequently used to protect the neck and head.

FORT SNELLING
NEAR ST. PAUL—MINNESOTA

HE historic post of Fort Snelling, Minnesota, for more than a generation after its establishment, in 1819, the most remote western outpost of the United States, is situated at the confluence of the Minnesota and Mississippi Rivers, eight miles southeast of Minneapolis by river and six miles from St. Paul. It lies in a region of rare natural beauty, in the vicinity of the Falls of Minnehaha, Bridal Veil Falls, and other points locally notable and is, itself, no mean attraction to the many visitors who are attracted to the locality every year. The old fort standing on its high bluff at the headwaters of America's greatest river is a most picturesque object.

The reservation of Fort Snelling contains 1,531 acres, though originally this tract was much larger than now. The fort structure which one sees from the river is an irregularly shaped bastioned wall conforming in outline to the high plateau of land upon which it is situated. It occupies the extreme end of the point of land formed by the juncture of the two rivers, and on the Mississippi side the bluff upon which the fort is situated descends abruptly to the water, the river there running almost in a canyon. On the Minnesota side the slope is more gradual and ends in a low marshy flat which ex-

OLD STONE TOWER AT FORT SNELLING, NEAR ST. PAUL, MINN.

Copyright, Detroit Publishing Co.

FORT SNELLING

tends from one-third to one-half a mile and is frequently submerged during high water. The altitude of the post plateau above the river is 300 feet.

The establishment of Fort Snelling was one of the fruits of the work of Lieutenant Z. M. Pike, the first American to explore and chart the peak which bears his name. In 1805 this officer was in command of an exploring expedition and held a conference with the Sioux Indians on an island at the mouth of the Minnesota River which now bears his name. He secured from the Indians for military purposes a strip of land nine miles on each side of the Mississippi River and extending from the conference island to the Falls of St. Anthony, near which Fort Snelling is.

It is to be remembered that in 1805 the settlement of the American nation did not extend beyond the Mississippi River. The country west of Lake Michigan and on the headwaters of the Mississippi River, though a part of the United States, thanks largely to George Rogers Clark, was in a state of nature with only the trails of Indians and traders and the remains of little French settlements as the foundation for the civilization which was to grow up within it.

The privileges which Lieutenant Pike secured from the red men were not immediately taken advantage of by the United States authorities. Time passed and the War of 1812 with England gave the War Department

QUAINT AND HISTORIC FORTS

of this country quite as much as it could take care of. Finally, in 1819, Lieutenant Colonel Henry Leavenworth, of the Fifth United States Infantry, was sent with his regiment to locate a fort upon the reserve selected by Lieutenant Pike. Colonel Leavenworth reached the headwaters of the Mississippi without incident and rendered his first monthly report in September, 1819.

Scurvy broke out now among the troops and this, added to the natural inclemencies of the climate here in winter, prevented any work being done until the spring of 1820. In May, 1820, Colonel Leavenworth moved his troops to a point on the west bank of the Mississippi River, about a mile and a half above the present location of Fort Snelling. The site chosen by him for the fort was the present military cemetery. He made preparations to commence the work, but Colonel Josiah Snelling assumed command in August and selected the location where the fort now stands.

Work actually commenced September 10, 1820, and went steadily ahead until October, 1822, when the post was first occupied. During this time Colonel Snelling was in command and his regiment was engaged in the work.

For two years after it had been finished the post was known as Fort St. Anthony—at Colonel Snelling's suggestion—after the falls which are near the place,

FORT SNELLING

but, in 1824, it was visited by General Scott, who suggested to the War Department that the name should be changed to that which it bears to-day as a compliment to its builder.

The defences and some of the store-houses and shops were built of stone, but the quarters for the soldiers were log huts until after the Mexican War. The huts have now given way to comfortable barracks of modern construction, but the stone construction and the shops remain to-day as they were when the fort was far distant from civilization.

During the Civil War the fort was a concentration point for volunteers. In 1878 a plan of enlargement to accommodate a full regiment was entered upon in accordance with the policy then inaugurated by the War Department of having the soldiers of the country concentrated at a few points rather than scattered through a number of small posts.

While Fort Snelling has never seen active service itself it has had an active existence as a distribution point for those posts which were in conflict with the enemy during the United States' occasional Indian Wars. During the serious Sioux outbreak of 1862 in Minnesota it was the head-quarters of the campaign against the Indians, though the fighting took place from subsidiary posts in contact with the red men.

For twenty years after its completion Fort Snelling

was in the midst of the Sioux with no white neighbors except traders, agents of fur companies, refugees from civilization and disreputable hangers-on. In 1837 an enlargement of the military reserve and the coming of the first tide of white settlers who were to develop this country caused the eviction of this last class of dependents. One of the nearby squatters took his grog-shop to a point not far away. Around this point a settlement grew up. This settlement is now the proud city of St. Paul.

FORT LARAMIE
AT THE FORKS OF THE PLATTE RIVER—WYOMING

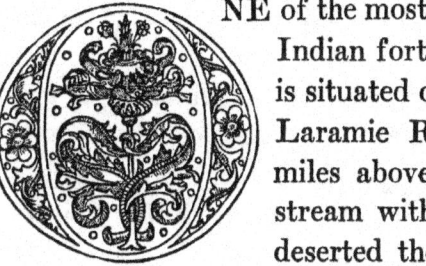

ONE of the most famous of the western Indian forts of the United States is situated on the west bank of the Laramie River, one and a half miles above the junction of that stream with the Platte. Though deserted the post is still a picturesque figure, recalling the days when it administered authority for seven hundred miles around. The property now comprises part of the ranch of Mr. John Hunton.

Before the white man had established a habitation where Fort Laramie stands the whole of the country of the North Platte River was a hunting-ground and battle-field for different tribes of Indians. Countless herds of buffalo roamed the land and it was rich in fur-bearing animals, as well.

In 1834 William Sublette and Robert Campbell, coming to this part of the country to trap beaver, found themselves obliged to construct some sort of protection against the roving bands of vagabond Crows and Pawnees which occasionally swept along the Platte, stealing where they could. They built in that year upon the present site of Fort Laramie a square fort of pickets 18 feet high, with bastions at two diagonal corners, and a number of little houses inside for their employés. In

QUAINT AND HISTORIC FORTS

1835 they sold out to Milton Sublette, James Bridger and three other trappers, who went into partnership with the American Fur Company and continued the beaver trapping business.

In that year the American Fur Company sent two men named Kiplin and Sabille to the Bear Butte and Northern Black Hills to persuade the Sioux Indians to come over and hunt their game and live in the vicinity of the fort. Their ambassadors succeeded so well that they returned with over one hundred lodges of Ogalla Sioux under Chief Bull Bear. This was the first appearance of the powerful Sioux nation in this part of the country, which they speedily overran, driving away Pawnees, Cheyennes, Crows and all others from its very borders.

Of course the fort speedily became a trading post where the Indians bartered a buffalo robe for a knife, an awl, or a drink of " fire water." Anything that the company had to trade was at least of the value of one buffalo robe. An American horse brought fifty of them; any pony was worth twenty or thirty. Any old scrap of iron was of great value to an Indian and by him would be speedily converted into a knife. Firearms he had none and his arrow-heads were all made of pieces of flint or massive quartz, fashioned into proper shape by laborious pecking with another stone. The Sioux then had no horses, but herds of wild horses were abundant on their arrival and it was not many years before they learned their use.

FORT LARAMIE

In 1836 the picket fort began to rot badly and the American Fur Company rebuilt it of adobe at an expense of $10,000. The people who lived inside of the fort at this time called it " Fort William," after William Sublette, but the name could not be popularized. The fort being built on the Laramie River, not far from Laramie Peak, the American Fur Company's clerks in their city offices labelled it Fort Laramie and by that name it was destined to be called.

It seems that Laramie was a trapper, one of the first French voyageurs who ever trapped a beaver or shot a buffalo in the Rocky Mountains. He was one day killed by a band of Arapahoes on the headwaters of the stream which has ever since been called by his name.

The American Fur Company retained possession of the fort until 1849 when it sold it to the United States government for four or five thousand dollars. Bruce Husaband was the last representative of the company who had charge of Fort Laramie.

The first United States troops which arrived here came in July, 1849, under the command of Major Sanderson of the Mounted Rifles. They were companies C and D of that regiment. Company G of the Sixth United States Infantry arrived in August of the same year under command of Captain Ketchum. In the summer and fall of 1849 a large number of additions were made to the buildings at the post.

In 1846, just prior to its occupancy by the United

QUAINT AND HISTORIC FORTS

States, Francis Parkman, the future historian, then little more than a boy, visited Fort Laramie and wrote a description of the place in that singularly vivid style which characterized his best work as a historian. His description may be abridged:

Looking back, after the expiration of a year, upon Fort Laramie and its inmates, they seem less like a reality than like some fanciful picture of the olden time; so different was the scene from any which this tamer side of the world can present. Tall Indians, enveloped in their white buffalo robes, were striding across the area or reclining at full length on the low roofs of the buildings which enclosed it. Numerous squaws, gayly bedizened, sat grouped in front of the rooms they occupied; their mongrel offspring, restless and vociferous, rambled in every direction through the fort; and the trappers, traders, and engagees of the establishment were busy at their labor or their amusements. . . .

Fort Laramie is one of the posts established by the " American Fur Company " which well nigh monopolizes the Indian trade of this region. Here its officials rule with an absolute sway; the arm of the United States has little force; for when we were there the extreme outposts of her troops were about seven hundred miles to the eastward. The little fort is built of bricks dried in the sun, and externally is of an oblong form, with bastions of clay, in the form of ordinary blockhouses, at two of the corners. The walls are about fifteen feet high, and surmounted by a slender palisade. The roofs of the apartments within, which are built close against the walls, serve the purpose of a banquette. Within, the fort is divided by a partition: on one side is the square area, surrounded by the offices, storerooms and apartments of the inmates; on the other is the corral, a narrow place, encompassed by high clay walls, where at night, or in presence of dangerous Indians, the horses and mules of the fort are crowded for safe keeping. The main entrance has two gates, with an arched passage intervening. A little square window, high above the ground, opens laterally from an adjoining chamber into this passage; so that when the inner gate is closed and barred, a person without may still hold communication with those within, through this narrow aperture. This obviates the necessity of admitting suspicious Indians, for the purposes of trading, into the body of the fort; for when danger is apprehended, the inner gate is shut fast and all traffic is carried on by means of the window. This precaution, though necessary at some of the Company's posts, is seldom resorted to at Fort Laramie; where though men are frequently killed in the neighborhood no apprehensions are felt of any general design of hostility from the Indians.

A train of emigrants encamped outside the fort for the night on their long journey across the plains.

A crowd of broad-rimmed hats, thin visages, and staring eyes appeared suddenly at the gate. Tall, awkward men in brown homespun; women, with cadaverous faces and long lank figures, came thronging in together, and as if inspired by the very demon of curiosity ransacked every nook and corner of the fort. The emigrants prosecuted their investigations with untiring vigor. They penetrated the rooms, or, rather, dens, inhabited by the astonished squaws. Resolved to search every mystery to the bottom, they explored the apartments of the men, and even that of Marie and the bourgeois (the commandant of the fort). At last a numerous deputation appeared at our door but found no encouragement to remain. . . . Having at length satisfied their curiosity, they next proceeded to business.

On the 19th of August, 1854, a Mormon train was encamped about ten miles below the fort on the Platte River. The Indians having killed a cow or ox belonging to the train had been complained of by the Mormons to the commanding officer, who sent Lieutenant Grattan, of the Sixth United States Infantry, with thirty men of Company G and two howitzers, to recover the cow and bring the thieves to the garrison. They met a large number of Indians (Sioux) under the leadership of a chief named Mattoioway about eight miles from the fort and a conflict ensued in which Lieutenant Grattan's command, with the exception of one man, was annihilated. The survivor was hidden in some bushes by a friendly Indian and brought to the fort that night where he died two days afterward. The bodies of the slain were buried in one grave where they fell and a pile of stones marks their resting place.

THE ALAMO AND FORT SAM HOUSTON
SAN ANTONIO—TEXAS

THE Alamo, which is famous for its heroic defence against the Mexicans by Travis and his men, is situated in San Antonio, Texas, and is the point of pilgrimage annually for many hundreds of the visitors to the southwestern part of the United States. On the outskirts of San Antonio is the modern great military plant, Fort Sam Houston, the Alamo's lusty successor.

The Alamo, as late as 1870, was used for military purposes by the United States government, but of recent years it has been preserved purely as a monument to those brave men who lost their lives in it fighting bravely to the last a battle which they knew to be hopeless from the first. Upon the front of the building has been placed an inscription which reads, " Thermopylæ had its messenger of defeat. The Alamo had none." The building, itself, is a low structure of the familiar Spanish mission type, and its main walls, though constructed in 1744, are almost as solid to-day as when new. The chapel of the Alamo bears the date 1757, but this was of later building than the rest of the place.

The city of San Antonio owes its foundation to the establishment in 1715 by Spain of the mission of San Antonio de Valero, which in accordance with the custom of that country combined priestly enterprise with military prerogative. The Alamo was a quadrangular, central court structure built to house the troops of Spain and to sound the call to worship. It was acquired by Mexico with the rest of the Spanish possessions when this southern neighbor of the United States, in 1824, finally secured its independence from the parent country.

At the time of the siege, San Antonio was a town of about 7,000 inhabitants, the vast majority Mexican. The San Antonio river which, properly speaking, is a large rivulet, divided the town from the Alamo, the former on the west side and the latter on the east. South of the fort was the Alamo village, a small suburb of San Antonio.

The fort itself was in the condition in which it had been left by Cos, the Mexican general, when it had been surrendered in the fall of 1835. It contained twelve guns which were of little use in the hands of men unskilled in their use, and owing to the construction of the works most of the guns had little width of range.

In command of the place at the beginning of the winter of 1835 was Colonel Neill, of Texas, with two companies of volunteers, among whom was a remnant of the New Orleans Greys. Early in 1836 Lieutenant Colonel William B. Travis, a brave and careful officer, was appointed by the Governor of Texas, which had as yet only a provisional government, to relieve Colonel Neill of his command.

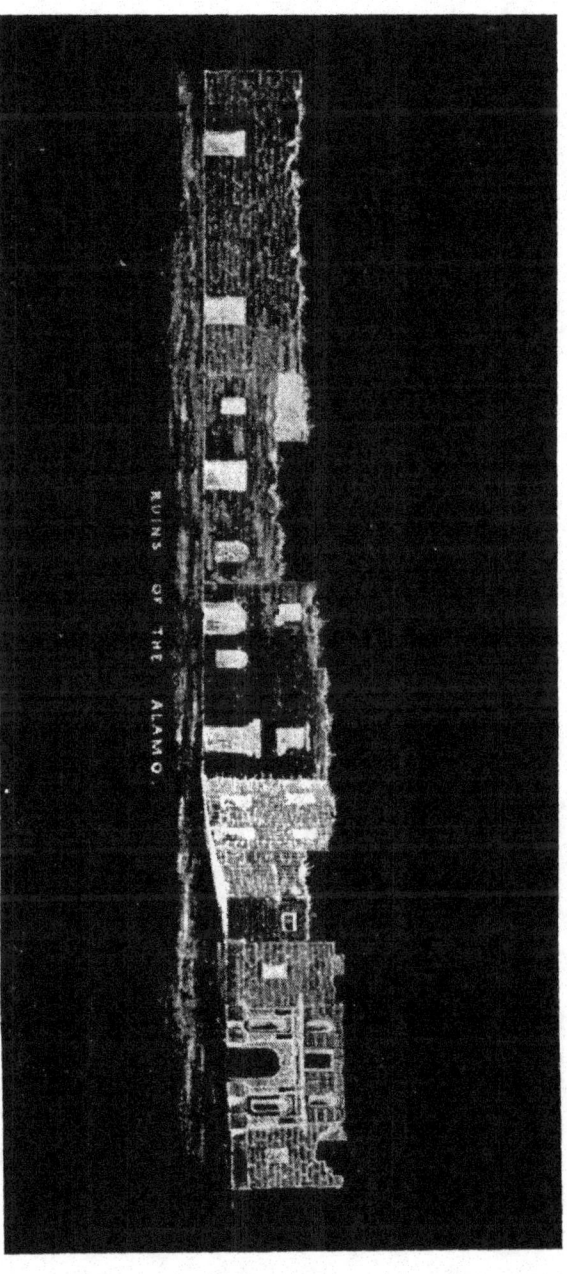

RUINS OF THE ALAMO IN 1845

From a sketch upon Map of the Country in the Vicinity of San Antonio de Bexar made by J. Edmund Blake, 1st Lieut. Topographical Engineers, U. S. A.

By courtesy of the War Department

THE ALAMO

The volunteers, a hard-headed and independent lot, wished to choose their own leader though they were willing to have Travis second in command, and called a meeting, where they elected as full colonel one of their number, James Bowie, a forceful figure of early Texan history. Bowie's name to-day unfortunately is chiefly remembered by virtue of the "Bowie" knife. Travis arrived at the fort early in February, just two weeks before the Mexicans under the detested Santa Ana came in view, and naturally enough refused to recognize the superior authority of the officer so informally placed in power, as did the men whom he had brought with him. There was thus divided authority in the Alamo at the time of the siege.

All disputes were dropped, however, upon the approach of the enemy. The advance detachment of the Mexican force which came in four divisions arrived in San Antonio on February 22, and was welcomed by an eighteen-pound shot from the little American garrison. Santa Ana procured a parley and demanded the surrender of the entire garrison, the terms to be left to his discretion.

A dramatic scene took place in the Alamo, tradition tells us, when news of this proposal came to the ill-starred place. Colonel Travis drew a line upon the ground. "All those who prefer to fight will cross this line," he is reported to have said. Every man crossed the line and Bowie, who had been stricken to his bed with pneumonia, roused enough to ask that his cot be carried with his men. It was well understood that the issue of the fray, if once Santa Ana succeeded in taking the post, would be the death of every man without mercy; and the chances of withstanding an attack were known to be weak.

When finally the Mexican host was assembled it numbered about twenty-five hundred men. The American garrison, which was swelled by a reinforcement of 32 men from Gonzales who managed to get through the lines of the besiegers into the fort, numbered altogether 188 men. The siege commenced on the 24th of February and continued without cessation until the morning of the 6th of March, when there was a grand assault.

The final assault occupied not more than half an hour. The blast of a bugle was followed by the shuffle of a rushing mass of men. The guns of the fort opened upon the charging columns which came from all directions. The outer walls were taken despite the efforts of the pitiful handful of their defenders, and the battle then became a series of desperate fights from room to room of the old structure. Travis fell with a single shot through his forehead and his gun was turned on the building. Bowie was found on his cot in his room at the point of death from the malady which had stricken him; with his last flicker of strength he shot down with his pistols more than one of his assailants before he was butchered where he lay, too weak to move his body.

The chapel was the last point taken and the inmates

THE ALAMO

of this stronghold fought with unremitting fury, firing down from the upper part of the structure after the enemy had taken the floor. Toward the close of this episode Lieutenant Dickenson, with his child strapped to his back, leaped from the east embrasure. Both were shot in the act.

One of the garrison was Davy Crockett, a well-known and beloved backwoodsman, known for his quaint sayings and homely wisdom. Crockett was found beside a gun in the west battery with a pile of slain around him.

The number of Mexicans killed has never been correctly estimated though it has been placed as high as a thousand. The most accurate estimate lies probably between 500 and 600.

A few hours after the engagement the bodies of the slaughtered garrison were gathered by the victors, laid in three heaps and burned. On February 25, 1837, the bones and ashes were collected by order of General Sam Houston, as well as could be done, and buried with military honors in a peach orchard then outside Alamo village and a few hundred yards from the fort. The place of burial was not preserved and the ground which contains the remains of these heroic men has long since been built over.

During the Mexican War the walls of the Alamo buildings were repaired and the buildings newly roofed for the use of the quartermaster's department.

Fort Sam Houston, the modern successor of the

QUAINT AND HISTORIC FORTS

ancient Alamo, was first located on Houston Street where one of San Antonio's great new hotels now stands. Its present ideal situation on a high plateau 762 feet above the level of the Gulf of Mexico was chosen in 1872 and the grounds first comprised 162 acres of land. The fort was built around a quadrangle 624 feet square, in the centre of which was erected a gray stone tower 88 feet in height. Of recent years large accessions of land have made the post over one thousand acres in extent and the buildings have been largely added to, over two and a half millions of dollars being expended upon the fort by the national government. It is now one of the most important of the United States' military possessions. During the Spanish-American war the place acquired celebrity as being the scene of organization and training of the Rough Riders.

Immediately before the outbreak of the Civil War the Alamo was commanded by that soldier who was to lead the armies of the Lost Cause and whose name is a household heritage in the south to-day, Robert E. Lee. Associated with him here was Albert Sydney Johnston. The house occupied by General Lee was situated on South Alamo street and here he wrote his resignation to the United States authorities before assuming command of the enthusiastic and untrained masses of Southerners.

During the Civil War San Antonio was the headquarters of the Confederacy in the southwest and the Alamo was used for storage.

OTHER WESTERN FORTS
FORT PHIL KEARNEY, NEBRASKA; FORT LEAVENWORTH, KANSAS; FORT FETTERMAN, WYOMING; FORT BRIDGER, WYOMING; FORT KEOGH, MONTANA; FORT DOUGLAS, UTAH

ONE of the most dreadful Indian fights in the history of the Middle West is associated with Fort Phil Kearney, on the Platte River, Nebraska, which was in 1848, at the time of its establishment, the only United States post between Fort Leavenworth, Kansas, 350 miles distant, and Fort Laramie, 420 miles to the west. It stood midway between the Mississippi River and the Rocky Mountains on the California Overland route and was established for the protection of west-bound emigrant trains from hostile Indians.

Fort Phil Kearney was a storm centre during the Sioux War, which began in 1863 and continued intermittently for nearly ten years, and the " Kearney Massacre" occurred during this time. On the morning of December 21, 1866, the fort received word that the wood train was being attacked by Indians and was in need of assistance. Immediately Brevet Lieutenant Colonel W. I. Fetterman with seventy-six men was ordered to protect the train.

Colonel Fetterman moved rapidly upon his errand, and the sound of heavy firing soon showed that he was in contact with the enemy. The firing continued so long that the commandant, Colonel Carrington, became alarmed for the safety of the detachment and sent out as many men as he could spare for reinforcement. These men were under Captain Ten Eyck. The rest of the story may be taken up in the words of Senate Document 13, 1867:

Colonel Ten Eyck reported as soon as he reached the summit commanding a view of the battle-field that the valley was full of Indians; that he could see nothing of Colonel Fetterman's party, and requested that a howitzer should be sent him. The howitzer was not sent.

The Indians who at first beckoned him to come down now commenced retreating and Captain Ten Eyck, advancing to a point where the Indians had been standing in a circle, found the dead, naked bodies of Brevet Lieutenant Colonel Fetterman, Captain Brown and about sixty-five of the soldiers of their command. . . . At about half the distance from where these bodies lay to the point where the road commences to descend to Peno Creek was the dead body of Lieutenant Grummond, and still farther on, at the point where the road commences to descend to Peno Creek, were the dead bodies of three citizens and four or five of the old, long-tried and experienced soldiers.

Our conclusion, therefore, is that the Indians were massed on both sides of the road; that the Indians attacked vigorously in force from fifteen hundred to eighteen hundred warriors and were successfully resisted for half an hour or more; that the command then being short of ammunition and seized with panic at this event, and the great numerical superiority of the Indians, attempted to retreat toward the fort; that the mountaineers and old soldiers who had learned that movement from the

OTHER WESTERN FORTS

Indians in an engagement was equivalent to death remained in their first position and were killed there; that, immediately upon the commencement of the retreat, the Indians charged upon and surrounded the party who could not now be formed by their officers and the party was immediately killed.

Only six of the whole command were killed by balls and two of these, Lieutenant Colonel Fetterman and Captain Brown, no doubt inflicted this death upon themselves, or each other, by their own hands for both were shot through the left temple and powder was burnt into the skin and flesh about the wound. These officers had also oftentimes asserted that they would not be taken alive by the Indians.

In its appearance Fort Kearney was typical of the Indian forts of the period, being little more than a stockade on the level prairie with the necessary houses inside. The parade ground occupied four acres and was flanked by a few straggly cottonwood trees. The post was deserted not long after the building of the Union Pacific railroad six miles away, which destroyed the reason of its being; after its desertion fell victim to its ancient enemy, for it was burned by the Indians.

Fort Leavenworth, Leavenworth, near Kansas City, Kansas, whose name occurs so often in the records of Indian warfare of the West, was established May, 1827, by Colonel Henry Leavenworth, commanding a detachment of the Third United States Infantry. At first the post was extremely unhealthy, a large part of the command being prostrated by malarial fever. It was evacuated in 1829 and reoccupied in 1830, then, and for several years, being known as Cantonment Leavenworth. Since the latter date the place has never been without United States troops and it is to-day the largest fixed post in the United States military service.

The first mission of Fort Leavenworth was to protect the emigrant trains which set out from St. Louis, several hundred miles to the east, and passed this point on the way to California, or Oregon, by the famous old Santa Fé Trail, the California Overland Trail or the Oregon Trail, each of which went by this place. As the years went on the fort became more and more a base of supply for the army posts established further west. Its central location, which made it ideal as a distributing point to any part of the West, is the factor which is at the base of its importance in the present day.

Fort Fetterman, Wyoming, was established in July, 1867, and named in honor of the officer who lost his life commanding the detachment destroyed by the Indians at Fort Kearney. In the following month the Indians of the vicinity were actively hostile. The old post was a most picturesque point in its day, being situated on a high bluff which shows its pointed palisade in fine relief against the sky. It is now deserted.

Fort Bridger, Wyoming, another of the Indian posts of the past, was one of the most important points on the Great Salt Lake Trail. It was located on the Black Fork of the Green River and was established in June,

FORT KEOGH, NEAR MILES CITY, MONTANA

OTHER WESTERN FORTS

1858. The immediate locality had long been known as Bridger's Fort because of the situation here of a trading post of James Bridger, one of the most noted trappers and guides of this section. In its establishment it was intended to be a base of supplies for the army of General Albert Sydney Johnston moving against the Mormons in Salt Lake Valley in 1857 to 1858. That winter the entire command encamped in the valley just above the site of Fort Bridger and upon its removal the permanent post was located.

Fort Keogh, Montana, one of the still existing Indian posts, was established, in 1876, on the right bank of the Yellowstone River, two miles above the mouth of the Tongue River, Custer County, on a high elevation above the river bottom, by General Terry during a campaign against the Sioux. It was named in honor of Captain Miles Keogh, killed in the battle of the Little Big Horn, popularly known as Custer's Massacre, June 25, 1876. The area of the post reservation is 90 square miles. In appearance Fort Keogh is typical of the other forts of its class.

Fort Douglas, Utah, is at the base of the plateau of the Wahsatch Mountains and is part of the suburbs of Salt Lake City. The reservation contains two square miles of territory, and the scenery from any part thereof is extremely fine. The post was established October, 1862, by Colonel P. E. Connor, of the Third Regiment of California Infantry.

FORT VANCOUVER
COLUMBIA RIVER—WASHINGTON

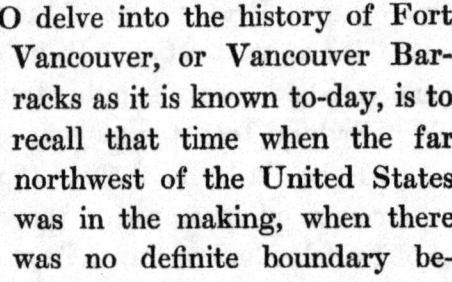O delve into the history of Fort Vancouver, or Vancouver Barracks as it is known to-day, is to recall that time when the far northwest of the United States was in the making, when there was no definite boundary between England, Spain, Russia and the American nation in this part of the American continent and when all of these great nations, with the addition of France and little Portugal, to boot, were claimants to the Columbia River and the wildernesses which it held tributary.

The first white men to descry the mouth of the Columbia from the sea were, no doubt, the Spaniards, for Heceta, in 1775, and Bodega and Arteaga in the same year and, again, in 1779, made brief excursions into the river. In 1792 Captain Robert Gray, of Boston, with the good ship " Columbia," ascended the stream for twenty-five miles and claimed possession of it for the United States. He named the river for his vessel. Several months after Gray had been on the stream the English nation, as represented by Captain Cook's lieutenant, ascended the stream for over a hundred miles, making careful record of his trip. The three great nations Spain, England, and the United States had each valid claims. Portugal, Russia and France were early eliminated from the struggle for possession which was thereupon fought determinedly by the first three countries.

In 1819 by the Florida treaty with Spain that country ceded to the United States all of her claims north of the 42nd degree of latitude and so, here, Spain gracefully stepped out of the ring.

The close of the War of 1812 with Great Britain saw that power in possession of the disputed country, but the Treaty of Ghent, 1815, provided that each nation should restore what it had taken from the other by force. Thereupon the United States resumed possession of the fort at the mouth of the Columbia which it had formerly maintained. In 1818 was signed the Joint Occupation Treaty between the two countries, by which it was provided that the northwest coast of America should be open to citizens of both powers for the period of ten years. Finally, in 1846, was signed the agreement between Great Britain and the United States by which the northern boundary of the Northwest was fixed at the line of 49 degrees, where it rests to-day. The United States received about 750 miles of the river and England about 650 miles. While there was much diplomatic jockeying and juggling and while the two nations came periously close to a resort to arms, the question, on the whole, was settled with great amicableness and the decision once arrived at was accepted with entire good nature by each party to the contract.

QUAINT AND HISTORIC FORTS

Now let us ask why was it that the Northwest of those days was considered so great a prize that six of the World Powers should contend for its possession? The domain, though a princely one, was not a necessity to a young nation—our own—which had illimitable leagues of arable soil still untilled. It was remote from all of the powers of Europe. The answer to our question is to be found in the one word, furs. The Northwest was a treasure house through virtue of the fur-bearing animals which it contained.

As early as 1806 a trading station was established in the valley of the Columbia River by The Northwest Fur Company, an English corporation. In 1810 the Pacific Fur Company, which was to found the fortunes of John Jacob Astor, was organized by that gentleman in New York and, in 1811, the first of Astor's ships arrived at the mouth of the Columbia River to erect the trading post of Astoria, whose fortunes have been so entertainingly told by Washington Irving in the book of that name. The Hudson Bay Company had also made entrance to this rich field.

During the War of 1812 the Pacific Fur Company retired from its positions in the Columbia valley and the Hudson Bay Company absorbed its English rival, the Northwest Fur Company. The English built a strong fort at Astoria which they called Fort George. But several years after the conclusion of the war between England and America, the Pacific Fur Company re-

FORT VANCOUVER

sumed possession of its posts in the Columbia, with the backing of the United States government, under the authority of the Treaty of Ghent and the Hudson Bay Company, and though events proved that it could maintain an amicable joint household with Astor's corporation at Astoria, began to look about for a site for headquarters of its own. Since the Columbia River at that time seemed destined to become the dividing line between English and American possessions, a site was chosen on the north side of the river, about 120 miles above its mouth. Here a strong post was established in 1825 and named Vancouver, in honor of the British mariner. The site was not deemed as suitable for the purposes of a fort as a situation a short distance away, so a second Fort Vancouver was built on the last chosen spot. This is the Fort Vancouver of the present day, and the site of the city of Vancouver, Washington.

The new post was made the Pacific head-quarters for the Hudson Bay Company and became a great mart of trade from California to Alaska and for innumerable little stations in the Rocky mountains and the hinterland thereof. The fort, itself, was an imposing structure with a picket wall twenty feet high, buttressed with massive timbers inside. It enclosed a parallelogram five hundred feet by seven hundred feet and contained forty buildings, including a governor's residence of generous proportions. The lands outside of the fort proper were cultivated and were exceedingly productive. The employees of the company were comfortably housed and formed a happy community, and to the point came red men in various garbs, hunters, trappers and woodsmen, a picturesque throng in craft of all description.

This is a sketch of the post in 1846, the year in which, through the treaty between England and America, it became a possession of the United States. In 1849 a company of United States Artillery, under Captain J. H. Hathaway, took possession of the place in the name of the republic and the stars and stripes waved where the lion of St. George had held the breeze. It is an interesting commentary of the times to remember that to reach their destination Captain Hathaway and his soldiers were obliged to sail around Cape Horn in a sailing vessel, the voyage consuming many months. In the Spring of 1850 a company of mounted riflers arrived at the post overland from Fort Leavenworth.

An additional interest is given Fort Vancouver by knowing that at various periods prior to the Civil War Grant, Sheridan, McClellan, Hooker, and other of the famous United States leaders of the Civil War were stationed here. It was in a campaign against the Indians not far distant from Fort Vancouver that General Sheridan fought his first battle.

FORT YUMA
AT HEAD OF NAVIGATION, COLORADO RIVER—CALIFORNIA

THE comedian of Uncle Sam's military posts is old Fort Yuma on the Colorado River at the southwestern extremity of California. To mention the name in a barrack-room where there are seasoned soldiers is to call forth a reminiscent smile and the old story of the hen that laid hard-boiled eggs. These and that other one of the officers, who when they die at Fort Yuma and appear before his Satanic Majesty (by some strange miscarriage of justice) shiver with cold and send back to the fort for their blankets.

Other posts in Uncle Sam's itinerary are hot, but Fort Yuma spends all of its time in heating up with a passion for its work and an unrelenting attention to detail that have become legendary. During the months of April, May, and June no rainfall comes, and the average temperature is 105° in the shade. Of course the post does much better on some occasions, and at other times it falls below this batting average.

The most active days of Fort Yuma as a military post were found just before and for a few years subsequent to the Civil War, though that great conflict had no part in Yuma's past. During the days that California was having its mind made up for it to become a part of the United States, and during the days in which it was beginning the great experiment indicated, Yuma was of much importance as a base for United States troops. In addition to this it exercised and has always exercised a restraining influence upon those restless spirits of the desert, the Apache Indians. Being situated on the border between the United States and Mexico, it has some little to do in seeing that the customs regulations of this country are preserved. And it has always secured importance from being one of the stations on the old Santa Fé trail.

After receiving the Gila at a point 100 miles from its mouth, the Colorado River turns suddenly westward and forces its way through a rocky defile, 70 feet high and 350 yards long and 200 yards wide, thus cutting off a narrow rocky bluff and leaving it as an isolated eminence on the California side of the river. Here stands Fort Yuma, grey and sombre above the green bottom lands of the river, which are covered with a dense growth of cottonwood and mesquite. Chains of low serrated hills and mountains limit the view on nearly every side—all bare and grey save when painted by the sun with delicate hues of blue and purple.

Before reaching the fort the traveller passes through a long road shaded by young cottonwoods and mesquite interspersed with an impenetrable growth of arrow-bush and cane. Then he comes to a bend of the river where the water loses the ruddy tint which gives it its musical

FORT YUMA, CALIFORNIA

By courtesy of the War Department

FORT YUMA

name of "Colorado" and, finally, he brings up at the fortification, which in the distance appeared heavy and forbidding but which near at hand resolves itself into a collection of substantial adobe houses inclosed by deep verandas with Venetian blinds which shut out every direct ray of sunlight.

All the buildings at the post are of sun-dried brick and neatly plastered within and without. They are one story in height, have large rooms with lofty ceilings and facilities for the freest ventilation. The roof and walls are double, inclosing an air chamber. Each house is surrounded by a veranda and adjacent houses have their verandas in communication, so that the occupants may pass from one to another without exposing themselves to the heat of the sun.

What entitles the post to the name of fort are certain unpretentious intrenchments scattered along the slopes of the bluff overlooking the river and commanding the bottom lands adjacent. They are not visible from the river and the visitor is not aware of their existence until he steps to the edge of the bluff and looks down upon them. The parade is a stony lawn. Not a blade of grass is to be seen and everything is of that ashy light-grey color so trying to the eyes. It is a relief to gaze out upon the green bottom lands through which one passed before ascending to the top of the eminence where stands the fort.

Being so excessively dry the air at this post plays

strange pranks with articles made for use in less arid climates, as many a young officer's wife has found to her cost when bringing trunks and other household paraphernalia to her new home. Furniture put together in the North and brought here falls to pieces; travelling chests gape at their seams, and a sole-leather trunk contracts so much that the tray must be pried out by force.

Ink dries so rapidly upon the pen that it requires washing off every few minutes and a No. 2 pencil leaves no more trace upon a piece of paper than a piece of anthracite coal would leave. To use a pencil it is necessary to have it kept immersed in water before calling upon it for service. Newspapers require to be unfolded with care, for if handled roughly they crumble. Boxes of soap that weigh twelve pounds when shipped to Fort Yuma weigh only ten pounds after having been there for several weeks. Hams lose 12 per cent. in weight and rice 2 per cent. Eggs lose their watery contents by evaporation and become thick and tough. The effort to cool one's self with an ordinary fan is vain, because the surrounding atmosphere is of higher temperature than the body. The earth under foot is dry and powdery and hot as flour just ground, while the rocks are so hot that the hands cannot be borne upon them.

"The story of the dog that ran across the parade at mid-day on three legs barking at every step may be correct," writes an officer who was stationed there, "though I have never seen it tried."

VALLEY FORGE—YORKTOWN—VICKSBURG—LOOKOUT MOUNTAIN—GETTYSBURG—THE "CRATER"

IN the nature of the case field fortifications are temporary erections, earthworks thrown up for an immediate emergency; but, occasionally some bright deed or some momentous consequence gives these defences a fame more enduring than walls of stone planned with deliberation and executed with leisured care.

Who has not heard of Valley Forge and the heroic winter of 1777-1778 which Washington spent there with his meagrely clad men? Valley Forge is now a public reservation about twelve miles north of Philadelphia, on the Schuylkill River. Excursion trains run out from that city to the park, so it is easy of access. The grounds cover hundreds of acres, but the principal points are plainly marked and may be quickly reached.

One of the most interesting souvenirs of Washington's immortal encampment at Valley Forge is the little stone house which the great commander used as his headquarters. An unpretentious, substantial structure of the typical style of building of the days in which it was constructed, it is in excellent preservation, strong and sturdy as on the day of its erection. The building contains numerous Washington relics and curios collected by the State authorities or presented to the park by men and women of various parts of the nation.

One of the most conspicuous objects of the reservation is the Memorial Arch erected by the United States government to the memory of the men and officers who shared the privations of that terrible winter at this spot. It is of Roman character and stands on a commanding eminence in the central part of the grounds. Near at hand is planned the Washington Memorial Chapel, which the Future may complete, or leave unbuilt, as it sees fit.

Fort Washington, a small redoubt or earth, is not far from the Arch and has been carefully preserved against the encroachments of Time. The lines of the earthworks may also be made out.

A historic site is Yorktown, Virginia, the sleepy little village on the peninsula between the James and York rivers Cornwallis surrendered to Washington and the French allies in 1781, thus making sure of American Independence, and where the Army of the Potomac encamped under McClellan in 1862, throwing up massive earthworks. The traces of both Cornwallis' and McClellan's encampments are easily to be made out to-day.

The American and French forces marched from Williamsburg, September 28, 1781, driving in the

National Memorial Arch

Washington's Headquarters
SCENES AT VALLEY FORGE

The Slaughter Hollow

The Entrance to the Tunnel
TWO VIEWS TO-DAY OF THE "CRATER," PETERSBURG, VA.

VICKSBURG

British outposts at Yorktown as they approached and taking possession of the abandoned outworks. Forming a semicircular line about two miles from the British intrenchments they completely invested the enemy, the York River enclosing his forces to the northeast. October 17, Cornwallis offered to discuss terms of surrender.

The beginning of the year 1863—to make a jump from the Revolution to the Civil War—saw the turning of the tide for the United States, and it was in this year that the decisive battles of Vicksburg, Gettysburg and Chattanooga were fought. The battle-grounds of each of these engagements have been created national parks and are maintained in such a fashion that the visitor may follow the movements of the troops in those great clashes.

After the capture of the posts north of Vicksburg, on the Mississippi, and the opening of the mouth of the river by Farragut's taking of New Orleans in 1862, Vicksburg was the only remaining defence of the Confederacy on the Missspipi, and the sole remaining link between the Confederacy's east and west portions. The principal works of the city were on a commanding eminence, giving a clear sweep of the river and the surrounding country, which was swampy and almost impassable. They were competently manned, capably officered and well supplied.

The place, altogether, was deemed almost impregnable. To follow out all of the steps by which its reduction was brought about is not the province of this chapter. The United States troops under the comparatively unknown commander, U. S. Grant, began to operate at the end of January, 1863, and on July 4 concluded their task in the unconditional surrender of the main fortification of the Confederates. The surrender of Vicksburg came one day after the conclusion of the battle of Gettysburg which occupied the first three days of July.

The reservation of the Vicksburg National Park contains 1,255.07 acres and was acquired pursuant to an Act of Congress approved February 21, 1899.

The grounds of the Gettysburg National Park, Adams County, Pennsylvania, comprise 2,054 acres and their acquisition was commenced in 1873. The scenes of the principal movements of the battle have been marked with suitable monuments. The battle of Gettysburg proved conclusively that the South could not invade the North. It was the last gallant attempt of a completely invested country to strike a fatal blow before the strangle-hold of its enemy should bring the end.

The largest of the national military parks is Chickamauga and Chattanooga National Park, which comprises 5,688 acres in the State of Georgia, in addition to nearly 150 acres in the State of Tennessee, the park being

THE "CRATER"

situated on the line between the States. In Tennessee is located Lookout Mountain. The acquisition of this reservation began under the provisions of an Act of Congress approved August 19, 1890.

On the outskirts of Petersburg, Virginia, the remains of Forts Haskell and Steadman, the scene of the "Crater" episode, and part of the defences of the capital of the Confederacy which fell before Grant in 1865, have been preserved as a private enterprise. For a small consideration the "Crater" and the earthworks will be shown to the visitor. The Federal forces opposed to Fort Steadman—at the suggestion of a miner from Chambersburg, Pa., it is said—constructed a long tunnel from their lines to beneath the Confederate stronghold. An enormous quantity of powder was here, and when it was set off a body of soldiers was to charge through the breach and take the Confederate positions.

The powder was exploded and the plan was successful in so far that it blew several hundred men into eternity, but when the attacking column reached the cavity in the ground its men became confused, giving the Confederates time to reform and to pour in a terrible fire upon the Union men concentrated in the broken ground below. The result was terrible carnage of United States troops. The "Crater" had become a death trap. Nearly three thousand men were killed in it in thirty minutes, the most disastrous loss the Federal forces suffered in so short a time during the war.

The " Crater " to-day is a peaceful spot glorified by tall trees which keep the scene in continual gloom. The depression in the ground is ten feet or more in depth and about two hundred feet in diameter. A short walk brings one to the entrance to the tunnel where the lines of the United States were stretched.

INDEX

Adams, Fort, Newport, R. I., 222-231
Alamo, Texas, 279-284
Allen, Ethan, 63, 70
Amsterdam, Fort, 37
Andre, Major, 156
Andros, Edmund, Royal Governor of Mass., 29, 107
Annapolis Royal, 2, 84-92
Arnold, Benedict, 64, 82; his treason, 154 et seq.; 169, 171, 238
Atares Castle, Havana, 206

Baltimore, Fort at, 180-189
Battery, The, New York City, 46
Belfast, Me., 99
Belle Rive, Louis St. Ange de, Commanding Chartres, 12; stationed at Vincennes, 14; surrenders Chartres to English, 14
Boston, Fort at, 25-35
Boston Tea Party, 31
Bourbon, Fort, on the Mississippi, 263
Bowie, James, inventor of Bowie knife, 281
Braddock, 18; his march and death, 19, 53, 127
Bradford, Wm., 106
Brownsville, Pa., 21
Burgoyne, General, 64
Burnet, Governor of New York, 122, 123, 124

Cadillac, La Moote, 132
Caen, Emery de, 75
Canseau, Nova Scotia, expedition against, 2; fleet arrives at, 7

Castine, Baron Vincent de, 103, 104
Castle Garden, New York City, 46
Castle St. Louis, Quebec, 72, 77, 82
Castle William, Boston, 25, 35
Castle Williams, New York Harbor, 46
Champlain, Memorial Light House, 67
Champlain, Samuel, 49, 50, 51, 52, 60, 72, 73; dies at Quebec, 76
Charles, Fort, Me., 107
Charleston, South Carolina, Fort at, 241-250
Chartres, Fort, site selected, 11; disastrous expedition leaves, 12; second fort built, 12; surrenders to English, 14
Chebucto Bay, 93, 94, 97
Chicago, Illinois, 21; Historical Society, 23
Cincinnati, Ohio, 24
Citadel of Halifax, 93-97
Citadel of Quebec, 72-83
Clark, Fort, Illinois, 24
Clark, George Rogers, 23, 24, 144, 145
Clinton, Fort, New York City, 46
Clinton, Fort, New York, 148, 149
Columbus, Fort, New York, 36-48
Constitution, Fort, New Hampshire, 161-166
Constitution, Fort, New York, 150

305

INDEX

Cornbury, Governor of New Amsterdam, 41
Covington, Fort, 187
"Crater," The, near Petersburg, Virginia, 303
Crevecœur, Fort, 15
Crockett, Davy, falls at Alamo, 283
Crown Point, 53, 66–71

Damariscotta, 3
Davenport, Captain Richard, 28
Davis, Jeff, cell at Fort Monroe, 235
Dearborn, Fort, 21, 22, 23
Dearborn, General, Secretary of War, 35
Defiance, Mount, 64
De Soto, 142, 201
Diamond, Fort, 45
Dieskau, 54, 55, 56, 69
Donop, Count, 177
Dorchester, Mass., 32
Douglas, Fort, Utah, 289 et seq.
Drake, Sir Francis, menaces Havana, 203
Duchambon, successor to Duquesnel, 8
Dufferin Terrace, Quebec, 72, 83
Dummer, William, Governor of Mass., 29
Dumplings, Fort, near Newport, R. I., 231
Duquesne, Fort, erected, 18; falls to England, 19
Duquesne, Governor General of Canada, 18
Duquesnel, Commandant of Louisburg, 2

Edward, Fort, New York, 57
Erie, Pa., 20

Falls of Minnehaha, 268
Federal Hill Fort, Baltimore, 188, 189
Fetterman, Wyoming, 288 et seq.
Franklin, Pa., 21
Frederick, Fort, Maine, 105–112
Frenchman's Bay, Me., 88
Frontenac, in command at Quebec, 77, 78, 79, 110
Frontenac, Fort (Kingston, Canada), 114, 127

Gage, Fort, 23, 24
George, Fort, at mouth of Columbia River, Ore., 292
George, Fort, Me., 98–104
George, Fort, New York City, 37
Gettysburg, 302
Governor's Island, New York Harbor, 36, 37, 41, 42, 43, 44–48
Griswold, Fort, Conn., 167–172

Hamilton, Fort, New York, 45
Havana, Cuba, Forts at, 201–206
Heald, Captain Nathan, 22, 23
Heights of Quebec, 72–83
Hennepin, Friar Louis, and his map, 114
Holmes, Major, 140
Holmes, Fort, Michigan, 131–140
Howe, Sir William, 59

Independence, Fort, Boston, 25–35, 148
Irving, Washington, 36

Jackson, Fort, Louisiana, 263–267

INDEX

Jay, Fort, New York, 36–48
Johnson, William, of New York, 53, 54, 55, 56, 69, 104, 117, 119
Johnston, General Albert Sidney, 284
Kaskaskia, Illinois, 143
Keogh, Fort, Montana, 289
Key, Francis Scott, 180, 187
Kirke, Admiral Sir David, attacks Quebec, 74
Kosciuszko, 151
Lafayette, Fort, 45
La Fuerza, Cuba, 201–206
Laramie, Fort, Wyoming, 273–278
Larrabee, Captain Lieutenant John, 30
La Salle, Robert Cavelier, 114, 131
Laurel Moat, Havana, 206
Leavenworth, Fort, Kansas, 287 et seq.
Le Bœuf, Fort, 20, 21
Lee, Robert E., 181; resigns from U. S. Army, 284
Lescarbot, Marc, 86
Louisburg, Nova Scotia, importance of, 1; incentives to attack, 2; preparations against, 4; a novel plan, 5; expedition sails, 6; strongest outlying work, 8; siege progresses, 10; restored to France, 10
Louis de la Mobile, Fort, Alabama, 257
McHenry, Fort, Maryland, 180-189
McHenry, James, Secretary of War, 184

McKenzie, Sir William's experiment in Nova Scotia, 88, 89
M'Lean, Colonel Francis, 100
Mackinac Island, State park commission, 140
Marion, Fort, Florida, 190–200
Marion, General Francis, 199
Marquette, Father, 131–132
Massac, Fort, Illinois, 21, 141–146
Matanzas Inlet, Florida, 192
Menendez, Juan, de Aviles, 193
Mercer, Fort, New Jersey, 175
Mermet, Father, 142, 143
Metropolis, Illinois, 141
Michillimackinac, Michigan, 131–140
Mifflin, Fort, Pa., 173–179
Monitor and Merrimac, seen from Fort Monroe, 240
Monroe, Fort, Virginia, 232–240
Montcalm, Marquis de, 57, 59, 60, 62, 69, 127, 128
Montgomery, Fort, Alabama, 212
Montgomery, Fort, New York, 148, 149
Montgomery, Richard, 82, 83
Montmagny, Governor of Canada, 76
Monts, Sieur de, discovers Annapolis basin, 82
Morgan, Fort, Alabama, 257, 262
Morro Castle, Cuba, 201–206
Moultrie, Fort, South Carolina, 200, 241–250
New London, Conn., 167 et seq.
Newport, R. I., Forts at, 222–231

INDEX

Newport Artillery Co., 222
Niagara, Fort, New York, 113–121
Nonsense, Fort, 170

Ontario, Fort, New York, 122–130
Ordre de la Bon Temps, 86
Osceola, Monument at Fort Moultrie, 244
Oswego, New York, 122, 130

Pell, S. H. P., of New York, restores Ticonderoga, 65
Pell, William F., of New York, acquires Ticonderoga, 65
Pemaquid, Maine, 105, 106, 111
Pensacola, Florida, Fort at, 207–214
Pentagoet, or Castine, 103, 105, 107
Peoria, Illinois, 24
Pepperell, William, of Kittery, Maine, chosen to head expedition, 5; home still standing, 5, 30, 125
Phil Kearney, Fort, 285 et seq.
Philadelphia, Fort at, 173–179
Phips, Sir William, 29, 78, 79, 90, 108, 109
Pickens, Fort, Florida, 213
Pike, Lieutenant C. M., secures Fort Snelling reservation, 269
Pipon, Captain John, 29
Pitt, Fort, Block-house at Pittsburgh, 17
Plains of Abraham, 81
Port Henry, New York, 68
Portsmouth, New Hampshire, Fort at, 161–166
Potrincourt, Baron, founds Annapolis Royal, 84, 85, 87

Presidio of San Francisco, Cal., 215–221
Presque Isle, a memorial of, 20
Principe Castle, Havana, 206
Pulaski, Fort, Georgia, 251–256
Putnam, Fort, 152
Putnam, General Israel, 148, 151

Quebec, 49, 51, 62; Historic Forts at, 72–83

Redstone Old Fort, 21
Renault, Phillippe Francois de, introduces negro slavery to Illinois, 11
Revere, Lieutenant Colonel Paul, 33, 100, 163
Ribaut, Jean, 192
Richelieu Cardinal, 73
Robinson, Col. Beverly, 156
Roxbury, Mass., 32

St. Augustine, Florida, Fort at, 190–200
St. Clair, General Arthur, 64
St. Denis, Juchereau de, 141, 142, 143
St. Frederic, Fort, New York, 67, 68, 69, 70
St. Louis, Fort, 14
St. Paul, Minn., foundation, 272
St. Philip, Fort, Louisana, 263–267
Sam Houston, Fort, Texas, 279–284
Samoset sells land at Pemaquid, 106
San Antonio, Texas, Forts at, 284–289
San Carlos, Fort, Florida, 207–214
Sandusky, Ohio, 21

INDEX

San Francisco, Cal., Presidio at, 215–221
San Marco, Fort, 197, 198
Scott, Fort Winfield, San Francisco, 220
Screven, Fort, Georgia, 254
Shippen, Margaret, 157–158
Shirley, William Governor of Mass., organizes expedition against Louisburg, 3; his list of instructions, 6; 53, 116, 125
Smith, Capt. John, sees Hampton Roads, 236
Snelling, Fort, Minn., 268–272
Stanwix, Fort, 129
Star Spangled Banner, 188
Starved Rock, Ill., 14
Stony Point, New York, 158–160
Sumter, Fort, South Carolina, 241–250

Ticonderoga, New York, 49–65, 147
Tracy, Uriah, 137
Travis Col. William B., of the Alamo, 280
Trumbull, Fort, Conn., 167–172
Turnbull, Col. John, 33

Valesca, Luis de, his settlement at Pensacola Bay, 207
Valley Forge, 179
Vancouver, Fort, Washington, 290–294
Van Twiller, Wouter, or Walter, Governor of New Amsterdam, 37, 38
Vauban, 1, 56, 79
Vaudreuil, last Governor of New France, 81

Vaughan, William, of Damariscotta, suggests attack on Louisburg, 2; his career, 3; captures grand battery, 8, 9
Venango, 21
Vicksburg, Miss., 301
Vincennes, Ind., 12

Wadsworth, Peleg, 100, 102
Walker, Admiral Sir Hovenden, 81
Warren, Fort, 35
Washington, Fort, Valley Forge, Pa., 300
Washington, Fort, Cincinnati, Ohio, 24
Washington, George, 18, 32, 33, 129, 155, 157, 168, 176, 226, 228
Waterford, Pa., 20
Wayne, "Mad" Anthony, 145, 159
Wentworth, Sir John, Governor of New Hampshire, 162
West Point, New York, 147–160
White Hall, New York, 55
Wilkinson, James, 145
William Henry, Fort, Mass., 109, 110
William and Mary, Fort, New Hampshire, 161–166
William Henry, Fort, New York, 54, 56, 57, 58, 59, 119
Winthrop, Fort, Boston, 26
Winthrop, Governor of Mass., 27, 34
Wolcott, Fort, Torpedo Station, 231
Wolfe, captures, Quebec, 81

Yorktown, Va., 64
Yuma, Fort, Cal., 295–298